Praise for *High Performers*

"Challenging times test even the best on their people skills. Leon Martel's research is a critical and timely reminder for all management."

> —Alfred C. DeCrane, retired chairman and
> CEO, Texaco, Inc.

"The unique insight of this book is that it focuses on two major changes affecting business everywhere—the changing nature of work and the changing values of workers. In clear and entertaining writing Martel tells us what these mean and how we have to respond to find and keep the employees we need."

> —C. R. Shoemate, retired chairman,
> president, and CEO, Bestfoods

"The author's long experience managing research programs at the Hudson Institute and The Conference Board serves the reader well. The useful practices he discovers and concisely describes will aid employers in every field."

> —John R. Hall, retired chairman and CEO, Ashland Inc.

"This valuable book tells you how great companies produce great employees. Asian readers will especially profit from this book because of its global approach. Martel takes us inside a wide variety of companies located in different regions of the world, showing how they motivate and reward high performance people."

> —Washington SyCip, founder, The SGV Group

"With workforce growth slowing in most industrialized countries, including many in Europe, while demand for high performers continues to rise, Martel's book is essential reading. All companies can benefit from what he has learned from the best of them."

> —Vittorio Tesio, Corporate University, Fiat Group

"Leon Martel's book is a unique opportunity for all HR professionals to fully understand how to develop the potential and motivation of their companies' most valuable asset: people."
>   —Hilmar Kopper, chairman of the supervisory board,
>   Deutsche Bank

"Every great leader knows that the key to success is surrounding yourself with talent. Committed, engaged, and appreciated employees are essential for businesses to succeed in the post-industrial area. Leon Martel provides a practical road map for hiring, retaining, and maximizing the potential of the folks who will determine the success or failure of your organization."
>   —Norm Coleman, mayor, St. Paul, Minnesota

"This is what we should be told, but rarely hear. Business leaders will benefit from the key principles (many of them counterintuitive) the author has drawn from the practices of the best companies of America, Europe, and Asia."
>   —Rahul Bajaj, chairman and managing director,
>   Bajaj Auto Ltd.

"Practices that work, not theory, is what distinguishes this book. HR officers everywhere will find the author's examples and conclusions both useful and insightful."
>   —Sharon Douglas, vice president, human resources,
>   chief people officer, AFLAC Incorporated

"We all know there is no silver bullet on keeping the best and the brightest. *High Performers* gives you an entire arsenal of ideas on how to make it happen."
>   —Bruce W. Ferguson, chief people officer, Exult, Inc.

"An insightful review of the current issues facing our workforce, and opportunities to make significant strides in understanding how to nurture, support, and retain high performers."
>   —Kathryn E. Johnson, CEO, Health Forum

High Performers

High Performers

How the Best Companies Find and Keep Them

Leon Martel

Foreword by Richard E. Cavanagh

JOSSEY-BASS
A Wiley Company
San Francisco

Published by

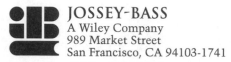

JOSSEY-BASS
A Wiley Company
989 Market Street
San Francisco, CA 94103-1741

www.josseybass.com

Jossey-Bass books and products are available through most bookstores. To contact Jossey-Bass directly, call (888) 378-2537, fax to (800) 605-2665, or visit our website at www.josseybass.com.

Substantial discounts on bulk quantities of Jossey-Bass books are available to corporations, professional associations, and other organizations. For details and discount information, contact the special sales department at Jossey-Bass.

We at Jossey-Bass strive to use the most environmentally sensitive paper stocks available to us. Our publications are printed on acid-free recycled stock whenever possible, and our paper always meets or exceeds minimum GPO and EPA requirements.

Library of Congress Cataloging-in-Publication Data

Martel, Leon
    High performers : how the best companies find and keep them /
by Leon Martel ; foreword by Richard E. Cavanagh.—1st ed.
    p. cm.—(The Jossey-Bass business & management series)
    Includes bibliographical references and index.
    ISBN 0-7879-5382-2
    1. Employees—Recruiting—Case studies.   2. Employee
retention—Case studies.   3. Employee motivation—Case studies.
4. Job satisfaction—Case studies.   5. Performance—Case
studies.   I. Title.   II. Series.
HF5549.5.R44 M369 2002
658.3—dc21   2001008160

FIRST EDITION
HB Printing   10 9 8 7 6 5 4 3 2 1

The Jossey-Bass
Business & Management Series

For Christopher and Jonathan,
High performers both

Contents

Foreword

The changing world of work and competition has clearly created a bull market for high performance employees.

In this lucid book our longtime colleague Leon Martel takes you inside twenty-five of the world's most successful companies, showing you how they hire, motivate, and retain high value employees. These uncommon companies clearly know something that many others don't—that high performance employees, not technology and capital, are the crucial drivers of growth. Based on real-life business experiences, not conjecture, this book provides a wealth of proven practices that can be adopted by all organizations.

Martel traces the growing link between high performing employees and productivity, profitability, and return to shareholders. The innovative ways these companies reward and recognize their best employees help explain why most of them deliver superlative results in both good times and bad.

Each of these twenty-five companies is distinctly different. They are based in various parts of the world and represent a cross section of industries. But they share a common strategic philosophy: they view their people not as costs but as critical assets. Although this may sound like simple, old-fashioned common sense, a lot of companies still don't get it.

You'll discover the innovative ways people are recruited, motivated, and rewarded at Microsoft, Sun Microsystems, Cisco Systems,

Harley-Davidson, Toyota Motor Corporation, Merck, Acer, Novo Nordisk, Amgen, AFLAC, Compuware, and Royal Dutch/Shell Group—and at Intel, MBNA, Ingram Micro, Taiwan Semiconductor Manufacturing, Capital One Financial Corporation, Genentech, CDW Computer Centers, Starbucks, BMC Software, Wal-Mart, LM Ericsson, Nokia, and Singapore Airlines.

You'll learn how Novo Nordisk dispatches experienced facilitators to improve performance throughout the company, why Microsoft does not encourage telecommuting, and why there is no executive floor at Sun Microsystems. And you'll go inside AFLAC, where people are not hired for specific jobs but for their individual knowledge and skills.

These firms recognize that their high performing people are the difference between winning and losing. They fully understand what Peter Drucker has told us all, that work has shifted from the tangible to the intangible, making employees a company's most important investment. At Microsoft, we learn that after management adds up all the corporation's hardware and software, all the land and buildings, and all the money in the bank, there's another $350 billion-plus in market value that doesn't show up on the balance sheet. That's the knowledge Microsoft employees carry around in their heads and the energy in their hearts.

Breaking new ground, this book warns that the things people value most are in flux. Citing significant new research, Martel notes that although employees want to be adequately compensated, they are more concerned with their overall well-being, their freedom to express themselves, and the quality of their lives. This is now true throughout the developed world. As this book declares, employees are moving from a *materialist* to a *postmaterialist* set of values. This shift in the things people care most about has vast implications for the way organizations reward and recognize people. In this changed world, many of the old-school motivators that once worked are likely to fail.

This book is far more than a pragmatic tour of the human resource practices of leading companies. It is a strategic primer on why companies succeed. Best of all, it forces us to reexamine some of our favorite theories about the way we structure work and recognize people. The companies examined in this book invest heavily in their people, constantly upgrading employee skills. They reject the still too frequent view that the more education and training you give to workers, the more likely they are to desert you for greener pastures.

Almost every executive has at one time or another paid homage to the importance of people. What makes the difference at the twenty-five companies you are about to visit is that they practice what they preach.

February 2002

Richard E. Cavanagh
President and CEO
The Conference Board

Preface

The purpose of this book is to briefly describe the practices that a select group of twenty-five outstanding U.S., European, and Asian companies use to find and keep the high performing employees that have made them successful. Unlike books that discuss specific employee management practice areas such as recruiting, compensation, supervision, and training or that tell the stories of individual excellent companies, this book provides a comprehensive review of all relevant practices in a wide range of companies. Thus its content and the conclusions it reaches—a number of them controversial and counterintuitive—will be of interest to everyone—including chief executives, chief operating officers, and line and staff managers at all levels—who plays a role in hiring, paying, managing, and training employees.

I selected these twenty-five companies to examine because each of them is highly correlated as a good employer and a good performer. This correlation does not imply cause and effect. Being a good employer does not guarantee that a company will be a good performer, and not all good performing companies are good employers. However, the correlation is striking: it suggests that there is a strong relationship between being a good employer and being a good performer and, moreover, that particular high performing companies are especially adept in the practices of choosing, developing, and retaining high performing employees.

To find out how they do so, I interviewed senior managers in the twenty-five companies, concentrating on those in human resource functions. To supplement these interviews, I examined the companies' annual reports, their Internet sites, relevant internal documents, and any secondary source literature I could find describing their employee management practices. My scope was deliberately broad and comprehensive in order to identify all practices that might contribute to finding and keeping high performing employees. My organization of my findings is by practices, under familiar headings, providing descriptions of how the twenty-five companies use each of them. For each practice, I also present a context, discussing, as appropriate, its origins, history, and overall use as well as commentary by leading experts and relevant survey data from polling organizations and consulting firms. In a few cases I have aggregated data from the twenty-five companies, but because their number is small, it would be misleading to suggest they represent a larger universe. Because they are a special group, I have more often sought to describe the individual activities that make them special.

What I have found, and what appears inherent in virtually all the practices I describe, is that these twenty-five companies understand what employees value and how they should be treated. These two guiding insights about employees rest in turn on two major structural changes that emerged in the second half of the last century and are continuing to evolve in this century. One of these changes is the profound alteration in the values of workers as more and more of their societies experience the security and benefits of economic development. The other change is the equally profound alteration in the nature of work as it shifts from predominantly tangible to predominantly intangible.

These two structural changes are discussed in Chapter One. This chapter also explains how I selected the twenty-five companies whose employee management practices demonstrate their understanding of the implications of these changes.

In the four central chapters of this book (Chapters Two, Three, Four, and Five), I then group and discuss the employee management practices that the twenty-five companies use to find and keep their high performing employees. At first, it seemed logical to begin the discussion at the chronological beginning, with hiring and recruiting practices. But my interviewees almost always wanted to begin by speaking about the meaningfulness of the work in which their companies were engaged and, at the same time, about the work environments they were creating to encourage and maximize the contributions of those doing that work. I came to see that the selected companies considered these matters prerequisites for recruiting and major attractions to recruits. So Chapter Two considers both the various aspects of work content and the environment in which work occurs, because executives of the twenty-five companies see these matters as a seamless whole. They know that the meaningfulness of their companies' work and the importance they place on the context in which it is done are two sides of the same coin.

Chapter Three then takes up hiring and recruiting. It begins with a brief section on the evolving labor market, addressing both that market's dramatically changing supply and its continually tightening demand. This is the context in which *all* companies, but especially those in developed countries, will soon be finding new employees. Very few employers understand this, but a number of the twenty-five companies are already preparing for it, adjusting their search methods, and creating and applying new tools and new techniques to their hiring and recruiting practices.

The fourth chapter moves on to compensation and benefits. It opens with a section on the unresolved and still evolving question of the relationship between pay, performance, and retention. On the one hand, in the changing value structure of contemporary workers, money no longer comes first, and it is of uncertain value in promoting either higher performance or longer tenure. On the other hand, there is no doubt that employees want to share in the financial rewards that their efforts make possible. The twenty-five companies are pursuing a range of compensation initiatives to respond to employee needs and simultaneously advance corporate goals, ends that in practice can be difficult to make compatible.

Stock options, for example, continue to be widely used, though recent economic developments have continued to expose their flaws, not the least of which is that they are taking a major part of an important corporate responsibility and cost—employee compensation—out of corporate hands. Benefit programs too are playing a changing role, especially in shaping the relationship between compensation and business strategy.

Chapter Five examines education and training practices. It is particularly concerned with the practices needed to respond to the steadily advancing structural change from tangible to predominantly intangible work. In the wake of this change, attaining high performance increasingly requires traditional education and training programs to give way to continuous learning, informal training, and knowledge management. It also requires paying greater attention to the "soft" skills of communication, leadership, and personal growth and to the knowledge-related competencies essential to postindustrial work. Many of the twenty-five companies are creating and adjusting education and training programs to respond to these imperatives. Most also recognize—as part of their understanding of what employees value—the new relationship developing between retention and corporate-provided and corporate-sponsored education and training.

The sixth and final chapter initially identifies general principles that derive from each of these four major employee management practice areas. Although these principles refer to specific practices and are keyed back to the chapters that discuss those practices, they are also informed by insights from and relationships with other practices. This chapter concludes with nine key themes that guide implementation of the general principles.

Readers may thus approach *High Performers* in one of two ways. They may read it straight through, obtaining a comprehensive grasp of the practices undertaken by the twenty-five companies and the principles derived from those practices. Along the way, they should find practices that are unique, instructive, or useful in new and different ways. Together with the principles, these practices may suggest courses of action that readers can take to improve performance and increase retention in their own organizations. Alternatively, readers may look at particular practice areas or individual practices within these areas by examining the appropriate general principles in Chapter Six first and then turning to the sections in the four central chapters where the relevant practices are discussed.

Finally, in any effort to find and keep high performers, it is essential not only to seek and work with people already identified as high performers but also to develop the potential of those who are not yet high performers. It is through the application to all employees of the practices discussed here that all organizations will be able to find, develop, and retain their own high performers.

New York, New York   Leon Martel
February 2002

Acknowledgments

I could not have completed this book without the generous assistance of many people.

My initial gratitude is to The Conference Board, which supported my writing and regularly provided administrative, logistical, and research assistance. In particular, I am indebted to Dick Cavanagh, the Board's president and CEO, for his interest and encouragement and for authoring the Foreword; to Jack Wirts, executive vice president, who generously suggested I pursue a project of my own choosing and gave me both guidance and free rein when I did so; to Al Vogl, editor of the Board's fine flagship magazine, *Across the Board,* whose early and wise editorial counsel influenced both my choice of topic and means of presentation; to Randy Poe, executive director of communications, who assisted with the Foreword and whose expertise has been most helpful in the book's promotion; to Tam Hernandez, administrative director of research, who supervised the transcriptions of my interviews and faithfully attended to numerous other logistical matters; to Charles Peck, who carefully read and helpfully commented on the chapter on compensation and benefits; and to Diane Shimek, senior information specialist, who tirelessly and speedily attended to my various research requests, both comprehensive and minutely focused.

I am especially grateful to Frances Hesselbein, chairman and founding president of The Drucker Foundation, whose wise and generous counsel gave direction to this book and provided an introduction to its publisher; to Frances Huessy, whose careful review of early parts of the manuscript both improved them and influenced the writing of all that followed; and to Martha Finney, who gave her enthusiastic endorsement to the finished product and, in the wake of the terrorist attacks of September 11, alerted me to the now even greater meaning of the book's conclusions on the importance of meaningful work.

My debt is particularly great to all those I interviewed at the twenty-five "best" companies. Without exception they patiently answered my questions, ferreted out useful items of information, and carefully reviewed what I chose to quote from my conversations with them. It is their candid and thoughtful responses to my many queries that give this book its substance.

At Jossey-Bass, my gratitude begins with Susan Williams, whose gentle but firm advice throughout the acquisition process gave this book its focus and its present form. The baton was then passed to my principal editor, Julianna Gustafson. From the very beginning her wise suggestions shaped and improved both content and structure, and in the end her patient and good-humored support proved critical to the book's completion. All the while, valuable editorial assistance was provided as well by Tamara Kastl. I am grateful also to Mary Garrett, who expertly shepherded the book through production, and to Elspeth MacHattie for her fine copyediting.

Finally, as always, my greatest debt is to my family. First, it is to my two sons, to whom this book is dedicated. Christopher, now a key player in Wall Street's high finances, has been an invaluable source of information and assistance throughout the book but most especially in the chapter on compensation, where he carefully reviewed and critiqued my discussion of the arcane subject of stock options. Jonathan, the family expert on information technology—now employed in the new world of e-commerce—has been equally valuable in taking me through the complexities of research on the Internet and computer formatting. Most important has been my wife, Marilee. Her thoughtful comments, both macro and micro, on all aspects of this book have greatly improved its organization and its flow, and her careful reading of every word has brought clarity and logic where it was most needed. I am grateful indeed.

All of the above have helped make this a better book. The faults that remain are mine alone.

The Author

Leon Martel is a senior fellow at The Conference Board, where he has also served as senior vice president for research, managing the Board's extensive studies program, and as senior vice president for international programs. Previously he was acting president, executive vice president, and director of the Research Management Council of the Hudson Institute, and a tenured member of the faculty of Hofstra University.

Martel is the author of *The Next 200 Years: A Scenario for America and the World* (with Herman Kahn and William Brown, 1976); *Lend-Lease, Loans, and the Coming of the Cold War* (1979); and *Mastering Change: The Key to Business Success* (1986), named one of the year's "10 outstanding business books" by *Best of Business Quarterly*.

A frequent lecturer on coming economic, political, social, and technological changes and how to manage them, Martel has made over 300 presentations as keynoter, featured speaker, or seminar leader to business audiences and professional association meetings in the United States and abroad. A retired captain in the U.S. Naval Reserve, he holds a B.A. degree from Dartmouth College and M.A. and Ph.D. degrees from Columbia University.

High Performers

1

The Twenty-Five Best Companies and What They Understand

Companies need high performing, committed employees. Recent research by consultants at McKinsey & Company, surveying 6,900 managers (including 4,500 senior managers and corporate officers) in fifty-six large and midsize U.S. companies, finds that high performers increase productivity 40 percent in operations roles, increase profit 49 percent in general management roles, and increase revenue 67 percent in sales roles.[1] The consulting firm Watson Wyatt Worldwide, in a 2000 survey on the attitudes of more than 7,500 workers, reports that "companies with highly committed employees had a 112 percent three-year total return to shareholders, versus a 76 percent return for companies with low employee commitment."[2] Further, Stanford Graduate School of Business professor Jeffrey Pfeffer has summarized and analyzed considerable evidence consistent with these findings, showing the good business results of practices that develop high performing, committed employees.[3]

However, not all companies understand this relationship. The McKinsey research just cited also finds that only 14 percent of the managers surveyed in 2000 strongly agree that their companies attract highly talented people—even less than the 23 percent of the 6,000 managers surveyed in 1997 who strongly agreed with this statement—and only 3 percent of the respondents in both 1997 and 2000 strongly agreed that their companies develop talent quickly and effectively. Corroborating these findings are the results of two recent surveys by the New York–based business research organization The Conference Board. In a 2001 survey asking CEOs to select their top issues from a list of fifteen management challenges, "engaging employees in the company's vision/values" and "developing and retaining potential leaders" were chosen by 20.8 and 20.0 percent, respectively, of the 506 responding CEOs, ranking these issues in only the middle of the list.[4] Similarly, in a 1997 survey, 40 senior executives were asked, "To what extent do you think senior management is willing to make the investment—in time and money—for employee development?" The highest response was "little," chosen by 37 percent, and the lowest response was "great," selected by only 13 percent.[5] The most successful companies feel differently and are acting differently. Who are they, and what are they doing to acquire, develop, and retain the workers that make them high performing organizations?

Identifying the Most Successful Companies

To find these companies, I began with the 1999 edition of the leading and best-known list of good employers in the United States, *Fortune* magazine's annual compilation "The 100 Best Companies to Work For in America."[6] A few weeks later, examining the *Wall Street Journal*'s 1999 Shareholder Scorecard of publicly held companies, I noticed a remarkable correlation. On this scorecard, the companies highest on the *Fortune* list had the most A ratings (top quintile) for average compound annual total return for the most of the four time periods (one, three, five, and ten years) examined. In fact, ten of the top twelve publicly held companies on the *Fortune* list received an A in every time period, one had a C in the three-year time period and A's in the other periods, and another had a B in the five-year period along with its A's.[7] This offered powerful evidence that good employers are also good performers. From these highly correlated U.S. companies, I then selected the top seventeen for research and interviews.

In further evidence of their overall managerial excellence, a number of these companies also appear on other well-known lists of "best" companies in 1999. Eleven were listed in the Business Week Fifty, a compendium of top performing companies in the Standard & Poor's 500 index,[8] and four appeared among the top ten in Fortune's "America's Most Admired Companies."[9] In addition, research by Fortune has separately confirmed that the publicly traded companies on its list of "100 Best Companies to Work For" had significantly higher returns to shareholder value in their five previous years than those in the Russell 3000, an index of large and small companies that mirrors the 100 Best list.[10]

Two "100 Best Companies to Work For" lists have appeared since 1999. Eleven of the seventeen U.S. companies have reappeared on both lists and four more have reappeared once.[11] In performance, several of the seventeen companies—in the slower growth environment of 2000 and 2001 that has affected most firms—have not had the same high returns reported in 1999, but each has continued to do very well in its own peer group.

Because good people practices are also followed by companies outside the United States, I wanted to include the best of them too in my research and interviews. Although there are no global lists of best companies to work for similar to Fortune's list for U.S. companies, several useful surrogates are available: "The World's 100 Best Managed Companies," compiled by Industry Week;[12] "Being a Good Employer," a section of a larger list titled "Asia's Most Admired Companies" (including companies based all over the world), compiled by Asian Business;[13] and "World's Most Respected Companies," compiled by the Financial Times and Pricewaterhouse-Coopers.[14] From these lists I chose the four companies in Europe and the four in Asia ranked highest as both employers and performers, confirming my choices with senior staff in The Conference Board's European and Asian offices.

Table 1.1 shows the distribution of the twenty-five selected companies by industry sector. Appendix A gives the companies' locations and summarizes data on their sales, net income, and number of

TABLE 1.1. The Twenty-Five Best Companies, by Industry Sector.

Automotive & Transport Equipment
- Harley-Davidson, Inc.
- Toyota Motor Corporation

Computer Hardware
- Acer Inc.
- Cisco Systems, Inc.
- Sun Microsystems, Inc.

Computer Software & Services
- BMC Software, Inc.
- Compuware Corporation
- Ingram Micro Inc.
- Microsoft Corporation

Drugs
- Amgen Inc.
- Genentech, Inc.
- Merck & Co., Inc.
- Novo Nordisk A/S

Energy
- Royal Dutch/Shell Group

Electronics & Miscellaneous Technology
- Intel Corporation
- Taiwan Semiconductor Manufacturing Co., Ltd.

Financial Services
- Capital One Financial Corporation
- MBNA Corporation

Insurance
- AFLAC Incorporated

Leisure
- Starbucks Corporation

Retail
- CDW Computer Centers, Inc.
- Wal-Mart Stores, Inc.

Telecommunications
- LM Ericsson
- Nokia Corporation

Transportation
- Singapore Airlines

employees. Henceforth, when I refer to these twenty-five as a group, I call them simply *the best companies*.

Examining the table, it is clear that *new economy* sectors (computer hardware and software, electronics and miscellaneous technology, and telecommunications) are strongly represented among the best companies. This is in part because these sectors have been leaders in economic growth during most of the 1990s, but it is also because companies in these sectors—that is, in innovative rapidly changing industries—are highly competitive and of necessity have been in the forefront in developing human resource practices to find and keep high performers. Most important, these companies strongly exemplify the shift in society's major value-creating resource—from energy and, earlier, human and animal labor to information—a shift that is increasingly affecting all industry sectors. Nonetheless, the list also includes a number of companies in more traditional, or *old economy*, sectors, like automotive and transport equipment, energy, and retailing. Facing the same tight labor markets and therefore also needing to create and replicate outstanding HR practices, they too are among those highly correlated as good employers and good performers.

Learning What the Best Companies Are Doing

I then researched each best company, focusing on its human resource (HR) practices, by examining its annual reports and other public documents, its Internet site and references to it elsewhere on the Internet, and material published about it in the business and general periodical literature. Following this research, I conducted face-to-face interviews at the corporate headquarters of twenty-four of the twenty-five companies and, owing to scheduling conflicts, telephone interviews at the remaining company. For all interviews, I requested and included the senior available HR executive.

My interview protocol followed two lines of inquiry. First, I asked about overall human resource strategy and its relationship to corporate strategy, including such matters as mission and vision statements and strategic and annual planning. Second, I asked about specific HR practices, focusing on recruiting and hiring, compensation and benefits, work environment, training and education, employee participation (communications and feedback, empowerment, and knowledge sharing), recognition and rewards, and performance management and counseling.

The general results of inquiring about overall strategy were not unexpected. Most of the best companies seek to align their human resource strategy with corporate strategies and business goals. In some cases, HR goals and objectives are explicitly included in corporate mission and vision statements; in other cases, corporate human resource groups have their own mission and vision statements, carefully composed to be consistent with overarching company statements. In all cases, senior human resource executives play important roles in both strategic and annual planning. Almost always they are participants in the corporate strategic planning process, providing input on the HR consequences of proposed actions. Similarly, they are involved in annual planning, usually shaping requirements for recruiting, compensation, and training, and frequently setting goals for retention.

However, although overall strategies provide useful guidance in acquiring, developing, and retaining high performing employees, it is through specific human resource practices that the best companies actually achieve these objectives. In colloquial terms it comes down to what happens when the rubber meets the road. Thus finding and keeping high performers comes about through implementing a wide range of HR practices in all the traditional employee-related management areas. For each best company it is the sum total of its practices that accounts for its success, and therefore the reasons for that success can be discovered only by examining those specific practices.

Structural Changes Affecting Workers and Work

Standing back from this comprehensive examination of practices and the general principles that can be derived from them, it is possible to see that two major insights, or understandings, inform what the best companies do. First, these companies understand what employees value; second, they know how employees should be treated to obtain their best performance and their commitment. Both insights recognize two major structural changes affecting workers and work that arise from the ongoing shift from industrial to postindustrial status as countries develop economically. The first change is a shift from the predominance of materialist values to the predominance of postmaterialist values. The second change is a shift in the nature of work and the role of workers.

A Change in Values

What employees value is changing. Research in the data from the *World Values Survey* (WVS), measuring values and beliefs during the past three decades in sixty societies representing almost 75 percent of the world's population, indicates a major shift from materialist to postmaterialist values as these societies develop economically, a shift that is strengthening as each new generation grows and matures. As Ronald Inglehart of the University of Michigan has shown in his extensive examination and analysis of the data from the WVS,[15] when countries are industrializing, their inhabitants are strongly materialistic, giving top priority to economic and physical security and the maximization of material gains. Then, as these societies begin to experience the security and benefits of industrialization and continue their development, becoming postindustrial countries, their people become postmaterialistic, shifting "toward an increased emphasis on self-expression, subjective well-being, and quality of life issues."[16] It is not, Inglehart points out, that inhabitants of postindustrial countries are *anti*materialist; they value economic and material security as much as anyone else. However, having grown up under conditions in which survival is taken for granted, they now give higher priority to values that are not explicitly material.

Analysis of the WVS data reveals two further findings that bear importantly on the future evolution of this major change in values. One is that the shift from materialist to postmaterialist values is not a uniquely Western phenomenon. It is found in a variety of societies, including Asian countries whose religious, social, and cultural traditions are very different from those in the West. The other is that the generational differences seen at first in this shift are steadily receding with the passage of time. Inglehart is among those who note that at the time of the first WVS surveys, in 1970 and 1971 (when memories of the Great Depression and World War II were still strong in the numerically dominant cohort groups), materialists outnumbered postmaterialists four to one. At the beginning of the twenty-first century, with post–World War II generations becoming numerically dominant, materialists and postmaterialists seem about equal in number, at least in most developed countries.

Several important conclusions can be drawn about this major change in values from materialist to postmaterialist:

- This is a structural change. Although economic setbacks from time to time slow or even reverse the development of postmaterialist values, their long-term trajectory shows a clear upward trend.

- The shift is occurring everywhere. As more countries pass through their industrial stages, more of their inhabitants will acquire postmaterialist values.

- The numbers who hold materialist views are steadily declining. As older cohort groups retire and depart the workplace, newer generations with postmaterialist views are filling their ranks. Soon, most likely within the next generation, the entire workforce in each developed country will be postmaterialist.

A Change in the Nature of Work and the Role of Workers

Complementing the structural change in values is an equally profound change in the nature of work and the role of workers. Throughout the preindustrial and industrial eras of history, most work centered on the manipulation of physical things and the products derived from them. These were tangible, their properties were known, and their responses under different conditions were generally predictable. Labor—aided by energy-fueled machines in the industrial era—altered and combined these tangible things. The result was a finished product, or a finished part for that product, with a fixed, known value.

In the current postindustrial era, in all developed countries, most work is very different. It deals less with the physical and more with the intellectual, especially with information, which is representational and intangible. In preindustrial and industrial work, labor constructs: things with things; however, in postindustrial work labor connects: information with information, funds with funds, people with people, and each with the other. In postindustrial work, often what is done is incomplete, left to be reworked by others in ways bearing little resemblance to the intentions of those whose work it once was, and almost always work's value is not fixed but variable.

These changes in the nature of work mean equally sweeping changes in the role of workers. The changes put a premium on worker innovation and creativity, flexibility and adaptability. They make it essential to see new connections that will increase value and maximize results—for customers, investors, and fellow employees. Above all, they underline how important it is for workers from the CEO to the plant foreman, line worker, and customer service representative to gather, understand, present, and share information and to develop knowledge of how best to use information.

As Peter Drucker, the father of modern management theory, has written, the shift of work from the tangible to the intangible has not only changed workers from costs to assets, it has also made them a company's most important asset, surpassing its capital and infrastructure.[17] It is the workers of a company who are the repositories of its intangible assets—the information and knowledge about its research, its products and processes, its customers, and its corporate experience of what works and what does not work. Further, it is the workers who create new information and new knowledge, the incubators of the company's future success. In fact the market value of nearly all of today's major corporations—most of them either technological or highly technology dependent—rests largely on such intangible assets.

Chris Williams, former vice president of Human Resources at Microsoft Corporation, the world's leading producer of computer software, made the following calculation for me when we met in mid-December 1999:

> Microsoft has a market capitalization of $450 billion, the largest in the world. If you add up every desk and chair, every computer, every building, every piece of land, everything we own, including the $17 billion or so we have in the bank, it comes to about $30 billion. If you then add in things like goodwill and other financial assets, maybe you'll come up with another $70 billion, if you really struggle. But that means that there is $350 billion more that people have given us credit for that is not there. What is it? Well, it's the stuff in smart people's heads.

Similar calculations could be made for many other large capitalization high-technology companies.

Effects of These Changes on Employment Management Practices

The change in values in the developed countries from materialist to postmaterialist and the concomitant structural change in the nature of work and the role of workers are having major effects on employment management practices. These changes are driving companies to be responsive to the changing attitudes of today's workers toward work content and work's relationship to the rest of their lives, they are mandating new approaches to recruiting and hiring, they are causing a comprehensive reevaluation of employee compensation, and they are revolutionizing corporate training programs.

Conveying the Importance of Work and Valuing Workers Are New Imperatives. Materialists and postmaterialists have different views of what they expect from work. Whereas materialists focus largely on the security and tangible goods they derive from work, postmaterialists want work to be meaningful and challenging, giving them a chance to exercise self-expression, feel a sense of accomplishment, and make a difference. And because economic security for many workers is a given, and because quality of life and subjective well-being have become more important, they seek a supportive work environment that will enable them to balance work with family and other outside interests.

Such expectations of the work environment, insistently arising in polls and surveys, eloquently testify to the dramatic changes occurring in the attitudes and aspirations of today's workers and to the responses expected of employers. These responses include

- Meaningful work, with an opportunity to make a contribution and have an impact
- Respect, and accommodation for nonwork activities
- Supervisors who lead, mentor, and inspire
- Communication, listening, and the opportunity for feedback
- Recognition for what is accomplished

Recruiting and Hiring Are Acknowledging a Changing Workforce and Changing Needs. Today's workforce is changing dramatically in structure and composition. Slowing population growth rates, especially in the developed countries, mean slowing growth, and in some cases a reduction, in workforces. At the same time, lengthening life expectancy means a workforce that is growing steadily older. The influx of immigrants in many developed nations is increasing these countries' proportion of nonnationals, notably in younger age cohorts. In the United States the faster growth of minorities will in time cause their number to exceed the number of non-Hispanic whites. Finally, the increasing participation of women in the workforce will eventually make them close to 50 percent of workers.

Nevertheless, despite these dramatic changes and the economic growth causing them, increased competitive demand for workers is having little effect on worker loyalty. Although multiple jobs have replaced a single job as the norm over a career, satisfaction and commitment remain high, and employee tenure has declined only marginally. What recent surveys show, and what employers need to recognize, is a growing gap between the loyalty workers feel toward their companies and the loyalty they believe their companies feel toward them.

At the same time, postindustrial, intangible work means new skills (abilities in particular activities) and especially new competencies (comprehensive bundles of skills needed for specific tasks). To staff for these needs requires new tools and new techniques for recruiting job candidates and selecting among those recruited.

Compensation Though Still Important Is No Longer the Primary Incentive. Noted management authority Charles Handy points out that "when laborers become assets, the underlying contract with the organization has to change."[18] Indeed, as workers come to understand that their changing roles in postindustrial work give them greater responsibility for making businesses grow and prosper, their views undergo important changes. In general, as in other aspects of life, where responsibility increases so too do expectations and rights. In particular, workers are developing new expectations and asserting new rights about the monetary rewards they receive. Base pay continues to play a leading role, but as workers—from the top down—exercise a greater influence on results, they expect a commensurate share of those results. There is also a growing feeling among employers that appropriate forms of compensation can strengthen employee feelings of *ownership* in an organization, reducing attrition and aiding retention. But the relationship between compensation, performance, and retention has been made more complex by the shift from materialist to postmaterialist values. Realizing this, companies have to know, first, how compensation can best be used to support business strategies and, second, which means of compensation—salaries, cash bonuses, stock shares, stock options—are most effective for which goals. Understanding the changing values of workers provides the surest guidance for managing both these aspects of compensation.

Continuous Learning Is Requiring Continuous Education and Training. Because workers are the repositories of the information and knowledge that make them increasingly every company's greatest asset, especially for intangible work, and because information and knowledge are changing and growing at near exponential rates, continuous education and training have become necessities. Although this varies by company, generally speaking, *training* refers to learning about specific tasks, and it usually occurs within the company, increasingly in informal, on-the-job contexts. *Education* has a much broader reference and is often applied to learning that occurs outside the company though frequently sponsored by the company.

Workers need training in new skills and education in new competencies and regular retraining and further education, and increasingly they are coming to expect it. Companies once feared that too much education and training might prompt newly qualified workers to move on; now companies are beginning to understand that too little will surely lead them to look elsewhere.

In my interviews with managers at the twenty-five best companies, I asked how they were responding in each of these major employment-related practice areas to the dual challenge of finding and keeping high performing employees. Their answers are presented in the following four chapters, which constitute the core of this book and which address:

- Work content and the work environment
- Recruiting and hiring
- Compensation and benefits
- Education and training

Finally, from the best companies' practices in each of these areas some general principles can be drawn, along with some themes that are key to implementing them. These principles and key themes are presented in the concluding chapter.

2

Work Content and the Work Environment

The shift from the predominance of materialist values to the predominance of postmaterialist values discussed in Chapter One means that the content of work and the environment in which it is done are of growing importance. Recent polls of workers make this abundantly clear.

In a 1999–2000 *New York Times* poll of more than 1,000 working adults, 70 percent responded "very important" to the question, "How important to you is having a fulfilling job?" and 27 percent responded "somewhat important," whereas only 2 percent said "not very important" and 1 percent "not at all important." In the same survey, when workers were asked, "If you had to choose between a job that paid very well but gave you little personal satisfaction, and a job that didn't pay very well at all but offered a great deal of personal satisfaction, which would you prefer?" 72 percent choose "low pay/high satisfaction," and 24 percent choose "high pay/low satisfaction."[1]

The Families and Work Institute's *1997 National Study of the Changing Workforce,* with a sample size of 2,877 employees, finds that "the quality of employees' jobs and the supportiveness of their workplaces are far more important predictors of these outcomes [job satisfaction, commitment, loyalty to employer, job performance, and retention] than earnings or fringe benefits."[2] A multinational survey in 1998, commissioned by Gemini Consulting and covering 10,339 workers in ten European countries, Russia, the United

States, and Japan, reported similar results. When ranking five "key attributes in a job," workers in all thirteen countries consistently identified "ability to balance work and personal life" and "work that is truly enjoyable" as the top two items.[3]

Similar conclusions have been reached by leading authorities in the human resource field. Jac Fitz-enz, founder of the Saratoga Institute and author of many books on human resource measurement and performance, lists "interesting challenging work" and "an exciting, fun place to come to every day" as two of the five essentials that create an employer of choice.[4] Jeffrey Pfeffer, exploring what it means "to put people first," writes, "Perhaps most importantly, putting people first entails ensuring that those in leadership positions have people-oriented values and manage in ways consistent with building high performance work environments."[5]

In the interviews I conducted in the twenty-five best companies, the managers with whom I spoke understood very well the implications of what these polls and studies are saying about what workers value and want. They know that to find and keep the high performing employees they need, they have to make clear the importance of the work they offer and the value they place on the workers doing it. What this means in practice is a wide range of activities, varying considerably from company to company but intended to convey the significance of the work the company is doing and to create a work environment that values, elevates, and recognizes those doing it.

As I listened to their descriptions of what they were doing, several shared themes emerged:

- The importance of meaningful work
- Respect for the individual and attention to work-life balance
- The critical role of supervisors
- The importance of communication and feedback
- The need for and value of recognition

The Importance of Meaningful Work

What are the practices that the best companies develop and implement to enable employees to feel that the work they do is meaningful? The most important and frequently mentioned are conveying the value and uniqueness of the company's products and services, giving employees autonomy and freedom in their work, permitting risk taking and tolerating mistakes, and using performance management processes.

Conveying the Value and Uniqueness of Products and Services

All companies have the opportunity to convey the value and uniqueness of their products and services, but they do so differently depending on what they are providing and for what purposes. For those best companies involved in the rapidly growing fields of information and communication technology, meaningful work means being able to participate in the development and growth of products that are affecting the lives of literally millions of people. At Microsoft, Chris Williams, former vice president of Human Resources, can say, "If you want your software to show up on 300 million desktops, there are very few places where you can make that happen; but that happens here quite regularly." These companies also offer unique opportunities for creation and innovation. At Sun Microsystems, a leading maker of workstation computers, storage devices, and servers for computer networks and web sites, Jim Moore, director of Workforce Planning and Development at the time of our interview, told me: "Most people who come here want to achieve. They want to be part of a winning team. They want to contribute to some new innovation. They want to be part of this great thing called the Internet."

One important way these companies, and companies like them, can convey the importance of what they do is older than the written word itself. They can tell stories of exemplary events and achievements, stories that in time take on the stuff of myth and legend, deeply woven into the fabric of a company's culture. At Cisco Systems, the world's number one supplier of computer networking products, Barbara Beck, the former senior vice president for Human Resources, spoke movingly about the role of stories in building Cisco's culture for its employees: "How do you get your senior management team to build the culture? If you have them tell stories about who we are, how we are trying to create this company, if you let them give examples—I think that is what is so critical. . . . It's about the management team finding the stories, building the stories, and telling them in new ways as often as they can."

In the same way, creating attractive exhibits of a company's past, as well as of its current products and services, conveys an impression of growth and accomplishment over time— even over a relatively short time—and helps demonstrate the importance and significance of the work it is doing. Before my interviews at the MBNA Corporation, the Wilmington, Delaware, financial services giant, I was taken on a tour of its beautifully designed museum, which proudly showcased the highlights in the history of a company not yet two decades old. In Toyota City, Japan, after I met with a group of senior executives at Toyota Motor Corporation, the country's largest automaker and number three in the world, I was escorted through a spacious exhibition hall, featuring not only the history of the company's early products but also models of what was on its drawing boards for the next decade, with vivid depictions of how these products would not only benefit those who bought them but preserve the environment as well.

At both companies these displays, which used state-of-the-art video and diorama technology, were being viewed by as many employees (often from the field and sometimes with families in tow) as visitors. When I asked about justifying the costs of these impressive exhibits, the replies were the same. Each company reckoned that its display cost far less than the value of the positive feelings it instilled in employees.

For the health care best companies, meaningful work is found in the creation of products and services that save lives, ease suffering, and improve the quality of life. Merck & Co., Inc., America's largest drugmaker, proudly and prominently reminds its employees of the credo of its founder, George W. Merck, "Medicine is for the people . . . not the profits," and from its headquarters, throughout its laboratories, and among its salesforce, it motivates its employees by reinforcing the role their work plays in helping people when they need help most.

At Amgen, the world's largest biotechnology firm, where meaningful work is considered a major attraction for new staff, that meaning is reinforced in part through visits from people who have been helped by Amgen products. In the words of Ilana Meskin, senior director of Human Resources, "At staff meetings, where we've actually had patients come speak to us, there is not a dry eye in the house when you hear about people who have been on our products and who have been helped by them to live a better quality life; and when you hear that, you feel you want to get up in the morning and come to work."

Even in more traditional blue-collar manufacturing industries, there are ways to convey the value and uniqueness of products. Harley-Davidson, of Milwaukee, Wisconsin, has been making its legendary "hogs" for nearly a century, and it deliberately seeks opportunities to link its employees with the unique lifestyle its products exemplify. There is, as might be expected, an attractive museum showing the evolution over the decades of the firm's famous motorcycles; there is a company store, with a 20 percent discount for employees on all products, including the bikes. Even better, the company pays for its employees to attend bike meets and roundups throughout the United States, coopting them as customers (approximately 50 to 60 percent are riders) and inculcating them with the Harley lifestyle.

Giving Employees Autonomy and Freedom in Their Work

There is a direct positive relationship between the amount of control employees feel they have over their work and how meaningful that work is to them. The more autonomy they feel they have, the more of a contribution they think they are making. With feelings of contribution comes pride, and with pride comes satisfaction. In 1999, a Roper Starch Worldwide survey that asked 1,122 college-educated working adults about expectations and reality in the workplace found that "people strongly associate those promises [of authority to define their work and power to make important decisions about it] with the ability to find meaning in their work."[6]

At Compuware Corporation, a longtime maker of testing, development, and management software for stand-alone mainframe computers, the "core philosophy" for employee involvement is summed up in this succinct phrase, "What would you do if it was your business?" As Denise Knobblock, executive vice president for Human Resources and Administration, explains: "All employees have input into the planning process for their areas. Each unit basically has meetings with its folks to determine what the strategy is going to be, let's say, for a particular product or a particular office. Then they meet and develop their own business plan, and then they take it forward."

At pharmaceutical companies, the development of drugs necessarily requires considerable freedom and autonomy, especially in laboratories. Amgen creates multidisciplinary "product development teams," each of which oversees the development of a particular drug over a four-, five-, or six-year period, from the start of trials through its submission to the Federal Drug Administration and ultimately its launch, when it is then handed over to marketing. David Kaye, Amgen's associate director of Corporate Communications, believes that such extensive empowerment of employees not only contributes to the meaningfulness they feel in their work but also is the most important contributor to both high performance and the retention of key employees. "The opportunity to have the kind of input that most staff at Amgen have into what they do and how they do it and to have the responsibility they are given is really what stimulates people here."

For Wal-Mart Stores, retail juggernaut and the world's largest private employer with more than one million workers, empowerment is

a way of life. The company describes its culture as one of "empowerment and open communication," and it proudly states, "Wal-Mart is
an organization whose strength lies in the belief that extraordinary
results can come through empowering ordinary people." Kevin
Harper, vice president, People Division, Wal-Mart Operations, told
me that empowerment starts at the first rung of the corporate ladder,
the retail store, where the store manager has considerable autonomy
in the purchasing and marketing of merchandise, and that it rises
from there through the ranks of the organization. Wal-Mart's goal is
to present opportunities to its employees—"associates" the company
calls them—that allow them to make a difference. Through this empowerment, the company gives meaning to their work.

In the airline business, empowerment is most visible on the front
lines, where employees come face-to-face with customers. Singapore Airlines (SIA), a perennial winner of number one ratings for
its excellent service, understands that an important part of its success arises from the autonomy and freedom it gives its employees,
particularly those with customer contact. Loh Meng See, senior
vice president Human Resources at SIA, says, "We train and develop our staff to have the attitude that if a decision is for the good
of the passenger, for the good of the reputation of the company,
they should proceed. . . . When they do, they have the opportunity
to flourish, the opportunity to excel, and that is all important to
their performance and to their retention."

Permitting Risk Taking and Tolerating Mistakes

When more employees have a degree of autonomy, the risk that
mistakes will be made spreads further into the organization. Thus
the necessary corollary to giving employees autonomy and freedom
in their work is tolerating mistakes, and this is what almost all the
best companies do.

At some of these companies, management simply believes that
risk taking is an attribute of the kind of person the company wants

to hire for its health and growth. Chris Williams at Microsoft says, "We hire people for taking risks. One of the things we screen for is people who are driven to do that. Now it is fair to say that when someone has a spectacular failure, sometimes that will hang over that person's head. But usually we've hired the kind of people who just get right back up on the horse and go at it again."

At MBNA Corporation, Ken Pizer, senior executive vice president, puts it succinctly, "People who don't make any mistakes are people who don't do anything." Ron Watson, Compuware's director of Human Resources, approvingly told me of the frequently noted words of company chairman and CEO Peter Karmanos questioning whether people who do not make any mistakes are really pushing themselves to do everything they can do. "If he sees that people aren't making mistakes," Watson says, "then he wonders if we are pushing the envelope, if we are trying things that are out of the norm."

For other best companies, permitting risks and tolerating mistakes are important parts of learning. At Intel Corporation, the world's top semiconductor maker, Tony Fox, manager of Intel University, told me: "We absolutely believe that it is important for people to try things and to take informed risks. We recognize that one of the primary ways that you learn things is by bumping into things." Amgen's Ilana Meskin said simply, "Failure is really just learning."

For Sun Microsystems, tolerating mistakes was the route to one of its most successful products. In the words of Jim Moore: "If you look at the history of Java [a programming language allowing users to write software across any operating system], it was a disaster, it was a total mess, lots of failures. But the CEO stuck with those who created it, and ultimately they turned out something successful."

At still other best companies, permitting risk and accepting failure is a way of showing that the worker is as important as the work, if not more so. At Cisco, where stories are valued for building the culture of the company, Barbara Beck tells the story of an employee working for her who, against her advice, was nonetheless permitted to pursue an initiative that indeed failed. When the distraught employee came to see her, Beck first consoled the employee, saying, "If you weren't doing that, you wouldn't be working hard enough. I don't want you here because you agree with me. I want you here because you add more than I do." Then Beck talked with CEO John Chambers, who promptly visited the employee in her office, reassured her about what she had done, and told her about some of the mistakes he himself had made.

Using Performance Management Processes

Performance management processes, widely used by companies around the world, can ensure that corporate goals are being met as effectively and efficiently as possible. When used with employees they typically involve setting goals, monitoring progress toward goal achievement, and evaluating results. These results are then fed back to the employees, usually with rewards or guidance or both, and new goals are set for the next time period. But the best companies do even more with performance management. In their hands it becomes a tool to show employees the connection between what they do and the strategic goals of the organization, demonstrating the importance of their work. At the same time, companies can learn from employees what they value in what they do. In the words of a leading writer on the subject, Dick Grote of the University of Dallas Graduate School, "organizations now see performance management systems as having tremendous power to transform the culture of the corporation."[7]

It was in my interviews with executives of the best companies outside the United States that I found the broadest use of performance management, including enabling employees to feel their work is meaningful. At the Toyota Motor Corporation, Mitsuo Kinoshita, managing director and member of the board, explains that each year "we let every employee write his or her own mission statement, and at the end of the year we do the appraisal, or the evaluation, and the result is reflected in the next year's mission statement and in the next year's activity of the individual person." Involving each worker in a discussion of his or her role in the workplace, Kinoshita points out, is a basic pillar in Toyota's human resource philosophy.

At the Taiwan Semiconductor Manufacturing Company (TSMC), the world's largest dedicated semiconductor foundry, S. H. Lee, vice president for Human Resources, describes the firm's performance management and development (PMD) process as "the very key for people management." The PMD process combines development, recognition, and compensation, and its objective is to maximize the employee's performance and potential and to align individual goals with company goals. It is seen as a "partnership between supervisor and employee," where responsibility for performance is shared and the employee is encouraged, and expected, to provide feedback. When I asked if this was happening, Lee replied, "It's going to take a lot of effort because of the Asian culture's emphasis on seniority and hierarchy and on face-saving. But we are doing better, and our belief is that the more we work on it, the more it will happen."

In the European best companies I also found extensive use of performance management. The Royal Dutch/Shell Group, the world's second-largest publicly traded oil company; LM Ericsson, a leading manufacturer of telecommunications systems; and Nokia, the world's number one cellular telephone maker all had comprehensive performance management processes that emphasized employee involvement and commitment to corporate goals. But the most comprehensive process was that of Novo Nordisk, a Danish company that is a leading maker of health products (primarily for the treatment of diabetes, including most of the world's insulin) and industrial enzymes. Novo Nordisk's performance management process, *The Novo Nordisk Way of Management,* is designed to ensure that the strategic and operational thinking of the company is accountably put into practice. In the words of Henrik Gürtler, corporate executive vice president: "All companies have beautiful value and policy statements. What is missing typically, and what we missed in our company earlier, is a credible way of following up, of saying to our personnel, 'We are not coming here to judge you but to help you realize you can improve year by year.'"

As described in *The Novo Nordisk Way of Management*, the unique vehicle for this follow-up is a group of fourteen high-level "facilitators"—experienced businesspeople recruited as best performers from the company's various divisions and affiliates. Appointed for three-year terms and reporting directly to Gürtler, they individually visit the company's business units and conduct an audit of performance in a number of specified policy areas. Working with the local management of the units they visit, they then evaluate what they find, measuring the results against company plans and criteria. And they do even more. "The reason why we call them facilitators," Gürtler explains, "is that their task is not just to come and say you're not performing well. They are expected to stay with the operating units, rectifying whatever shortcomings they find and helping them improve step by step. In this way we make damn sure we walk the talk."

Respect for the Individual and Attention to Work-Life Balance

In many of the best companies, respect for the individual is set forth in policy statements asserting the dignity and value of the employees. Some companies go even further, fostering an egalitarian ethic by giving all employees a common title and by eliminating hierarchical perquisites. In a few, employees are made the company's first priority, on the assumption that this focus will ultimately best serve all the other stakeholders. In most, respect for the individual is then explicitly implemented through work-life balance programs, special facilities to accommodate and ease dealing with nonwork matters, and company events and activities.

Policy Statements

For many of the best companies, valuing employees begins with a policy statement that makes such respect a key vision or goal. Here are a few examples from some of the best companies:

- Harley-Davidson: "Respect the individual" (one of five core values).

- Starbucks: "Provide a great work environment and treat each other with respect and dignity" (the first of six guiding principles in the mission statement).

- Shell: "Honesty, integrity, and respect for people are our three core values."

- Singapore Airlines: "Concern for staff" (one of six core values). The description of this value states in part, "We value our staff and care for their well-being. We treat them with respect and dignity."

For others among the best companies, the high value placed on employees emerges strongly, and often spontaneously, in the words of their senior executives:

- Capital One Financial Corporation's David Willey, senior vice president for Corporate Financial Management and treasurer: "Having the right people is the key to Capital One's success."

- Microsoft's Chris Williams: "When you get good people, they attract other good people."

- Cisco's Barbara Beck: "I really believe that one of the things that keeps great people is working with great people."

- Novo Nordisk's Mads Ovlisen, president and CEO, says the strong values that drive his company "reflect the belief and confidence we have in each employee, which day after day turn out to be justified through the results we achieve."

- Toyota's Mitsuo Kinoshita: "The company cannot survive without the best human resources, and for this reason we respect and we cherish our employees."

Some of the best companies demonstrate their respect for their employees by deliberately referring to them, individually and collectively, with a single term. In this way, they seek a feeling of equality that puts everyone on the same level and that is often proudly reinforced by the absence of such symbols of status as reserved parking spaces, titles on doors, executive dining rooms, and dress codes reflecting ranks. "Language is powerful and it telegraphs a lot about your beliefs," says Coleman Peterson, executive vice president of the People Division at Wal-Mart. "Everyone [here] is an associate; hierarchy never made anyone feel good, except the people at the very top."[8] Capital One and Ingram Micro also conspicuously refer to all their employees as "associates"; at Starbucks, the preferred term for the company's people is "partners."

At CDW Computer Centers, a leading U.S. direct marketer of computer products, employees are called "coworkers" and are considered the company's first priority. In the words of Art Friedson, vice president of Coworker Services, "CDW believes that the level of engagement and enthusiasm of our coworkers is our competitive advantage." CDW backs this up in ways that range from the vital to the symbolically memorable. "If we have to look at cost cutting, we don't even discuss the likelihood of layoffs," says Friedson; "major executive pay cuts would come before any rank-and-file jobs are lost." And when CDW had no choice but to pass on higher medical costs with higher health care premiums, it softened the blow by hand delivering to each coworker a crisp new one hundred–dollar bill. This employee-first philosophy echoes the view of a well-known maverick among senior executives, the chairman, president, and CEO of Southwest Airlines, Herb Kelleher: "You have to recognize that people are still most important. How you treat them determines how they treat people on the outside";[9] and it endorses the corollary advice of the popular management writer Bob Nelson: "If you're treating employees badly, eroding their self-esteem, they'll turn around and do that to customers."[10]

Work-Life Balance Programs

It was Sigmund Freud who suggested that the prescription for a healthy person should be *Lieben und Arbeiten* (love and work). The contemporary version is probably best expressed as *work-life balance* and, as the following examples illustrate, recent surveys of worker attitudes, both within and outside the United States, consistently show the steadily growing importance of making work-life balance a high corporate priority:

- The Heldrich *Work Trends Winter 1999 Survey*, employing 1,000 telephone interviews with U.S. adult workers in the forty-eight contiguous states, reports as its first key finding that "workers rate the ability to balance work and family as *the most important aspect of a job with 97 percent of workers indicating that it is important* and 88 percent indicating that it is very or extremely important."[11]

- The 2000 *Randstad North American Employee Review*, in a study of more than 6,000 North American employees, finds "62 percent prefer a boss who understands when they need to leave work for personal reasons over one who could help them grow professionally," and "51 percent prefer a job that offers flexible hours over one that offers an opportunity for advancement."[12]

- In the United Kingdom, a survey of 5,500 managers, carried out by work-life consultants WFD in conjunction with *Management Today*, reports that "the secret of real employee happiness is not a big paycheck, it is finding a successful balance between work life and home life."[13]

- In 1998, Citibank surveyed 2,400 of its employees in fifty-three cities and thirty countries to determine their attitudes toward their work environment. What it found was "a consistent theme in each of the countries surveyed: the need for better balance between people's work and personal lives."[14]

Yet in 1999, The Conference Board found that 656 CEOs of major corporations around the globe ranked "helping employees achieve work/life balance" dead last on a list of fifteen management challenges, tied for fifteenth place with "community relations across multiple regions," with only 1 percent selecting it.[15]

Each of the twenty-five best companies whose senior managers I interviewed for this book recognizes the high importance of work-life balance to employees, and most have comprehensive programs, within well-defined strategic frameworks, to put that recognition into practice. These programs generally focus on two kinds of activities: flexibility in work hours and workplaces, and employee assistance programs.

Flexibility in Work Hours and Workplaces. Several factors are spurring the increase of flexibility in work hours and workplaces. The first is simply that more employees, seeking greater discretion in the time they spend on nonwork activities, are demanding it. This is especially true as more women—particularly those with young children—join the labor force. Second, in a steadily tightening labor market, employers are finding that to stay competitive in hiring they must be more flexible. Finally, and notably with regard to workplaces, advancing telecommunication and computer technologies are rapidly creating new opportunities for flexibility.

Flexibility in work hours usually means either *flextime*, in which employees work a set number of hours per day but vary their starting or ending times, or *compressed work weeks*, in which a full week's work is accomplished in fewer than five days. In the United States, according to the Bureau of Labor Statistics (BLS) of the Department of Labor, the share of full-time workers with flexible schedules has increased dramatically, from 12.4 percent in 1985 to 27.6 percent in 1997.[16]

The best companies offer wide tolerance for flexibility in work hours but exhibit considerable range in implementing this tolerance and have different rationales for doing so. Kevin Harper explains that it is Wal-Mart's policy to have a lot of flexibility, especially in its stores, where work schedules can be arranged to be helpful to associates (employees). Microsoft's policy is even more explicit and universal. The "jobs" page of the company's Web site states: "Microsoft also recognizes that our employees have lives outside the workplace—whether they are parents juggling multiple responsibilities or musicians in bands that play into the wee hours of the morning, employees design their work schedules based on their lifestyles."

Cisco's policy on flexibility, more narrowly defined and also stated on its Web site, is to support "flextime, flexwork, and part-time work schedules, depending on the particular work requirements in the department and the manager's discretion." MBNA's *Guide to Employment and Benefits* states: "It's sometimes possible to allow for flexibility in scheduling work to help people meet personal and family responsibilities. You may be able to arrange a temporary or permanent alternate or a reduced work schedule." Wendy Yarno, Merck's senior vice president for Human Resources, says, "If an employee needs a flexible work arrangement and you [the manager] can do it and still get the job done, then try to do it," and David Kaye, alluding to Amgen's less formal flextime policy, states, "It's really done on a case-by-case basis."

At some best companies the rationale for flexibility in work hours is explicit. Dennis Liberson, executive vice president for Human Resources at Capital One, says, "We do a lot informally . . . we tend to encourage employees to work through arrangements that allow us to retain our good performing people," and CDW's Art Friedson points out, "We certainly want all these flextime and part-time arrangements available to [the employees] because retaining them is hugely important to us." At BMC Software, one of the world's leading software vendors, Johnnie Horn, senior vice president for Human Resources, says, "Flexibility in our market is an absolute necessity."

Although there is widespread agreement on the need for flexibility in work hours, flexibility in physical workplaces is more controversial. Here the differences center especially on telecommuting, particularly from home, a practice made increasingly available by the proliferation of personal computers, laptops, and wireless telephones—an availability that will grow further as more plentiful bandwidth emerges.

The arguments supporting telecommuting are undeniable:

- Reduction in infrastructure costs, especially real estate and office occupancy costs.
- Increased sense of independence and control by employees over their work-life balance.
- Potential edge in hiring and retaining desired employees, including tapping such worker pools as the physically handicapped and primary caregivers of young children.
- Elimination of commuting time and—a social benefit—a possible reduction of the environmental costs associated with commuting.
- Elimination of office environment distractions.
- Potential for increasing productivity.

But there are also downsides to telecommuting:

- Loss of direct interaction traditionally important to managing and evaluating performance.
- Elimination of frequently vital physical adjuncts to communication, including tone of voice, facial expression, and body language.
- Loss of visibility and of direct supervisory and peer relationships, often critical to promotion and advancement.
- Increased difficulty of inculcating the mores of company culture.

- Costs of equipping alternative workplaces and of training people to operate in them.
- Distractions of home or nonoffice environments.
- Potential loss of productivity.

Hence it is not surprising that among the twenty-five best companies, telecommuting has received only a limited and sometimes wary acceptance.

At Microsoft, where one might expect the practice to be widespread, Chris Williams says: "One of the things we like to be able to do is to go down the hall and open the door and sit down and have a frank discussion about the problem we've got. So, although some people are doing [telecommuting] a couple of days a week, it is not widespread, and it is not something we are going out of our way to make an important aspect of how we operate." But he adds that "because of advances in technology and DSL," the attitude toward telecommuting "probably has a better chance of changing sooner than other flexibility practices." Similarly, at another major information technology player, Sun Microsystems, Jim Moore says: "We do allow people to work at home; but we don't encourage it. We don't have a formal policy on it. But one of the things we do have that is quite popular is called 'drop-in centers,' all around the Bay Area in our different campuses, where you can go and log on to your workstation and do your e-mail."

At MBNA, Terri Murphy, formerly in Human Resources and now director of Marketing, explains that one reason telecommuting has not gone very far is that the company must limit access to proprietary customer data; "also the nature of where we have come from is face-to-face working with people, rallying around the goal, building esprit de corps." CDW's Art Friedson states, "We're not doing [telecommuting] yet, with the exception of a couple of IT people occasionally. Such a big part of our company is our culture, and until recently we were always under one roof." Then he adds, almost wistfully, "We just took office space downtown. So one of the only founding philosophies that has really fallen by the wayside is the one-roof philosophy, and another pillar of that philosophy will be falling when we start doing work at home."

In the best companies outside the United States, there is even greater ambivalence about telecommuting. In Denmark, Novo Nordisk makes limited use of telecommuting, which Henrik Gürtler explains by saying, "People find this rather awkward, because every-thing that makes this company tick is really personal interaction." He does use telecommuting to stay in touch with the company's fourteen globe-trotting facilitators who report to him, but he notes, "If we did not meet three times a year to touch each other, so to speak, it would not work." At Ericsson, in neighboring Sweden, Pär-Anders Pehrson, vice president for Leadership and Culture, says, "Given the kind of company Ericsson is, to take an approach on telecommuting wouldn't be appropriate." But he adds a prag-matic caveat: "It's very much dependent on the work you do. If you need to meet with other people, of course you need to be more pre-sent in the office. If you have a more independent job, where your work is actually done on the computer, then who cares where you sit? If you want to sit in your kitchen or if you want to sit in your office, it's your call."

In Asia, as might be expected because of the traditional impor-tance of direct personal interaction, there is even less use of tele-commuting. When I asked S. H. Lee of TSMC about the practice, he replied: "For two reasons we do not do that. One is that our kind of work requires a lot of collaboration; the other is that the average home in Taiwan is small, and with extended family living together, it is not conducive to telecommuting." Loh Meng See's answer to my question whether Singapore Airlines had people who were telecommuting was, "Not yet." Those with personal computers at home, he and his colleagues explained, used them to "build up their knowledge . . . and also to access information." In Japan—where very limited and very expensive residential floor space will probably inhibit the growth of home offices for some time to come—Mitsuo

Kinoshita explained that Toyota has not "implemented telecommuting" because most of the company's employees live close by and because most of its offices and buildings are concentrated in one area. Figure 2.1 summarizes the state of telecommuting in the twenty-five best companies.

So here is a work-life balance program, the *virtual office* of telecommuting, that is certain to be increasingly implemented and that is also uniquely challenging for both company performance and employee independence. As Charles Handy has written, "Paradoxically, the more virtual an organization becomes, the more its people need to meet in person."[17] A similarly thought-provoking contrast is presented in management consultant Mahlon Apgar IV's *mobility paradox:* "we are moving from an era in which people seek connections with one another to an era in which people will have to decide when and where to disconnect—both electronically and socially."[18] It may be that just as telephones supplemented but did not end personal interaction (as some nineteenth-century forecasters had feared), telecommuting will become simply another means for people to communicate, without removing either the desire or the need to meet in person.

FIGURE 2.1. Telecommuting in the Best Companies.

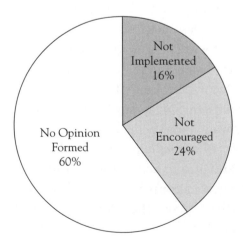

Employee Assistance Programs. Employee assistance programs (EAPs) began in the United States in the 1940s, principally to deal with alcohol abuse. Since then they have expanded to help employees deal with a wide range of matters—usually outside the workplace—that can affect their work. Often combining both in-house and outsourced resources, EAPs work to identify and resolve workers' problems by providing short-term counseling, referral to specialized professionals or groups, and follow-up services. According to the Employee Assistance Professional Association, Inc., in Alexandria, Virginia, the number of EAP providers has doubled in the last decade to more than 20,000, up from 10,000 in 1991.[19] Increasingly, EAPs can be accessed through the Internet, a medium that some experts believe will be more comfortable for employees seeking help, further extending EAP utilization. The BLS, in its most recent *Employee Benefits Survey* reports that 61 percent of full-time employees in medium and large private U.S. establishments were offered employee assistance as a benefit in 1997.[20]

Like most corporations, each of the best companies offers some form of employee assistance program or plan. Several of these are unusually broad and comprehensive, demonstrating a deliberate strategic commitment to the support of family and work-life balance.

AFLAC Incorporated, the leading provider of supplemental insurance sold at the work site in the United States and the largest foreign insurer in Japan, emphasizes family in its mission and gives it pride of place as the first of five main goals: "To maintain a family-oriented corporate culture." In keeping with this goal it has an employee assistance program that holds regular information sessions (including a monthly "lunch and learn" led by outside professionals) and is a resource that can be tapped for aid on any matter affecting family well-being and work-life balance.

Compuware also speaks of itself as a family-oriented company. It has created LifeWorks, a comprehensive, toll-free call-in service "for information and/or counseling on just about anything that makes work life and personal life difficult to balance," according to the company's benefits pamphlet. Denise Knobblock says that LifeWorks is "not just an employee assistance line for typical issues that one might deal with; it's for your whole life. We care about the individual, about what happens at home, whether it's your refrigerator breaking down or whether you're having problems with your child or your car. If it's an issue that will affect you in your daily life, we try to make it easy for you to deal with it."

At MBNA, employees are given the company's *Life-Events Guide*, designed to help answer the question, "What do I do if . . . ?" from a benefits perspective. The guide addresses marriage, divorce, birth or adoption, a transfer or move, disability, and death in the family. For each of these six categories, a chart lists (1) the applicable benefit area, (2) options the employee may want to pursue, and (3) what to do. The last page of the guide contains contact information, including various hot lines to call. BMC's generous Employee Assistance Plan takes yet a different approach, providing "up to six free counseling sessions per family member per calendar year as well as referral services for legal and work/life consultations."

An even more comprehensive effort has been undertaken by Intel, where the HR department has its own dedicated research staff of about ten people. Part environmental scanners and part problem solvers, these researchers examine all issues affecting human resources, doing both benchmarking and targeted research. With a broad charter to cover matters both inside and outside the workplace, they are particularly attentive to work-life balance issues, seeking to identify well in advance those likely to have a future impact. As Tony Fox describes the unit's proactive aim, "You may not be feeling the pain about this right now, but we think we need to put some plans in place to help the organization be positioned for success in the long run."

Special Facilities

One major way that corporations respond to employees' desires to achieve better balance between their work lives and their home lives is to create special facilities, usually on site. Often these are facilities for dependent care, but such facilities are also established for physical fitness and sports and for many kinds of routine services that consume nonwork time. Usually they are found at corporate headquarters or high-employment sites, but more and more companies are, of necessity, making them available at smaller field locations.

Dependent Care. To date the major emphasis in dependent care has been on children, especially as more young mothers enter the labor force. Recent Conference Board publications indicate that 65 percent of U.S. women with children under five are employed, and that the demand for child-care services in the United States and Canada, although slowing in rate of growth, will continue to rise in absolute numbers. Also rising, in *both* rate of growth and absolute numbers, will be demand for elder care. By 2005, 37 percent of U.S. workers are likely to be more concerned with caring for a parent than for a child.[21]

Outside the United States, particularly in Western Europe, child-care programs tend to be government sponsored. In America, child care is mainly private, and most of the U.S. best companies offer child-care assistance in some form. The question of whether to use on-site facilities, however, calls forth strong, even passionate, arguments both for and against.

David Kaye describes the thinking behind Amgen's new child-care facility, twice as big as its previous one: "One of the things we've recognized is that employees with kids often live twenty-five to thirty miles away, and when their kids get sick their mothers or fathers have to run home to pick them up. It's much better to have the children right here. A lot of our employees go over and have lunch with their kids, or they stop in during the day and read stories or participate in their classes. This way they know where their kids are; they don't have to worry about them, and they can be far more productive at work."

Wendy Yarno supports Merck's three on-site child-care facilities on grounds of recruiting as well as productivity: "It's one of our biggest advantages for a lot of people. . . . [Employees] think they are extremely well run and that the care is outstanding. We're probably going to add two more because in recruiting scientists we've found it can be difficult to get the ones we want if they don't have a place to put their children." Moreover, for employees, "Just knowing that their kids are close, being able to bring a cake in on their birthdays, being able to go take care of them if they get sick—I think that contributes a lot to their peace of mind and their productivity."

Genentech, the West Coast biotech giant, boasts "one of the largest corporate-sponsored day-care centers in the country." MBNA was noted by *Fortune* in its January 2000 "100 Best Companies to Work For" compilation for its six child-care centers. AFLAC cites its child-care center (with a "parents advisory council") as one of the features of its "supportive work environment," and in October 1999, CDW proudly announced the opening of its 33,000-square-foot, onsite child-care and fitness center.

But several of the best companies just as vigorously argue against on-site child-care facilities. Johnnie Horn points out that BMC provides child-care assistance to its employees, but for several reasons she strongly opposes creating an on-site center: "First," she says, "day care has a very limited appeal, only until children reach school age because most of our children live miles from BMC. Second, there are a number of liabilities associated with it. Third, day care is not our core business."

Microsoft also has chosen not to have an on-site day-care program. "It is something we examine literally every six months," says Chris Williams, "partly because the business is changing so much. But frankly we're not a day care company; we write software for a living. Also, if we built a center here [in the King County's East Side corporate headquarters area], we could expect to serve perhaps 200 to 300 children if it was a good, large facility; but with 16,000 employees in the area—many of them of childbearing age—we would have a [significantly larger] obligation [than that]. So instead, we have invested a great deal of time and energy into quality referral services."

Intel, with its in-house HR research group, has reached a similar conclusion. "We did benchmarking," says Tony Fox, "and one of the things we found was that many times companies with day-care facilities had huge waiting lists. It could be buying us more problems and frustrations than it provides [benefits]. So we work within the community to ensure that our employees have access to good day care; that seems like a better use of our energy." Sun Microsystems, which enables its employees to use pretax dollars for child-care expenses, has an even more pragmatic reason for not providing either on-site or outsourced facilities: "We keep looking at it and we keep deciding not to do it," says Jim Moore; "we just don't think the investment would produce a return for us. It wouldn't help stockholder equity."

Elder care, for several reasons, is potentially a much greater dependent-care need than child care. Aging parents are likely to need care longer than small children, and their needs likely will grow with age. These needs will be less predictable, more erratic, probably more repetitive, and more expensive to meet. Responding to them will take an increasing toll on family members who are caregivers. By 1999, according to a survey by Hewitt Associates, 47 percent of large companies were offering elder-care programs, up from only 20 percent in 1993.[22]

In most of the best companies, although elder-care programs are just beginning, they have management's attention. CDW, despite its employees' low average age, is probably furthest along. Art Friedson explains: "We hire a vendor who will work one-on-one with any of our coworkers, at that coworker's request, to help find elder-care arrangements. It costs us $245 a head whenever we use it; but there is no limit on the number of times you can use it. If the demand surfaces for elder care on site, we'll certainly look at it."

AFLAC, in a community where there are good elder-care centers, offers a referral service. Through Harley-Davidson's Dependent Care Spending Account, employees can use pretax dollars (with definitions and restrictions set by U.S. law) to obtain elder-care services. Genentech's retiree health care allowance can also be used for elder care, but Judy Heyboer, now retired from her position as senior vice president for Human Resources, thinks "elder care is probably something that we need to look at further." Similarly, Compuware finds elder care one of the "hot subjects" among employees who call the company's LifeWorks service. Table 2.1 summarizes the incidence of dependent-care programs in the U.S. best companies.

Fitness Centers and Sports Facilities. Fitness and sports centers are also very popular on-site attractions with both employees and management of many of the best companies. First, they are usually well equipped, have no enrollment fees, and are very convenient in terms of both location and hours. Second, management frequently sees them as important adjuncts to corporate wellness or preventive health plans, offering potential savings in medical benefit costs.

Fitness centers and health clubs are the most popular facilities in the best companies, but specific sports activities are occasionally appended. Starbucks, Genentech, and Amgen all offer on-site fitness centers to their employees; Amgen's is open seven days a week. CDW boasts a "state-of-the-art health club," and Dennis Liberson of Capital One speaks glowingly of what he calls "probably the world's greatest amenities complex" in Tampa, Florida. It offers "a gym with two basketball courts, volleyball, weights, and an aerobics room complete with treadmills, cycles, and StairMasters." Compuware adds "spinning" to its fitness offerings, and BMC features outdoor activities such as volleyball, bocce, and putting.

Such facilities are also popular outside the United States. At Nokia, Juhani Hokkanen, senior vice president for Human Resources, says, "In almost every building nowadays we have a fitness center where people can exercise during their breaks and after office hours or before." Singapore Airlines has a sports club and many small-scale fitness clubs at its various office premises. Toyota proudly speaks of its "Toyota Sports Center, a 610,000-square-meter complex of permanent facilities for many sports activities," as well as the "recreational facilities located in and around each of the Toyota plants."

TABLE 2.1. Incidence of Dependent-Care
Programs in U.S. Best Companies.

On-site child-care available	41%
Child-care assistance, but not on site	59
Elder-care assistance available	47
No elder-care assistance available	53

Service Facilities. Many of the best companies provide a variety of service facilities, and even products, as conveniences to save both the time and the pocketbooks of their employees. Some of these offerings are related to the companies' businesses (Harley-Davidson offers an oil change service, Starbucks gives each employee a pound of coffee or box of tea weekly). Others reduce the time employees might otherwise have to spend traveling to do routine errands. Many companies provide food and other consumables, either in subsidized cafeterias or in discount stores. Here are a few examples, illustrating the variety offered:

- Compuware provides laundry service, manicure and massage service, and film processing.
- At Amgen, there is a photo processing center, a floral shop, a gift shop, dry cleaning and shoe repair shops, a subsidized cafeteria, take-home dinners, and a concierge service.
- CDW has a dry cleaning service, free bagels and doughnuts twice a week, and the "Mom's Corner" for new mothers.
- AFLAC employees can eat at a subsidized cafeteria, shop at a fresh fruit and vegetable market every Tuesday, and get precooked holiday meals.
- Toyota's Co-op Association offers Toyota employees and their families various lines of daily necessities at discount rates.

The goal these companies seek is appreciative employees who will perform better and be reluctant to leave. BMC goes the furthest in this effort. The company's "new workplace is not just a place to work," says *Fortune*. "It's a place to live. It's where you can eat, nap, swim, shop, pray, kickbox, drink beer, run your errands, start a romance, get your dental work done, wield plastic lightsabers, and sculpt nude models." Roy Wilson, former BMC senior vice president for Human Resources, says: "I know this is hard to believe, but you do feel like you can get away while you are here. It gives you a balanced life without having to leave."[23]

Company Events

Most of the best companies bring their employees together frequently. Often they hold annual events built around holidays, anniversaries, or seasonal changes. Occasionally they celebrate the achievement of major milestones. Always they seem to highlight traditions—customs that may have begun casually but that now are enduring and anticipated. These company events serve to develop and maintain a favorable work environment in several ways. First, by bringing together all employees, from the highest to the lowest ranking, they build camaraderie and communicate the idea that everyone is responsible for the company's success. Second, they reinforce the company's values and goals, and they contribute to the growth of its corporate culture. Finally, they are a means of thanking employees and in turn earning their appreciation.

At CDW, says Art Friedson, "We gear our celebrations towards families because we understand what an important part people's families play in our success." The biggest of these celebrations are the holiday party, with spouses and significant others (whether opposite or same sex), and the annual picnic, focusing on kids but also including extended family members like aunts and uncles and grandmothers and grandfathers. CDW also holds steak and lobster dinners served by members of the executive committee, who themselves eat franks and beans. There is also a "mid-winter hug" and a "spring hug" with either CEO John Edwards or President Gregory Zeman; and when the company reached the $2 billion mark in annual sales for the first time, it hired a jazz band and a caterer and had a big party extending from the lobby to the cafeteria to the warehouse.

AFLAC also involves employees' families. On the first Thursday in December, it hosts a ceremony lighting its tower (the tallest building in town) and offers rides and other activities for children. Its annual Employee Appreciation Week features big breakfasts, dozens of drawings and giveaways, and a day at Six Flags amusement park for family members—all paid for by the company. Compuware has holiday parties too and company picnics geared to families. These events are run by the separate offices, each of which is given a budget and makes its own arrangements. The company celebrated its twenty-fifth anniversary with commemorative t-shirts for employees, and every year since 1980, it has given each employee a gift of cashew nuts.

Amgen, says David Kaye, tries to provide staff with family events "that make people want to continue to work here." There are holiday parties for families and annual trips to Disneyland and other nearby attractions, such as the Santa Barbara Zoo. There are also regular Friday night beer blasts and an annual chili cook-off, the company's most widely attended event. Wal-Mart brings its store managers together for twice-a-year conventions that combine awards and fervent exhortations to achieve new heights in sales; and Harley-Davidson holds weeklong fifth anniversary parties (2003 will see the company's big centennial celebration) that draw over 100,000 riders and submerge a good part of Milwaukee in cacophonous "hog" culture.

Not all the best companies put major efforts into annual or special events, however. Some concentrate instead on the creating a particular everyday work environment. For several the key word defining that environment is *fun*. The seventh of the seven core competencies of its culture that BMC lists on its Web site states: "Last, but not least, our employees truly enjoy what they do. And we've created many opportunities within the workplace for them to have fun." At Sun Microsystems, Jim Moore says: "One of the things that we traditionally have focused on here is having fun. And this is the one work-life matter our CEO tries to talk about a lot. His phrase is 'kick butt and have fun.' So humor is a big thing at Sun; but work-life balance is not something we spend a lot of time on." And Barbara Beck explains that to Cisco's people, "The fun component . . . is not parties. We don't invest a whole lot of time in parties. What matters more is the feeling that we're doing something important."

The Critical Role of Supervisors

At the best companies there is strong and unanimous agreement that supervisors and midlevel managers play a critical role in employee performance and the retention of high performing employees. Ron Watson of Compuware states the performance view unequivocally: "Managers are the ones that touch the employees. We really believe that managers are the key to their performance." Terry Lu, associated vice president at Acer, agrees that supervisors have the most important impact on employee performance—and on employee behavior in general. When it comes to retention, David Finley, senior vice president for Worldwide Human Resources at Ingram Micro, is equally categorical: "The single largest cause for turnover is how I was treated by my boss. That's always the number one category. Money is way down in the middle of the list." CDW's Art Friedson is even more forceful: "The single biggest correlate you can find to turnover is how people feel about their immediate supervisor. No matter what you do, that's the relationship that matters most. If we don't have good supervisors, we've lost the war!"

Opinion polls support the views of these executives; but they also show a gap between expectation and reality and hence the distance companies still have to go in working with their supervisors. The Heldrich Center's *Work Trends Fall 1998 Survey* reports that

75 percent of those polled see "relationship with supervisors" as "extremely important" or "very important,"[24] and the 2000 install-ment of Aon Consulting's United States @Work® survey (called America@Work® in previous years) shows that immediate super-visors have a very strong influence in helping build employees' company spirit and sense of pride in their organization.[25] However, an August 1999 Gallup Poll finds that although 67 percent of respondents were "completely satisfied" with their relations with their coworkers (and only 3 percent "not satisfied"), when asked about a boss or immediate supervisor, the percentage who are "com-pletely satisfied" drops to 47 (with 11 percent "not satisfied").[26] Fur-thermore, Aon Consulting's survey also finds that one in four workers do not think their companies are doing a good enough job of devel-oping managers and supervisors.

Leading management authorities concur on the importance of the supervisory role. Marcus Buckingham and Curt Coffman, au-thors of the best-seller *First, Break All the Rules: What the World's Greatest Managers Do Differently*, examined findings from two major research studies by the Gallup Organization undertaken over a twenty-five-year period. Surveying "over a million employees from a broad range of companies, industries, and countries," they say their research yielded many discoveries, of which the most powerful was that "talented employees need great managers. The talented em-ployee may join a company because of its charismatic leaders, its generous benefits, and its world-class training programs, but how long that employee stays and how productive is he while he is there is determined by his relationship with his immediate supervisor."[27] This finding leads Buckingham and Coffman to the corollary proposition, practically a mantra in their many commentaries on their research: "People join companies, but leave managers."[28]

In the United Kingdom a recent "remarkable and authoritative" study drawing on the work of the Sheffield Effectiveness Program reaches a similar conclusion. "[It] shows decisively that the way peo-ple are managed has a powerful impact on both productivity and profitability. Moreover, the study shows that other management practices commonly associated with performance—such as competitive strategy, technology, market share, Total Quality Management, or R&D strategy—do not have anything like the same effect on performance as people management."[29]

Given the critical role of supervisors, it is revealing to examine what some of the best companies do to select, develop, and retain them.

Selection

Ingram Micro's selection process for new supervisors makes sure that those involved in that process are themselves good supervisors, says David Finley, "rather than just the persons who have been here a long time or the persons who are nice or the persons who are the best technical performers." The foundation for the process is a list of technical-functional and leadership competencies that Ingram Micro has developed through independent research and its own focus groups. It is now in the process of developing an assessment test battery to measure these competencies in entry-level managers. For appointments to higher supervisory positions, the company has a well-tested evaluation tool in the form of an associate (employee) survey with two indices. One measures overall satisfaction; the other, called a "coaching index," enables employees to rank their bosses on eight specific aspects of leadership.

Training and Development

Compuware, according to Denise Knobblock, puts strong emphasis on training line managers and investing in their growth as "the key to adding value for the company." At Sun Microsystems (SMI), goal one (of six) in its human resources "playbook" for fiscal year 2000 is to "improve SMI management effectiveness." The goal is accompanied by this strategic vision: "Build an environment that highly values people management and increases the effectiveness and accountability of Sun's managers. By increasing the effectiveness of people managers, we will positively impact all Sun employees and improve retention and employee satisfaction, stimulate increased productivity, and gain competitive advantage from worldwide recognition as a great place to work."

At a number of the best companies the training that is emphasized for supervisors is leadership training. Raymond V. Gilmartin, chairman, president, and CEO of Merck, has made emphasis on leadership a top priority, believing that it "sets us apart from other companies and gives us a competitive advantage in all aspects of our business." As part of implementing this priority, Merck has established two major leadership training programs—one involving 360-degree feedback—that in two years will extend through all levels of the organization. At Ingram Micro, David Finley explains, leadership development involves "finding truly competent leaders and having them model that competency for the people working for them." Some of the fastest-growing best companies have had an especially acute need for a steadily increasing number of good supervisors. To meet this challenge, CDW, for example, has created Project Lead, a training program it conducts with the Kellogg Graduate School of Management at Northwestern University.

Communication and Engagement

At Genentech, supervisors who talk with their people and provide feedback are the key to effective performance and retention. In the words of Judy Heyboer, "All the things we do to make this a wonderful place to work are background to the fact that you have an individual in your manager who talks to you." At Compuware, having managers "who foster communications, with open dialogue and feedback" is considered critical to high performance. At Shell, John Hofmeister, director of Human Resources, states emphatically that the most important practice for both improving performance and aiding retention is one-on-one engagement between supervisors and those they supervise; and at Ericsson, the sole purpose of the

Ericsson Assessment Center is "to assess, develop and provide feedback from experienced managers to selected high potential young managers on their capabilities and individual capacities for general management positions."

Mentoring

To create better supervisors and improve the way they deal with those they supervise, mentoring has become an important practice in a number of the best companies. Diana Root, director of Human Resources at BMC, believes mentoring is one of the important factors in developing managers; Chris Williams of Microsoft considers "support and mentorship" among the main reasons the company is able to keep high performing people. One of the eight key features of TSMC's performance management and development process is "partnership between supervisor and employee." At AFLAC, the training department is working on a formal mentoring program that will enable supervisors to mentor not only within their own divisions but across divisional lines as well. Finally, Wal-Mart encourages an atmosphere of "support for its associates, by its associates." In the words of Kevin Harper, this unique form of mentoring, "not found elsewhere," means that people in effect "lift each other up." As a result, "they really tend to work one or two levels above their norm."

Rotation

BMC believes that rotating managers through the organization leverages their skills and competencies and produces strong supervisors. Johnnie Horn says she is "a perfect example. I was in HR management, then moved to PM&D [Performance Management and Development] operations management, and now I'm back in HR." Diana Root adds that people at BMC are "looking at what we are doing as a company to grow our top talent and make sure we've got the bench strength, and we know we've got to make planned efforts to move people within the organization." CDW also believes that rotating jobs is a good way to develop supervisors and expose them to different skills. Informal rotation has been so successful that a team is now working on a formal program.

Retention

When companies have good supervisors they want to keep them, and this has led several of the best companies to try to understand better why good supervisors leave and to take steps to keep them. At Compuware, Ron Watson points out that "so many times when people are ready to leave the organization, voluntarily or involuntarily, you sit down with them and you find it's due to the fact that managers haven't had some of the hard discussions they need to have with their employees." To facilitate the retention of valued managers and other employees, Compuware has taken several steps. One is establishing a training program, currently at the pilot stage, on how to have tough conversations with employees. Another is retaining an outside firm to obtain information about reasons for leaving that employees may be reluctant to divulge to company people. "Once our feedback on that is formalized," says Watson, "we plan to do some education and training on what we are learning."

The Importance of Communication and Feedback

The best companies understand that their employees need to be informed and want to be heard, and so they develop and implement communications policies for these purposes. Furthermore, they also understand—explicitly or implicitly—the wisdom of the great communications theorist Colin Cherry, who pointed out that the very word *communicate* means "share," and that in communicating we create unity and are "of one mind."[30] It is this unity, achieved in part through communication, that can be a company's greatest asset in achieving its goals.

Communications theorists explain that at its simplest, communication has three principal elements: a message, a means of transmitting the message, and a network through which the message passes and through which responses can be made. It is appropriate then to organize this discussion of the best companies' communications practices around these three elements.

The Message

Companies have many important messages to communicate to their employees. Some convey information about the firm—such as news of reorganizations, administrative changes, acquisitions and mergers, and new product and service introductions. Others supply employment information—such as news about job postings, benefit and compensation plans, training and education programs, and other services and facilities. Still others are instructional, providing guidance and setting out company expectations for employee responses to important changes, such as reorganizations and the introduction of new technologies. Companies also send celebratory and exhortatory messages, marking milestone achievements and awards and urging the attainment of ambitious goals.

Among the best companies three categories of messages seem especially important for high performance and retention: (1) messages about the company's mission, goals, and business strategy; (2) messages about performance; and (3) messages that build company culture.

Mission, Goals, and Business Strategy. Management experts and the managers they survey agree on the importance of communicating a company's strategic vision to employees. A recent study by the human resource consulting firm Watson Wyatt "offers evidence that an organization's communications planning and programming are critical factors contributing to the success of its business strategy. The results identify a definite correlation between high performing organizations and strong communications practices. Respondents agree that comprehensive communications programs help motivate and align employees with the goals of their organizations."[31]

Novo Nordisk presents thirteen basic policies in its guide to its strategic and operational thinking and the very first is its Communication Policy, stating in part that "Novo Nordisk will communicate with one voice as one company with one vision and shared values," and that any unit "must always communicate to staff at the same time or before any other audience is addressed." At Compuware, Ron Watson explains, "We try to make sure that our people around the globe understand our mission, our vision, our goals, our morals, and how we want to treat people." Similarly, Diana Root says that communications at BMC are focused on "what's important for employees to know" about the company's strategy and goals as well as "what they want to know"; and MBNA's *Guide to Employment and Benefits* says that employees can expect to "receive ample information about the company's plans, activities, and results."

Performance. Consistent with Watson Wyatt's finding that high performing organizations do a better job of communicating with their employees, all the best companies make providing organizational and individual performance information one of their corporate communications practices. Most have communications policy provisions intended to ensure that the information employees need to accomplish their work is widely shared. In addition, information about results is widely disseminated. MBNA promises that its people will "know what is required of them and be kept candidly informed of their performance and progress." At other companies, such as AFLAC and Harley-Davidson, similar information is disseminated at regularly scheduled division and department meetings devoted to performance results. Harley-Davidson's partnership agreements with its unions (PACE International and the International Association of Machinists and Aerospace Workers) set specific goals in this area and periodically track progress in achieving them, but the company has made deliberate efforts to go even further by including union leaders in discussions about important decisions—such as plant site selection—affecting union members. As a result, a leading authority on corporate loyalty concludes, "Unlike many of its counterparts in the transportation business, the motorcycle manufacturer enjoys cooperative and mutually respectful dealings with its unions."[32]

Several of the best companies also use their performance management processes to communicate specific results to teams and other smaller groups of employees. Dennis Liberson explains that the "core" of performance information and feedback at Capital One, "is our competency model and our performance." At TSMC, performance information, through "ongoing engagement and communication," is one of the key features of the performance management and development process. The fourth of ten "fundamentals" laid out in *The Novo Nordisk Way of Management* states that "every team and employee must have updated business and competency targets and receive timely feedback on performance against these targets." And at Toyota, as at most Japanese companies, the annual "spring offensive" in April is a time for communicating results and setting new goals at each level in the organization.

Creating and Building Company Culture.   In his landmark study of corporate culture, Edgar H. Schein wrote: "Through stories, parables, and other forms of oral and written history, an organization can communicate its identity and basic assumptions—especially to newcomers, who need to know what is important not only in abstract terms but by means of concrete examples that can be emulated."[33] More recently, James J. Collins and Jerry I. Porras, in their thought-provoking book, *Built to Last,* have written about the importance of "cult-like cultures" in making great companies great.[34]

At Cisco, Barbara Beck sees the telling of stories about the company, "about who we are, what we're trying to create" as critical to creating its culture. Such messages build "open communications, teamwork, and trust," all key elements of Cisco's culture. For Intel, building an "internal culture based on open communication" is a continuing goal; and at Sun Microsystems, another information technology (IT) company, a similar notion is expressed through the explicit creation of a "culture of sharing."

Juhani Hokkanen of Nokia sees messages about the company's record of constant innovation playing a culture-building role. They become "success stories for the company," and thus key elements in Nokia's culture, helping it retain high performers by giving them "the opportunity to grow and develop with the company's growth." Ericsson, considering its "strong corporate culture" one of its most important assets, regularly uses communications to stress its values of professionalism, respect, and perseverance. It feels that these values are not only key elements of Ericsson's corporate culture but also have worldwide applicability. TSMC considers "coaching on its history, culture, and business model" to be one of the four main responsibilities of its managerial mentoring program.

The Means of Transmission

The principal means of communicating messages are print media, electronic media, and in-person exchanges. All are widely used by the best companies. Each has advantages and disadvantages, and the use of each—especially electronic media—is undergoing rapid change.

Print Media. Messages in print come in a variety of formats, from posters to periodicals to employee handbooks. Most print media have the advantages of being long-lived and portable, readily available for reading anywhere and for future reference. Compuware, for example, makes use of a wide range of newsletters. *News for Managers* contains information about matters such as acquisitions and new product releases that the company expects managers to share with their staffs. *The Connection* disseminates various kinds of news to all employees. Among a variety of special purpose newsletters are one on health (part of the employee wellness program), one exclusively for administrators, and one that reports new developments for the decentralized human resource staff.

MBNA publishes *MBNA This Week* to highlight upcoming education and health services programs, volunteer opportunities, and other work-related information and *MBNA This Month* to focus on company and community events, education, and entertainment. Amgen's sixteen- to twenty-page company newspaper appears at least ten times a year; a special one- or two-page edition is put out for urgent breaking news. In Taiwan, Acer uses both monthly and weekly publications to inform its employees. AFLAC has official company bulletin boards in every area of the company and publishes *Family Album*, a monthly periodical that presents schedules of events and important company information and also recognizes employee achievements. BMC gets the word out with posters and easels, and Genentech, although it has a preference for electronic media, also finds, Judy Heyboer says, "that posters on bathroom doors are good in a pinch too."

Electronic Media. Supplementing print, and in many cases supplanting it, are electronic media. Amgen alerts its people by voice mail, links all conference rooms in the company with a closed-circuit television network, and uses videoconferencing throughout Europe, Asia, and Australia. BMC has its own television channel and links its worldwide operations via live satellite transmission. Harley-Davidson also has its own TV system, Eagle Network News (ENN); and Sun Microsystems' chairman and CEO, Scott McNealy, hosts his own radio show every four to six weeks, a show that Jim Moore describes as "awesome."

However, the fastest-growing and most ubiquitous electronic communications medium is by far the computer. All the best companies use e-mail. Some, like Genentech, have seen it rapidly replace voice mail; others, like Intel, agree that many employees "are more comfortable with e-mail." Most important, the computer has made it possible for any organization to create its own internal analog to the worldwide Internet, an intranet.

Intranets enable organizations to rapidly post and easily update virtually any information, such as company news, corporate directives and guidance, training and development opportunities, job postings, descriptions of compensation and benefit plans. Furthermore, because intranets are usually structured as interactive networks, feedback is possible, and participants at any level can often publish information and exchange it across divisions and departments regardless of functional specialties and hierarchical barriers. Throughout the world, intranet use is growing rapidly for both general and specific communications to employees. Watson Wyatt Worldwide has reported that in 2000, in the delivery of human resource services alone, fully 79 percent of 295 surveyed companies used their intranet as the chief means of transmission, up 50 percent from two years earlier.[35]

Microsoft, says Chris Williams, makes "almost every announcement" over its intranet. At Cisco, where the HR team runs the internal Web pages, Barbara Beck notes: "We get two million hits a month, and we change [the home page] twice a month. At the top of the page it says here's what's going on in the company, here are some things we think you need to know; and then you can drill down. It's a critical part of our communication." In the recent business environment of slowing economic growth and downsizing, Cisco has also deployed a "transition" intranet that features job listings from over 430 companies, including Cisco customers, partners, and vendors, and allows employees to post profiles that potential employers can search. It also offers information on career networking events, résumé writing, and interview preparation.[36]

Amgen offers a "biotech" intranet with company-wide information and announcements on the main site and separate sites dedicated to departmental matters. AFLAC finds that its newly developed internal Web site not only enables more information to be transmitted to more people more quickly than before but is also saving the company money. At the time of my visit to Harley-Davidson, its system, Rapid Intranet Information, was in the pilot stage, but staff were looking forward to its launch, candidly admitting that they had come up with its informal name first, R.I.D.E.

Outside the United States, intranet development in the best companies started out more slowly, with less emphasis on its interactive features, but is now growing rapidly. The Royal Dutch/Shell Group reports wide use of its Web site by staff, noting four million hits during the twenty-four months since it was launched. Singapore Airlines is using an electronic bulletin board to post announcements and in-house newsletters for staff. Acer has used its intranet as a major tool for communicating with its employees for a number of years, and TSMC sees its employee Web site as a vital infrastructure for communication and collaboration.

However, electronic media share some of the disadvantages of print media and add some drawbacks that are uniquely their own. First, as with print media, information overload may be a problem, along with the corollary difficulty of getting the attention of viewer-readers. Watson Wyatt's *1999 Communications Study*, for example, points out that although e-mail's popularity jumped 37 percent since the *1994 Communications Study*, "its relatively low effectiveness rating (55 percent) shows that it is not a magic communications pill for organizations. With all of the e-mail 'clutter,' an organization cannot be sure that its employees are really taking the time to process and understand their electronic messages."[37]

As BMC's Diana Root says, "You don't like to get buried with e-mails." BMC's "intranet and its use have been enhanced significantly over the last six months," but "the bigger challenge is how to get people to apply the tool; and that's one of the things we're still working on." Pär-Anders Pehrson at Ericsson was even more candid: "People are suffering more from information overload than from insufficient information."

Second, once anyone has the potential to publish anything electronically, there is likely to be not only information overload but also increasing interest in regulating what is published. Companies with extensive interactive intranets are finding that they need to establish protocols for what can be published by whom and to set up gatekeepers to both monitor and control their electronic media. Finally, no electronic media provide the means of transmission that all the best companies still feel is vital to high performance and retention—in-person exchanges.

In-Person Exchanges. In a recent *New York Times* symposium featuring four of America's top chief executives, Charles B. Wang, chairman, chief executive, and founder of Computer Associates International, said: "I don't have e-mail. I force my people to get in touch with me. And it takes effort. And it must be important, then, too." Shelly Lazarus, chairman and chief executive of Ogilvy & Mather Worldwide, said, "I also think there is no substitute for face-to-face," and Lawrence A. Bossidy, chairman and chief executive of Allied Signal, agreed.[38] Consistent with this view and with Charles Handy's insistence on the increased importance in this era of electronic communications of meeting in person,[39] all the executives I interviewed at the best companies spoke of the critical role of direct exchanges.

In these companies, in-person exchanges take place on and across many levels; often they are facilitated by office and floor layouts, and frequently they include senior management, notably chief executives. However, the most important of these exchanges involve supervisors at all levels and those they supervise. As communications consultants TJ Larkin and Sandar Larkin report, "In general, research conducted with frontline employees (blue-collar or clerical workers) shows that communication with supervisors has the greatest impact on frontline performance, that supervisors are the preferred source for information, and that employees perceive supervisors as good communicators."[40]

The best companies keep supervisors at all levels informed. They also facilitate communications between them and those they supervise by locating them together and reducing physical barriers between them. Here are a few examples from best U.S. companies. At MBNA, Terri Murphy notes, "The nature of where we have come from is face-to-face working with people. Every person will have at least one one-on-one meeting with his or her supervisor monthly, in some cases weekly." Throughout the gleaming, spotless buildings I toured at MBNA, supervisors were located with those they supervised, there were more partitions than doors, and all conference rooms had windows, with no drapes. Amgen holds biannual meetings of all employees for company updates, and, according to Ilana Meskin, "Most people are really located with their work units." At Cisco members of the small senior team have offices close to one another and to CEO John Chambers, and the rest of the company's vice presidents are housed with their own teams. Tony Fox told me that Intel "managers are physically located with the groups they manage, as opposed to sitting with a bunch of other managers," and "all Intel employees, from the CEO to interns, have similar cubicles, with no doors." And in nearby Palo Alto, at Sun Microsystems, the leveling of senior management has gone about as far as it can go. "There's no executive floor, there's no executive area," says Jim Moore; "we don't even have a concept of headquarters."

In the European best companies the emphasis on in-person exchanges is even stronger. Shell follows a policy of locating managers with those they manage and keeping doors to a minimum. At Ericsson, Management Planning Director Anne-Christine Carlsson says, "We believe very strongly in people meeting and getting to know each other, across units, across departments, across borders." In the company's London offices, where I met Carlsson, she pointed out how the décor and furnishings carried out this philosophy, and also Ericsson's Swedish heritage, using blond woods and glass to fill a formidable, old St. James Square structure with light and open space. Nokia stresses the importance of face-to-face exchanges, especially for performance evaluation, target-setting, and development discussions. Face-to-face meetings are also considered vital when team members start working together, because, Juhani Hokkanen says, "it helps them communicate later using different media." Novo Nordisk's Henrik Gürtler says, "It is too easy to write the perfect e-mail; to convince you, I have to sit with you."

In Asian companies, in-person exchanges are just as pervasive though more structured. Toyota makes wide use of direct personal communications but at regularly scheduled times and in a descending hierarchical pattern, with supervisors initiating meetings with

those they supervise. At TSMC, where one of the ten "business principles" in its Business Philosophy is "keeping communication channels open," there is a wide range of communication forums, from
the chairman's weekly lunch with his vice presidents to the VPs'
quarterly meetings with their managers to the managers' meetings
with those on the front line. When it comes to office space, with its
important influence on the opportunity for in-person exchanges,
TSMC "would like to move toward more of an open concept," says
S. H. Lee, but it does "not push very hard on that because people
are still sticking to the concept that a room is important, for private
conversation, and also because it is intangible recognition of a person's status and achievement." Acer favors "an open environment,"
with face-to-face communications in the form of periodic meetings
among top management followed by meetings throughout the managerial structure to the lowest-level employees. Singapore Airlines
holds half-yearly business meetings to inform staff of the company's
performance; it also has "communications facilitators" who arrange
in-person exchanges.

At many of the best companies, particularly in the United States,
members of top management regularly participate in in-person exchanges with employees, making clear their interest in them and
what they are doing and in return earning greater commitment and
loyalty. Intel holds open-forum sessions— described as "very well
attended"—where senior managers are available to talk with employees and answer their questions. At Genentech "you can sign up to
have lunch with a VP outside your area."

Best company CEOs are especially involved. Harley-Davidson
chairman and CEO Jeffrey Bleustein conducts town hall meetings at
each of the company's sites, and Amgen CEO Kevin Sharer has
monthly meetings with new employees. Cisco CEO John Chambers
attends new manager orientation sessions and also hosts popular
"birthday breakfasts" once a month, inviting those celebrating birthdays that month to join him for questions and candid discussion—
"no presentations and no pontification." AFLAC chairman and CEO

Daniel Amos seeks to meet each new employee with a greeting and a gift, and both he and company president Kriss Cloninger III speak to every employee during Employee Appreciation Week. CEO Amos also attends each division's quarterly meetings to hold an open question-and-answer period, and he makes himself available to any employees who feel normal channels are not adequate for what they want to say. CDW founder and former CEO Michael Krasny and President Gregory Zeman hold luncheons once a month with a randomly selected group of coworkers. Krasny has also been known to pitch in to help stack boxes during peak times in the company's warehouse.

Direct CEO participation in communications with employees is also catching on in Asia, albeit more modestly and tentatively. TSMC employees can sign up for the opportunity to participate in the company's Lunch with the President program. Periodically about twenty employees are chosen to join the president for lunch. He usually says a few words about new developments, then goes around the table soliciting questions and comments. At the end of senior staff core training programs at Singapore Airlines, dialogue sessions with the CEO and top management give senior staff an opportunity to speak directly with them about key issues and business strategies

It has often been said that one "can't communicate too much." But the danger of communications overload is real for all forms of communication and especially for the high-speed and ever more capacious electronic media. As the number of messages increases so does the risk that employees will tune out, missing or downgrading not only the trivial but also the relevant and even the urgent. The challenges are daunting, and organizations are just beginning to face them. Today the best companies understand that they can indeed talk too much to their employees, but they also know that they cannot *listen* enough to them. Enhanced interactive networks are tools that enable companies to improve that essential listening.

The Network

Interactive networks using any of the three means of transmission—print, electronic media, and in-person exchanges—enable companies to carry out their most important communications responsibility to their employees—to listen to them and to respond to what they hear. Companies that do so clearly benefit. A 1998 Gallup survey of 1,135 U.S. businesses "showed a consistent link between the level of agreement with statements such as, 'at work my opinions seem to count,' and profitability, productivity, employee retention and customer satisfaction." Companies with a high level of agreement with such statements "enjoy up to 27 percent higher profit and 22 percent higher productivity than average."[41] Watson Wyatt's *1999 Communications Study* agrees: "More respondents from high-performing organizations than from all others rated their channels of upward communication as effective and reported that employee input was used in decision making."[42] McKinsey & Company's extensive management surveys also stress the importance of employee feedback to high performance. Its 1997 survey of 6,900 managers reports that 71 percent of them believed feedback on their performance to be essential or very important to their development. This percentage rose to 89 in a 2000 survey. However, McKinsey surveys also show the low percentage of firms providing such feedback effectively, 32 percent in 1997, and 39 percent in 2000.[43]

Leading authorities concur. A recent book by professors Richard Freeman of Harvard University and Joel Rogers of the University of Wisconsin, based on an extensive workplace survey, concludes that more than anything, workers want their voices to be heard.[44] In *The Knowing-Doing Gap: How Smart Companies Turn Knowledge into Action*, Stanford University professors Jeffrey Pfeffer and Robert Sutton argue for the critical role of employee opinion in corporate progress;[45] and management guru Rosabeth Moss Kanter writes that one of the four things on which building long-term commitment depends is "the chance to speak up and be listened to."[46]

The best companies implement network communications practices in a number of ways. Many establish listening and responding as general policies, in published statements or as clearly understood components of their corporate cultures, and then create a variety of means to carry out these policies. Some also use more formal feedback mechanisms, such as employee satisfaction surveys and suggestion programs. But all take care that the means chosen are truly interactive, that the company listens and that it responds; for only when employees receive feedback do they know they are being heard.

Listening and Responding.   Coleman Peterson of Wal-Mart says, "There's no question that listening can take a great deal of time, but it gives you all that you need to fix things and make good decisions. You'll get a very strong and healthy culture, and culture is your best path to retention."[47] At Amgen interactive communication is a core value, specifically focused on building consensus, "a process where diverse opinions, conflicting views and other input are sought and seriously considered." "We engage in frequent timely and open communication with each other," is one of Shell's seven "people principles for working together," and John Hofmeister made a strong point of telling me that throughout Shell "interactive communication is particularly important." S. H. Lee notes that effective feedback, especially to managers, has been inhibited at TSMC by Asian culture and occurs comparatively slowly. Now TSMC has created an ombudsman system to aid the process. To give it appropriate stature, it is staffed with a vice president who reports directly to the chairman and is regularly available by appointment "in each location of the company" to speak with employees "in private, secure areas."

At several best companies dispute resolution is an important function of interactive communication and feedback. At AFLAC, as at most organizations, employees are told to discuss any problems first with their immediate supervisors. "But if they do not feel comfortable going to that supervisor," says Angela Hart, senior vice president and director of Human Resources, explaining the company's open-door policy, "then we provide other resources for them."

At Ingram Micro the dispute resolution process is somewhat more formal. "If I have a problem," David Finley says, "and it hasn't been resolved, I can kick it up to the next level. Not satisfied with that, I can kick it up another time. Altogether I can kick it up three times, and it can end up being at the CEO level if it is perceived as being important enough." Intel has "constructive confrontation," a unique process that Tony Fox characterizes as "feedback real time . . . where, for instance, we expect people to confront in a positive way any discussion that they think is not supported by good data."

Compuware stresses its executive-level open-door policy, which is implemented both electronically (through accepting and responding to e-mails) and face-to-face and which includes CEO and cofounder Peter Karmanos. As Ron Watson puts it, "If an employee wanted to talk to Peter right now all he would have to do is walk into his office." CDW, whose mission statement encourages two-way feedback, has "communication groups" of managers in each major department. Each manager in each group has the responsibility for getting answers to particular kinds of questions, and when a question is e-mailed, "answering is what you do first," says Art Friedson, "you don't let them wait." BMC, which is "trying to make more things interactive [and] give employees the opportunity to provide feedback, especially via e-mail," has recently taken electronic communications one step further by creating "think e-rooms." As Diana Root relates, "In all major locations there is one room that is sort of like a creative think tank. At first it strikes you as kind of comical, because it has beanbag chairs, dim lava lamps, and beads, and you sit on the floor. But it has a PC, and you can send an anonymous e-mail, about anything to anyone, and get a response. Employees like it because it's a neat room, it's fun and different, and out of our normal work environment. We can have little meetings in there, and hopefully it stimulates creativity and innovation."

Merck emphasizes 360-degree feedback as a critical factor in the practice of its company-wide core leadership principles, and Capital One does frequent road shows with "town meetings," where Dennis Liberson finds "it is better listening than actually talking."

He says he learns "a lot from the questions they are asking about how they feel about what is going on." When I concluded my interview of Judy Heyboer at Genentech by asking which practices, in the final analysis, are most important to performance and to retention, she said: "I think it is the same answer for both. I think it is paying attention and talking to people, it's providing feedback."

Formal Feedback.   Among the best companies, two of the most common ways of obtaining formal feedback are employee opinion surveys (often called employee satisfaction surveys) and suggestion programs. Employee opinion surveys are widely done. Although conducted under different titles at different intervals for a variety of corporate groups and on a variety of subjects, all seek feedback from employees with the goal of making changes that will improve operations. Executives at Capital One are "pioneers" in soliciting employee opinion, according to Daniel Liberson. The company conducts surveys every six months, and the results—for the company as a whole and for each department—are quickly analyzed and acted upon. Liberson says:

> I look at the analysis and see the two or three things we need to do to improve associate [employee] satisfaction. If you're a department, you do the exact same thing. You develop an action plan saying we're going to do things to try to respond to what is needed. Then you communicate the results to your people and tell them what they are going to do about it. We let people respond locally to the issues, and we turn them around in a matter of weeks. Our associate survey process allows us to really know what's going on, not anecdotally but against a really good set of databases.

Microsoft's annual employee satisfaction survey is conducted by a third party to provide anonymity for those responding. "It's a complete census," says Chris Williams; "we ask every one of the 48,000 employees to participate. We got almost 70 percent participation this last year, and it gave us a ton of valuable information." Nokia also does an employee survey every year, and "every single person in the company participates in it," completing either a paper form or an electronic form on the company's intranet. Nokia hopes to make the survey entirely electronic once all employees have either a personal computer or access to a computer kiosk. Toyota also uses an employee satisfaction survey, and Mitsuo Kinoshita told me the company was very proud that the level of employee satisfaction has been steadily rising in comparison to the levels at other Japanese companies, even during Japan's continuing economic downturn. About 80 percent of all employees said they were satisfied with the company, and he attributed that result to the variety of measures Toyota had taken in response to prior surveys.

Sun Microsystems' *Employment Quality Index* is administered to a sample of the workforce every month and to 100 percent of the employees every quarter. Intel's *Global Employee Survey* is revised and conducted every eighteen months. Wal-Mart conducts its *Grass Roots* associate survey annually at the store level—giving stores their local results first—and then aggregates the store results for the corporate picture. Shell carries out an employee satisfaction survey every eighteen months, Compuware every two years, and Genentech roughly every four years. Acer last did one in 1997 but since then has been using focus groups to collect employee opinion.

AFLAC does its employment surveys after big events, such as its annual Employee Appreciation Week, in order to evaluate these functions and to determine what is effective and what is not. Amgen's climate survey, deployed every two years, asks people what their most useful sources of information are. BMC does "massive worldwide surveys focused on specific topics" like employee communications.

Ericsson, according to Pär-Anders Pehrson, prefers to use its employee opinion surveys for "looking at the way the business is doing rather than asking employees how satisfied they are." As he explains it, "We will check and find out if they are pleased with the leadership, if they feel they are empowered, and measure that in terms of indexes; because at the end of the day what we are shaping is generic behavior amongst managers." Similarly, TSMC uses its employee survey to assess its practices with regard to its ten business principles. For the ultimate in employee feedback, one item that Ingram Micro determines with its annual employee opinion survey is an employee "confidence factor." Explains David Finley, "We survey them on their level of confidence that the company is going to respond to the issues raised in the survey."

Suggestion programs are more popular in the best companies outside the United States, especially those in Asia, than they are in the U.S. companies. However, MBNA is one U.S. company that looks to its employees for ideas and has a suggestion program that enjoys a measure of success because of the way it is run. According to Ken Pizer, many suggestion programs "collapse under their own weight; but this one never has because there is a lot of attention paid to it from the top." Called the MasterPiece Program, it encourages employees to submit ideas "for enhancing Customer satisfaction or about how to save time, effort or costs." Each Tuesday these ideas are considered at a MasterPiece meeting, and if any one of them is turned down, says Pizer, "we're tasked with going in there and challenging the person who turned it down as to why it was turned down." Thus care is taken to consider all ideas submitted. Cash awards are also made, with $15,000 going to the individual and a similar amount to the team with the year's best idea.

Among the Asian companies, TSMC has an "electronic suggestion box" that employees can use to make suggestions and communicate to management. Toyota, very proud of its suggestions program, regularly reports on the overall status of the program, noting that for 1997, for example: "Suggestions submitted = 727,884, Percentage adopted = 98 percent, Suggestions per employee = 10.3." Singapore Airlines' suggestion program, Staff Ideas in Action, was launched in 1982. It invites original ideas from all employees, focusing principally on ways to improve productivity, reduce waste, and increase revenue but also looking for ideas to enhance customer service, improve staff safety, and boost the company's image. The company gives Initiative Award Certificates to employees whose ideas are adopted, and employees can accumulate certificates to win prizes. Depending on the merits and benefits of an idea, as much as US$30,000 can be won.

Finally, CDW—which furthers informal personal relationships by sorting its corporate directory by first names—has a single formal feedback program: "All new hires get five stamped envelopes addressed to CEO John Edwards—with new batches each successive year," says Art Friedson, and CDW encourages employees to use these envelopes "to send any ideas they may have for the business, or just to bitch, if that is what they want to do."

The Need for and Value of Recognition

Employees need recognition. Mary K. Ash, founder of Mary K. Cosmetics, put it succinctly: "There are two things people want more than sex and money . . . recognition and praise."[48] A 1996 Louis Harris and Associates survey of 1,502 working adults found that one of the four most common responses to the question "What makes you feel successful at work?" was "Recognition from coworkers/supervisors."[49] However, Gallup Poll surveys of 1991 and 1999 showed that between those years the percentage of employees satisfied with the recognition they received at work dropped from 76 to 73, and the percentage dissatisfied rose from 22 to 25, with the largest change being among those "completely dissatisfied," who increased from 5 to 11 percent.[50] Confirming the need for attention to employee recognition, a 1999 study by the Hudson Institute and Walker Information lists "appreciation of employee ideas/contributions" as one of six work factors that have the highest priority for action by employers.[51]

In all the best companies, recognition programs have high priority. Furthermore, in keeping with the changing attitudes and aspirations of today's workers, these programs are undergoing major changes. Time of service awards, the hoary mainstays of most employee recognition programs, are declining in importance at many companies; some no longer give them at all. Instead, companies are putting more emphasis on performance awards, and to encourage better performance all around, they are giving performance awards even to average workers. In addition, as many people seek greater balance between work and life outside the office, more companies are recognizing events of personal importance in employees' lives. Finally, among the current important trends in employee recognition are a shift to nonmonetary awards; a greater emphasis on public presentations, especially before peer groups; and an increased use of immediate, informal, and personal awards.

Time of Service Awards

A recent Conference Board report points out that although three-fifths of sixty-four surveyed companies once honored career milestones, "only one-third do so now, and less than one-fifth expect such events in an employee's career to figure prominently in future recognition programs."[52] Consistent with this trend, a number of the best companies either do not honor career milestones or have significantly reduced their efforts to do so. Capital One offers no service awards, Dennis Liberson explains, "because it does not fit our culture. We want to reward for performance, and we find that rewarding someone for just being here is inconsistent with that." Harley-Davidson does have service awards, but its executives point out right away that the company does not focus on them—it is not a donor of pins and plaques. As retired Director of Human Resources Staffing Flip Weber told me, "Our service awards are nominal. I mean, I've been here forty years; I didn't get anything!" And although Ingram Micro uses service awards, David Finley says it places "far more emphasis . . . on recognition than on the tangible award."

Nevertheless, a number of the best companies still feel there are important benefits to recognizing employee tenure, not the least being the reinforcement of feelings of loyalty and belonging. Here are a few examples:

- MBNA awards 14k gold service pins to acknowledge each individual's years of service with the company.

- As part of its Employee Appreciation Week, AFLAC celebrates employees who are reaching milestones of five, ten, fifteen, twenty, and twenty-five years of service.

- Compuware recognizes service anniversaries of one, three, five, ten, fifteen, twenty, twenty-five, and thirty years, sending a plaque and presentation suggestions to each award recipient's manager, and also holds an annual recognition dinner at a local country club to honor employees of ten years or more.

- Wal-Mart associates' nametags are colored silver or gold and numbered to indicate years of service.

- Sun Microsystems, in keeping with its fun-loving culture, presents service awards at parties featuring "fairly wacky, bizarre kinds of things."

- Microsoft gives awards for tenure in five-year increments. Fifteen-year-plus people were recently feted at a big dinner at Chairman Bill Gates's new house.

- Acer recognizes years of service at the five-, ten-, fifteen-, twenty-, and twenty-five-year marks, and "a very substantial gift is given with each award."

- Merck, feeling its service award program "had fallen a little behind and lost some of its importance," is now in the process of revamping it.

Performance Awards

Awards tied to individual performance have advantages for both companies and individual employees. Companies can use awards for performance both to underline the importance of missions, strategic goals, or specific objectives and to stimulate people to achieve those aims. For individuals, an emphasis on good performance is both satisfying and encouraging of further high performance. In the words of Bob Nelson, "When you recognize performance, not only will you get more of that behavior, but that's also when it means the most to employees."[53]

The best companies have taken these points to heart and are rewarding different kinds of performance with a variety of awards:

- Merck presents four major awards—for excellent performance, sustained excellent performance beyond what is expected, strategic contributions, and outstanding scientific or business accomplishments—that all support the company's Strategy for Growth and Leadership Principles.

- Starbucks's Warm Regards recognition program offers three awards—The Mug (for "moves of uncommon greatness"), Bravo (for partner [employee] achievements); and The Spirit of Starbucks (to honor passion and spirit)—all embodying the company's "guiding principles, mission and goals."

- Ingram Micro has Associate of the Month and Partners in Excellence programs that support the company's Mission-Vision Values. Ingram Micro also makes a once-a-year award, with a grant of $10,000, to the one person who has made the most outstanding contribution to the firm.

- MBNA's MasterPiece Program recognizes (with cash awards of $300) ideas from employees that will enable the company to grow and provide better service.

- Ericsson, seeking to foster a culture that shares knowledge, has a program that rewards employees who share.

- Intel has two major corporate awards: the Intel Quality Award goes to organizations that have demonstrated outstanding performance on particular quality goals, and the Intel Achievement Award is presented to individuals and small teams for outstanding achievement in particular business results.

- Any Genentech officer can write a "Genen Check" for up to $3,000 at any time to recognize a specific accomplishment.

- CDW, to encourage a company-wide effort to achieve its goal of being the world's number one reseller of computers and peripherals, has created the CEO's 1–99 Challenge, promising every CDW coworker (employee) a three-day trip for two in the continental United States if the goal is met.

But not every best company is inclined to reward individual performance. Feeling that the practice may be at odds with their corporate culture or the culture of their domicile, some downplay such rewards or eschew them altogether. Microsoft, Chris Williams explains, "does have a program that gives everyone who ships [that is, completes the development of] a piece of software a plaque, but for the most part such programs are not a large, endemic part of our culture." At Novo Nordisk, it is difficult to determine which criteria say, "this guy is better than the other guy." Henrik Gürtler thinks "the culture suppresses it in a way. You have to do your stuff, then you'll get word that you're good."

Personal Milestone Awards

Some companies have always recognized important events such as weddings, the births of children, and the earning of academic degrees in the personal lives of their employees. Today, with work-life balance an increasing preoccupation of greater numbers of the workforce, more are doing so. As three practitioners recently wrote in the *Harvard Business Review,* "a small but growing number of managers . . . recognize and support their employees as 'whole people,' open-mindedly acknowledging and even celebrating the fact that they have roles outside the office."[54]

Many of the best companies are following suit, recognizing and honoring the personal milestones of their employees:

- Harley-Davidson CEO Jeffrey Bleustein personally signs birthday cards to each employee, usually adding a short note.
- CDW celebrates employees' birthdays by flashing their names on a huge electric sign along the highway.
- Capital One gives its departments "fun money" to buy birthday cakes and hold birthday parties for employees.
- TSMC gives employees gift vouchers on their birthdays (and on major holidays like the Chinese New Year and the Mid-Autumn Festival).
- Singapore Airlines gives newlywed employees "matrimony leave."
- MBNA provides a limousine on an employee's wedding day, plus $500 and a week of paid vacation.
- Acer regularly recognizes personal milestones, some with cash gifts.
- Cisco recognizes employees' families with its New Baby Gift Program.
- Compuware sent a box of cookies and a note to keep trying to an employee who failed a certification exam; when he did pass, he received 500 stock options.

But here, too, there are dissenters. One senior executive at a high-technology best company told me, "We don't go out of our way to recognize family because it's really none of our business." Table 2.2 compares the percentages of best companies that think particular recognition awards are important with the percentages that do not emphasize these awards.

Current Trends

A number of important trends are currently under way in employee recognition, influenced by surveys of employee preferences, results of focus groups, and the writings of management authorities and consultants. Companies are offering more nonmonetary awards,

TABLE 2.2. Recognition Awards in the Best Companies.

Type of Award	Important	Minimal or Not Emphasized
Time of service	68%	32%
Performance	80	20
Personal milestone	90	10

highlighting the significance of awards by presenting them on public occasions, and finding more opportunities for immediate, informal personal awards.

Shift to Nonmonetary Awards. Many senior executives believe that well-thought-out compensation plans, including salaries and bonuses, are more effective than spot cash awards for rewarding good performance monetarily. In addition, cash is usually quickly spent, often simply to pay bills; thus spot cash awards have little legacy value. When effectively tied to the performances they are rewarding, nonmonetary awards can have more enduring value than cash awards, reminding employees of the performance that earned the recognition, encouraging further similar behavior, and reinforcing commitment to the organization. Many of the best companies appear to agree.

Merck has a comprehensive program of monetary awards but also makes widespread use of nonmonetary awards, as does Nokia. Capital One's Circle of Excellence award, given to "groups or individuals that really do something great," is entirely noncash. At Amgen, where "team clothing has always been a big deal," says David Kaye, managers make wide use of commemorative t-shirts, sweatshirts, and baseball caps. Harley-Davidson offers perhaps the ultimate in nonmonetary recognition by encouraging all employees to staff bike rallies and roundups throughout the United States, at company expense. "They get to meet other employees," says Brenda Brimage, director of Diversity, "learn the business, and experience the real world of Harley."

More Public Presentations.   Recognition in public validates the significance of the achievements being honored. At the same time, it makes those achievements known to others, boosting the pride and self-esteem of recipients. Presentation of awards by members of senior management also reinforces their importance, and the participation of peer groups in choosing those honored and in witnessing the presentation ceremonies contributes to feelings of belonging and contributing.

Capital One strives to have one of its senior executives make its coveted Circle of Excellence awards. AFLAC's CEO and two executive vice presidents personally present milestone awards before the award recipients' peers during Employee Appreciation Week. At Intel, winners of the awards for quality and achievement receive them from the company chairman and CEO in a ceremony at a black-tie dinner. Amgen holds peer-group parties to celebrate the conclusion of important labor-intensive events like the completion of Food and Drug Administration submissions for a new drug. Singapore Airlines sees presentation of its customer service awards as cause for public celebration before the "entire network" of the recipients' peers because, in the words of senior manager of Human Resource Development Lam Seet Mui, "We want all of them to practice TCS [Transforming Customer Service], we want to empower them so that they become real ambassadors for the company."

Immediate, Informal, Personal Awards.   More and more companies are discovering that the most effective means of employee recognition are often immediate, informal, and personal—a brief handwritten note, a short phone call, even a simple verbal thank-you. These gestures are perceived as genuine and sincere, often more so than the products of even well-structured and well-intentioned corporate recognition programs. Employees learn right away that they and their work are valued, and bonds of cooperation and mutual support between them and their supervisors are strengthened.

Management authorities agree. In *Encouraging the Heart: A Leader's Guide to Rewarding and Recognizing Others*, James Kouzes and

Barry Posner speak of the importance of personalizing recognition and devote their final chapter to "150 ways to encourage the heart," many of which are immediate, informal, and personal.[55] Helen Axel's recent Conference Board survey on employee recognition programs finds that "informal/spontaneous awards are present in just over one-fifth of the [surveyed] companies, but comments from survey participants indicate this practice is gaining ground. At least half of the companies . . . [say their recognition programs are] moving toward informal/spontaneous events . . . [and] paying attention to personalizing forms of recognition."[56]

In several of the best companies these practices are already common. At Intel, awards range from formal recognition at the corporate level to spontaneous employee-to-employee awards presented at the department level. Merck, in its comprehensive pamphlet *Appreciation at Merck*, devotes a whole page to "quick and easy ways" to show informal appreciation. Ingram Micro makes 0.5 percent of its payroll available for spontaneous personal awards; the example David Finley gives is, "I caught you doing something right and I'm going to give you an award for $100; so take your spouse out to dinner." Wal-Mart gives out "Great Job!" buttons. Every time an associate (employee) amasses four buttons, he or she can exchange them for a share of Wal-Mart stock. CDW supplies each executive with Bravo Cards with the executive's name printed on them. The executives then give the cards, with handwritten notes, to people who have just done something good. Says Art Friedson, "This is the most effective recognition device we have at the moment; people really value them."

These then are practices the best companies are using to respond to the higher value workers now put on the importance of the work they do and the equally high value they now place on a work environment that engages them, recognizes their achievements, and acknowledges the importance of their nonwork lives. It is in part by using these practices that these companies have been able to develop and retain the employees that have made them high performing organizations. Next, it is necessary to examine what the best companies are doing to find and hire the employees who will be their future high performers.

3

Recruiting and Hiring

Recruiting and hiring are the most critical practice areas for finding and keeping high performers. If companies make good hiring decisions, their efforts in other practice areas (work content and work environment, compensation and benefits, and education and training) will reinforce those decisions, but if they do not hire well, no amount of effort in the other practice areas is likely to significantly improve performance or increase retention. In the words of the highly regarded chairman and CEO of AlliedSignal, Lawrence Bossidy, "I am convinced that nothing we do is more important than hiring and developing people."[1] Underlining his view is a recent Conference Board study of 516 human resource and line executives from 373 companies in thirty-three countries. It concludes that second among thirteen HR goals for future business success is "recruiting and retaining a quality workforce" (the first is "developing leaders").[2]

Recruiting and retaining good employees have demonstrably measurable results. The importance of recruiting is addressed by the *Human Capital Index* of the consulting firm Watson Wyatt (derived from a survey of more than 400 large U.S. and Canadian publicly traded companies). It groups thirty key HR practices into five major dimensions and reports the changes in shareholder value that may be expected with improvement in each dimension. The dimension associated with the highest increase (a 10.1 percent boost in market value over the five-year period from 1994 to 1999) is recruiting excellence.[3] One indication of the value of retention is a study by Towers Perrin consultants of the performance of seventeen large insurance companies (accounting for more than one-third of the U.S. market). This study "suggests that a company with employee turnover of 10 percent or less has as much as a 10 percent customer retention rate advantage over a company with employee turnover of 15 percent or more."[4] In addition to boosting shareholder value and fostering the continuity that retains customers, good recruitment and high retention also contribute to developing and maintaining a positive corporate culture, yet another important attribute of high performing companies.

Successful recruitment and retention also mean important cost savings. According to a survey of more than 1,700 HR professionals across the United States, conducted by the Society for Human Resource Management (SHRM) in partnership with Aon Consulting, "at the fiftieth percentile total cost-per-hire estimates range from $800 for clerical and administrative positions to $15,000 for executive positions."[5] Total replacement costs—which add in such items as the fees of outside recruiters, the value of lost leads and contacts, the cost of training replacements, the loss associated with new hires' initial lower productivity, and the cost of the time spent by in-place colleagues in offering guidance to newcomers—are even higher. Depending on the level and responsibilities of the personnel involved, these costs have been estimated to run from roughly one-half to as much as 150 percent of annual salary.[6] Looking at losses from the departure of professional and managerial employees, studies by the Saratoga Institute, a human capital performance research organization, show that a company loses about $1 million with every ten employees who leave.[7]

Still, most companies find recruitment and retention large and implicitly unmet challenges. Participants in the SHRM survey cited earlier reported that the greatest employment challenge facing their organizations was simply finding candidates, and the second greatest was retaining those hired.[8] A comparison of surveys done in 1995 and 2000 by Management Recruiters International reveals that finding and keeping qualified employees remains the top anxiety of executives.[9] According to an equally comprehensive survey of 614 U.S. organizations by Watson Wyatt Worldwide, 86 percent are experiencing difficulty attracting employees, and 58 percent are having trouble retaining them; yet only a little more than half of these companies have a formal strategy for employee recruitment, and a mere 35 percent have a plan to retain workers.[10] And a recent study of 7,000 corporate officers and managers by McKinsey & Company finds that only 7 percent think their companies have enough talent to pursue the most promising business opportunities. Despite this perceived weakness, only 7 percent said their companies were updating recruiting and retention strategies.[11]

In contrast, executives of the twenty-five best companies interviewed for this book say their companies are successfully meeting the dual challenge of recruiting and retaining, and described a number of their approaches. From their responses, I identified four areas of activity important in securing employees who will be high performers and who will remain with their organizations:

- Understanding the evolving labor market
- Recruiting desired job candidates
- Selecting among those recruited
- Evaluating recruiting and selecting practices

Understanding the Evolving Labor Market

In order to recruit desired job candidates and select effectively among those recruited, companies must understand the profound changes that are occurring today and will increasingly occur in the labor market. These changes are taking place especially in the supply of labor and in the demand for it. Contrary to popular opinion, however, there has been little change in the commitment and loyalty workers feel toward their employers.

Labor Supply

Workforces are growing more slowly, aging, and changing in composition. As will be seen, these changes are structural, not to be reversed, and are occurring or eventually will occur in all countries. But they are furthest along in the developed regions, notably in the industrialized economies of Japan, Europe, and North America.

Slowing Workforce Growth. In 1997, Peter Drucker made this startling prediction: "The dominant factor for business in the next two decades—absent war, pestilence, or collision with a comet—is not going to be economics or technology. It will be demographics. The key factor for business will not be the *over*population of the world, which we have been warned of these last 40 years. It will be the increasing *under*population of the developed countries—Japan and the nations of Europe and North America."[12]

This worldwide slowing of population growth, in time likely to be recognized as the most important change in the history of the planet, is permanent and irreversible. It is due in the first place to economic development, which has reduced the need for large families and simultaneously brought about the technology and fostered the education that enable people to carry out decisions to have fewer children. It has been further spurred by public policy programs in some countries, by urbanization in most countries, and by the increased entrance into labor markets of women, who then often defer having children and usually bear smaller numbers than women of previous generations. Finally, it is self-reinforcing, for each generation of women produces fewer daughters, who in turn produce still fewer.

Slowing rates of population growth mean slowing rates of workforce growth and—increasingly in developed countries—zero and eventually negative rates of growth. The number of people in the prime working years of twenty to sixty-four, which stood at approximately 491 million in 1950 in all developed countries, rose to more than 717 million by 2000. For the next decade it will continue to rise, reaching a projected peak of nearly 740 million in 2010. Then it will start falling, to just below 590 million by midcentury, a drop of over 20 percent from its peak.[13] (Appendix B presents some population projections. For workforce changes in the United States, Germany, and Japan, see Figure B.1.)

Workforce Aging. Two important changes are steadily increasing the median age of the world's people, especially in the developed countries. One is the slowing rate of population growth; the other is the rising life expectancy. The slowing of population growth means that the numbers of people in the younger cohorts are not rising as rapidly as they did in prior generations, and where population growth is zero, or below zero, these numbers are actually smaller than they were in prior generations. In the developed countries as a group, the number of people aged zero to nineteen is already falling and is projected to continue to do so in the future. Meanwhile, at the other end of the population age scale, rising life expectancy is continually adding to the numbers of older people.[14] When rising life expectancy is combined with slowing population growth, the result is a steady increase in the median age and dramatic shifts in the relative sizes of population cohorts. (See, for example, Figure B.2 in Appendix B.)

Also important will be the fluctuations among working age cohorts due to cyclical baby booms and baby busts. In the United States, for example, the largest working-age cohort currently consists of people in their thirties. In a few years, the largest working-age cohort will be people in their forties. This group will continue to be the largest through the early 2010s; then it will be succeeded in 2015 by the cohort of people in their fifties. In each period the other cohorts, especially the younger ones, will be smaller, meaning much greater competition for the shrinking numbers of those in their prime working years.[15] In the meantime the fastest-growing cohorts will consist of people in their sixties and seventies, traditionally considered postworking individuals, but since the late 1980s, retiring later and remaining in the U.S. labor force as both part-time and full-time employees.[16] In fact, the combination of slowing growth in the younger working cohorts and rising life expectancy (with an attendant increase in active, healthy years) is already being translated into a rising demand for those in their sixties and even seventies who are qualified, experienced, and willing to work.

It is clear from these trends that companies must fashion their recruiting and hiring strategies to pay careful attention to both the slowing growth and the aging of the workforces, preparing for more competition for younger people and greater availability of older people. In addition, they have to be aware of the changes occurring in workforce composition.

Changing Workforce Composition. Throughout the world, but again especially in the developed countries, the composition of workforces is changing and will continue to change in two important ways. First, their racial and ethnic makeup is changing, due to the slowing growth or in some cases decline in the numbers of whites and the increasing growth in the numbers of nonwhites and nonnatives in working-age cohorts. Second, their gender makeup is changing, due to the increasing participation of women.

Numbers of whites are decreasing and numbers of nonwhites are increasing because these groups have different population growth rates. Numbers of nonnatives are increasing due to continuing immigration. In the United States both these trends are visible. Higher growth rates are steadily raising the percentages of African Americans, Hispanic Americans, and Asian Americans in the total population. In 2000, non-Hispanic whites constituted 71.4 percent of the population; by 2050 their percentage is expected to fall to slightly over half of the total, at 52.8.[17] Since 1970, immigrants have been a steadily increasing percentage of the U.S. population, constituting 12 percent of all U.S. workers by 1999. For the period from 2000 to 2050, net migration to the United States is projected to continue at just below a million persons a year.[18] (See Figure B.3 in Appendix B.)

In other developed countries, it is immigration more than rising growth rates of nonwhite groups that is changing workforce composition. Even with increasing emigration and immigration restrictions in many countries, the number of immigrants is steadily increasing. They move for many reasons, but the predominant one by far is to seek better economic opportunities. Thus their countries of choice are the industrialized developed nations, especially in Europe and North America. Because many of these countries, especially in Europe, now have relatively slow growing or even declining populations, even modest streams of immigrants (often with higher fertility rates than the existing population) are significantly raising these countries' percentages of nonnatives. Furthermore, because most of these immigrants come looking for jobs, they tend to be of working age, increasing the percentages of immigrants in the younger cohorts

The other major change in workforce composition is in gender. Especially in the developed countries, women are becoming a steadily increasing proportion of all employees. This is happening for a number of reasons, most of which apply simultaneously: the growth of service-producing work in the developed economies, creating more jobs available and attractive to women, especially in offices and in the professions; the urge for a more affluent lifestyle or simply the need to make ends meet, causing more families to seek second incomes; the desire to pursue a fulfilling and rewarding career, spurred in many countries by movements for women's liberation and equality; and finally, the improved ability through increasing options for birth control to defer childbirth and plan smaller families, enabling women to both maximize and optimize their workforce participation.

In the United States the participation of women sixteen years and older in the civilian labor force rose steadily from 33.9 percent in 1950 to nearly 60 percent in 1998. It is now projected to level off at about this same percentage for the next quarter century. During this same period the participation of men sixteen years and older declined from 86.4 percent to 74.4 percent, from which it is projected to drop still further, to 68.8 percent in 2025. These changes mean that the proportion of the U.S. civilian labor force sixteen years and older made up of women has risen from just under 30 percent in 1950 to

46.3 percent in 1998. Currently, it is projected to rise slightly to 48 percent in 2015 and then level off.[19] Thus it seems that the difference between the percentage of men and the percentage women in the workforce of the world's largest developed country—after prolonged change—is likely settling at about 4 to 5 percent, a not implausible benchmark for the future course of other developed and developing countries.

As a result of all the changes just described, employers need to take into account the following traits they are currently finding in the labor supply and will increasingly find in the future:

- Slowing growth of the total number of people in the prime working years (ages twenty to sixty-four); and in many developed countries, declining numbers in these ages.

- Rising median ages, leading to steadily older workforces; and rising life expectancies, leading to an increasing number of active people in what traditionally have been considered postworking cohorts.

- Changing relative sizes of the age cohorts as the bulges and shrinkages of baby booms and baby busts pass through the working years of a country's population, severely reducing the numbers of younger people who typically have filled entry-level and junior positions.

- Changing composition of workforces, emphasizing, first, the increasing percentages of nonwhites (especially in the United States) and nonnatives (especially in the developed countries of Europe) and, second, the increasing participation of women in labor forces, eventually rising to nearly 50 percent of all workers.

Labor Demand

In addition to labor supply, employers also need to be attentive to the likely future demand for labor. A rough idea of labor demand can be obtained from examining projections of future employment in the various industrial and occupational categories. Among the most detailed are the ten-year projections by the Occupational Outlook Program of the Bureau of Labor Statistics (BLS) of the U.S. Department of Labor.

The most important industrial projection of the BLS is that the long-term shift from goods-producing to service-producing employment will continue. Jobs in all service-producing industries combined are expected to account for approximately 19.1 million of the 19.5 million new wage and salary jobs generated in the United States over the 1998 to 2008 period. The services group (a subset of service-producing employment that excludes transportation and public utilities; finance, insurance, and real estate; wholesale and retail trade; and government) alone will add 11.8 million new jobs by 2008, nearly three-fourths of which will be in three sectors of services—business, health, and professional and miscellaneous.[20]

When numbers of people required in different occupations are projected for 1998 to 2008, the five fastest growing all turn out to be computer related, the core group of the *knowledge workers* (to use the felicitous phrase coined by Peter Drucker nearly four decades ago) who will be the twenty-first century's most valuable employees:

1. Computer engineers: 323,000 new jobs (a growth of 108 percent)

2. Computer support specialists: 439,000 new jobs (a growth of 102 percent)

3. Systems analysts: 577,000 new jobs (a growth of 94 percent)

4. Database administrators: 67,000 new jobs (a growth of 77 percent)

5. Desktop publishing specialists: 19,000 new jobs (a growth of 73 percent)

Further down the list of fastest-growing occupations but fourth in the total number of new jobs (551,000) expected to be generated from 1998 to 2008 are general managers and top executives.[21]

Job openings may result from either growth or replacement needs. Three major occupational groups are projected to experience as many or more than as many job openings to meet growth needs as they experience to meet replacement needs from 1998 to 2008. These groups are (1) professional specialty, (2) executive, administrative, and managerial, and (3) technical and related support.[22] Particularly important will be the growth of demand for executives. McKinsey & Company points out that the executive population in the United States has been growing roughly in line with GDP, suggesting that an annual economic growth rate of 2 percent for the next fifteen years would increase demand for executives by about a third.[23] But there may not be a large enough supply to meet demand overall. Altogether, the BLS estimates that during the next ten years there will be a shortfall of 23 million employees for approximately 52 million new jobs.[24]

Although similar occupational outlook projections do not exist for other developed countries, for most of them the Organization for Economic Cooperation and Development (OECD) publishes both historical statistics showing the percentage of employment in different industrial categories and more recent data about civilian employment broken down by major activities. These data show trends similar to those in the United States in the shift to service-producing industries and the growth of business-related jobs, and they suggest similar projections for the future. For example, employment in services as a percentage of all civilian employment rose in Germany from 39 percent in 1960 to nearly 60 percent in 1997 and in Japan from 41 percent in 1960 to over 62 percent in 1997.[25]

Looking to the future, a 2000 International Data Corporation study commissioned by Microsoft indicates that European demand for skilled professionals in telecommunications and computers will exceed supply by as much as 13 percent over the next three years. Hardest hit by the shortage will be Germany, the leader of the European Internet business, where demand for professionals in these two sectors is expected to exceed supply by as much as 15 percent, the equivalent of more than 400,000 jobs.[26]

Projections of future employment in the United States, and inferred similar projections for other developed countries, indicate a proportionally higher number of jobs to be filled in business-related occupations. They suggest that demand, often growing faster than supply, will continue to be high—notwithstanding periodic declines in economic growth—and that prospective employers will find a far more competitive environment for recruiting and hiring. When combined with the changes in labor supply described previously, these projections make it clear that companies will have to expand and change their search strategies to find the candidates they want.

Commitment and Loyalty

Although the 1990s were years of unprecedented prosperity in the United States and of substantial growth in many other developed countries, they still carried the legacy of the downsizing and layoffs of the more turbulent and troubled 1980s. In fact, as data from the *General Social Survey* show, workers during the 1990s were more pessimistic about losing their jobs in the next twelve months than workers were during the 1980s.[27] At the same time, many new businesses were created in the 1990s, greatly increasing labor market volatility. In the view of many analysts these developments were certain to have diminished workers' commitment and loyalty to employers, leading to dramatic reductions in employee tenure. However, both polls and government employment data show that this view is greatly exaggerated.

Even though lifetime jobs are a tradition of the past and multiple jobs over a lifetime the likely prospect for the future, job satisfaction remains high. A recent Harris Poll, *The Mood of American Workers*, finds 54 percent of respondents declaring themselves "very satisfied" with their current jobs and 37 percent "somewhat satisfied," leaving just 6 percent "not very satisfied" and only 3 percent "not satisfied at all."[28] Similarly, a 1999 issue of *Work Trends*, the John J. Heldrich Center for Workforce Development's multiyear public opinion series on U.S. workforce attitudes, reports that 88 percent of workers are at least "somewhat satisfied" with their jobs, and over half (54 percent) are "very satisfied."[29]

This high satisfaction also appears to translate into high commitment. Aon Consulting's 1999 America@Work survey shows that the commitment of American workers—as measured by Aon's *Workforce Commitment Index*—has continued to grow, even during the recent period of tight labor markets. In the words of Aon's David Stum, "There is no question we are in a seller's market for labor, yet employees remain basically loyal to their employers and the most sought-after employees—highly educated, high-income professionals—are more committed to their employers this year than last year."[30] The *Randstad North American Employee Review,* in its 2000 survey of more than 6,000 workers, confirms that 7 in 10 feel loyal to their employers.[31] Goldfarb Consultants, in a survey of 1,100 Canadian workers, reports what it considers even stronger support than is found among U.S. workers, with a national average of 88 percent committed to employers.[32]

Data on employee tenure in the United States support these poll findings of job satisfaction and commitment. The BLS reports that the median tenure with the current employer for all employed wage and salary workers was the same in February 2000 as it was in January 1983—3.5 years. For men the median tenure declined modestly during this period, from 4.1 to 3.8 years, and for women it increased slightly, from 3.1 to 3.3 years. The BLS also reports that the percentage of employed wage and salary workers twenty-five years of age and over who had 10 years or more of tenure with their current employer declined only slightly during the 1983 to 2000 period, from 31.9 to 31.7 percent. Again, for men there was a decline, from 37.7 to 31.7 percent, and for women there was an increase, from 24.9 to 29.9 percent.[33] For executives alone, the numbers are even higher. According to a survey of 3,000 managers by outplacement firm Challenger, Gray, & Christmas, tenure in 1999 was 9.8 years, up from 6.5 in a 1991 survey. In addition, in 1999 slightly over 18 percent reported working for just one employer, compared with 5 percent in 1991.[34]

This pattern of stability in employee tenure is consistent with the shift in employee values from predominantly materialist to predominantly postmaterialist, meaning the pattern is likely to continue. Moreover, two additional factors support this stability. One is that job mobility declines with age. The other is that Hispanics tend to be more committed to their employers than non-Hispanics,[35] and women, as the numbers just given indicate, tend to be more committed than men. Thus, with higher percentages of older workers and Hispanics in the U.S. labor force in coming years and the continuing high percentage of women, employee tenure is unlikely to decline and may possibly increase. Even at the younger end of the worker-age scale, where tenure has always been shorter and has become moderately more so recently, accounts of rampant job hopping also appear to be exaggerated. In the *1997 National Study of the Changing Workforce,* the Families and Work Institute reports: "Though most Gen Xers do not expect to stay in the same jobs forever, they are not a generation of job hoppers. Indeed, only 22 percent of young workers in both 1977 and 1997 said it was very likely that they would leave their employers within the next year."[36]

However, even though satisfaction and commitment remain high, and tenure is relatively unchanged, surveys of employee attitudes show a considerable gap between the loyalty workers feel toward their companies and the loyalty they believe their companies feel toward them. The Heldrich Center's *Work Trends Fall 1998 Survey* reports that "only 27% of American workers strongly agree that the company or organization for which they work feels a sense of loyalty toward them, while nearly half (49%) of American workers strongly agree that they feel a sense of loyalty toward the company or organization for which they work."[37] In a corollary finding from a 1999 survey of approximately 2,300 full-time workers, the Hudson Institute and Walker Information report that only 42 percent feel that their employers deserve their loyalty.[38]

In looking at the evolving labor market, it is clear that companies need to recruit and hire from a workforce that is slower growing, aging, and changing ethnically and in gender, and they must do so also in the midst of rising demand, especially for increasingly important knowledge workers. It is also clear that they will be more successful in reducing turnover and increasing retention if they recognize and reinforce workers' continuing strong feelings of satisfaction, commitment, and loyalty, rather than assume these feelings are weak and declining.

Recruiting Desired Job Candidates

Basically, recruiting desired job candidates involves two steps. The first is understanding what a company needs in the context of the evolving labor market. The second is searching for candidates, using both internal and external sources. The best companies have responded to the challenges posed by dramatically evolving labor markets with a range of successful recruiting practices covering both these steps.

Understanding Needs

To understand their needs the twenty-five best companies consider, first, their business plans and business strategies. Doing this in the context of the evolving labor market, they find both challenge and opportunity. The challenge is a pool of candidates whose composition is steadily changing from the pool that was previously available. The opportunity is being able to find employees representative of the populations for whom the companies are creating and marketing their goods and services. Second, even though the companies are looking for specific expertise and experience for many of the positions they seek to fill, they also understand that future high performance—given the changing nature of work—depends as much, if not more, on an employee's attitude and on the "soft" skills of communication, leadership, and interpersonal relations. Thus, in effect following the advice of management authority Jeffrey Pfeffer for selective hiring to build a high performance organization, they "screen for cultural fit and attitude—not for skills that can be readily trained."[39]

Matching Business Needs with Evolving Workforces. When companies align recruiting efforts with their business plans, they realize evident financial benefits. Among the six critical recruiting practices with a positive correlation to market value in Watson Wyatt's *Human Capital Index,* the two most important are hiring well-qualified professionals and designing recruiting efforts to support business plans. Each of these is associated with a 2.3 percent gain in market value.[40]

For many of the best companies, global competition and the rapid growth of postindustrial, intangible work mean that creativity and constant innovation are critical business needs. Thus the reach for new employees must be very wide, across nationalities and across gender lines, leaving no potential sources untapped. No one ethnic or national group has a monopoly on new information or new ideas. Each makes its own, often unique, contribution. Likewise, the search for new markets must be continuous, and once in new markets, the need to develop and successfully sell competitive products and services is paramount. Success in both activities requires building global workforces, hiring from abroad as well as at home, including employees whose heritage gives them the languages, the experience, and the knowledge of other lands. In the same manner, many of the best companies are attentive to the changing populations of their home countries, mindful of the need to hire from their ranks to maintain and grow domestic markets. Experience is also a critical business need, especially in the face of slower-growing younger workforce cohorts, and leads often to the hiring of older workers and the fashioning of flexible part-time and job-sharing employment to accommodate them. And because many business needs respond to evolving populations, meeting these needs requires taking advantage of the changing workforces within these populations.

At Intel, a global corporation with over 85,000 employees in forty-five countries, Tony Fox, manager of Intel University, says: "We really want human resources to be a central thread of the organization, woven right into our overall business objectives. . . . [W]e really try to map out what are the business needs of the company and how human resources can provide effective support to meet them." Because these business needs require both a constant stream of new products and ever-growing markets to consume them, the human resource response has been to develop programs and create practices that have led to a global workforce that is 36 percent outside the United States, 31 percent minorities, and 27 percent female.

The financial goal of Merck & Co., with operations around the world, is to perform in the top quartile of leading health care companies. To meet that goal, states chairman and CEO Raymond V. Gilmartin, "we need people who can discover and develop important new medicines and market them effectively around the world."[41] Finding these people, says Wendy Yarno, Merck's senior vice president for Human Resources, means "looking at the entire talent pool, down all the different avenues where you can find talent. The overall philosophy," she emphasizes, "is to hire the best people, regardless of what they look like or who they happen to be." The result is a workforce that is global and diverse, that is "representative of the general population," not because that was Merck's explicit goal, but because it was the outcome of focusing on its business needs.

Business needs also drive the recruiting efforts of best companies in the retail sector. Kevin Harper, vice president, People Division, Wal-Mart Operations, told me that Wal-Mart's human resource policies are based on the characteristics of the communities in which its stores are located. The goal, he explains, is to achieve a balance in each store appropriate to the demographics in the surrounding area in terms of ethnic groups and nationalities. He also spoke of the challenges posed by a shrinking labor market and pointed out Wal-Mart's response of employing increasing numbers of part-time and senior employees, the latter (defined as individuals over fifty-five years old) accounting for over 15 percent of its

900,000-member U.S. workforce. Similarly, the seemingly ubiquitous stores of Starbucks Corporation reflect the demographics of the
neighborhoods in which they are sited. Sharon Elliott, senior vice
president for Human Resources, states: "We embrace diversity as a
standard way of doing business. To us it means everything that
encourages different opinions, which in turn fosters innovation and
stimulates entrepreneurism." Like Wal-Mart, Starbucks is also a
strong employer of part-timers. Moreover, says Elliott, with their
diverse staffs, "our stores are our best form of marketing."

Harley-Davidson, the nearly century-old manufacturer of America's most famous motorcycles, sees human resources as a natural
adjunct to its business goals. When I asked Director of Diversity
Brenda Brimage to explain Harley-Davidson's diversity policies, she
said: "As we put together our diversity strategies and initiatives, we
really try to base them on business needs. And that means focusing
on who we want to buy our bikes and to ride our bikes in order to
keep our business going. The focus is to reach widely and to be as
inclusive as possible. Currently and traditionally, our customer base
has been dominated by white males." Moreover, workforce diversity at Harley, Brimage told me, is more than a matter of race or na-
tionality or gender—or even salaried versus hourly, or tenured versus
less tenured. It is also a matter of riders versus nonriders: "For the
record, being a rider is not a requirement to be hired or to work here.
But there is a difference between those who ride and those who
don't. Those who ride experience Harley differently than those
who do not."

Outside the United States, there is a similar awareness of the link
between business needs and workforce development. Novo Nordisk,
based in Denmark but with operations in sixty-one countries, knows
that to continue to innovate and to continue to serve old markets
and enter new ones it must build a workforce inclusive of all those it
wants to reach as customers. So attentive is it to the cultures and attitudes of those in the countries in which it operates, that it asked them
to participate when it drew up the list of values for its new vision
statement. Henrik Gürtler, corporate executive vice president, who

had the assignment to modernize the management and value systems of the company, explained that he approached the general managers in each country with this goal for the new vision statement: "We want to take out everything that is either inapplicable or not optimal in your culture and see what's left." He also asked them to "give us the basic business conduct principles that apply in your country and the list of values you would like to see appear in our new statement." Out of this process came a list of six "core values" and ten "fundamentals" that today provide the basic guidance for Novo Nordisk's conduct in all the countries in which it has operations.

In Japan, Toyota also sees both challenge and opportunity in the connection between its business needs and evolving workforce populations. The challenge is in Japan itself, where Toyota employs 70,000 in a national workforce whose numbers have already peaked and are now declining. Mitsuo Kinoshita, managing director and member of the board, explained that each April a new policy is established for the coming fiscal year. "This fiscal year" he said in February 2000, "the upcoming issue is the aging society," and the challenge is "how can we fully and effectively utilize the human resources we have." Among the options being discussed in public policy forums in Japan and already being tried in some Japanese businesses are extending employment beyond the traditional retirement age of sixty, bringing more women into the workforce, allowing more job sharing and part-time work, and making better use of current employees (that is, ending the still prevalent but inefficient practice of lifetime employment). Encouraging immigration, an option once rarely spoken of, is also now beginning to appear on policy agendas, at least for discussion.

Although the domestic challenge for Toyota is very strong, its greatest opportunity lies outside Japan, where it sells 60 percent of its cars, a proportion that is steadily growing. Its response to this opportunity has been particularly interesting. Known for its success in the 1970s and 1980s in meeting the automotive needs of maturing baby boomers, especially in the United States, Toyota in the early 1990s, as it stuck with its earlier models, picked up the appellation "stodgy." To shed this image it has turned in part to the design preferences of its younger more global workforce, and the result has been a burst of stylish, offbeat small cars, with names like Fun-Cargo, Vitz, and the Will Vi, the last a funky little vehicle that Toyota's president has likened to a pumpkin.[42] Toyota's goal in growing a worldwide workforce that will innovate and market for it is not to arrive at a distillation of the attitudes and values of the countries in which it operates—in the manner of Novo Nordisk—but instead, taking a different tack on the course of globalization, to find and nurture what Kinoshita calls a "global mind," an increasingly shared worldview that will guide the creation and promotion of products for markets everywhere.

In matching needs with evolving workforces, the best companies are paying more attention than they formerly did to nonwhites, nonnationals, older workers, and women. They know not only that these are the fastest-growing components of today's and tomorrow's workforces but also that they are the fastest growing components of their marketplaces. Many also realize the added bonus that these groups contain the employees with the strongest loyalties, the longest tenures, and the highest retention rates.

Identifying Skills and Competencies. For many of the best companies, the skills most desired as they search for new employees are not those of technical expertise. These they may consider necessary but not sufficient. In an era when intangible work will continue to predominate and to grow, desirable job candidates also need to have skills in communication, leadership, and interpersonal relations, including those that have been identified as components of *emotional intelligence* in the path-breaking research of Daniel Goleman.[43] Employers' high regard for these skills is seen in the 1994 *National Employer Survey* of the National Center on the Educational Quality of the Workforce. In one part of the survey, respondents at more than 4,000 establishments ranked on a scale of 1 to 5 (with 1 being "not important or considered" and 5 being "very important") the factors they considered in making hiring decisions. The top two, well ahead of the other nine factors on the list, were "applicant's attitude" (at 4.6) and "applicant's communication skills" (at 4.2).[44]

At Cisco Systems, high on many lists during the last several years as both a best employer and a best performer, Barbara Beck, the former senior vice president for Human Resources, says, "We're looking more for competency areas . . . for people who are interested, passionate, good team players . . . than we're looking for a specific skill set." Chris Williams, former vice president for Human Resources at Microsoft, puts it this way: "Occasionally we need someone who is an expert in, say, TCP/IP protocols. But more often than not, the kinds of people we're looking for are people who are flexible, open, willing to take on a challenge, have a certain amount of passion in their eyes, want to do things, want to make a difference, want to change the world." Howard Schultz, the man who transformed Starbucks from a small Seattle coffee retailer to a household name, wrote in his aptly titled autobiography, *Pour Your Heart into It:* "Whether I'm hiring a key executive, selecting an investment banker, or assessing a partner in a joint venture, I look for the same kind of qualities most look for in choosing a spouse: integrity and passion. To me, they are just as important as experience and abilities."[45]

At Nokia, the world's number one cellular telephone maker, Juhani Hokkanen, senior vice president for Human Resources, has drawn up a pie chart titled "Competency Profiles—Success Factors." "Value based skills (behavioral)" take up about 70 percent of the pie, "process skills (know-how)" about 20 percent, and "professional skills (knowledge)" only about 10 percent. In Japan, Mitsuo Kinoshita points out, graduates of universities have not studied special fields in depth. "Thus when we [at Toyota] look at applicants, we look at their very basic abilities, and when we receive newcomers, we do not characterize them as management or specialists. Only later, after they join us, will they gradually be divided."

Many of the best companies, focusing their recruiting efforts on candidates with desirable soft skills, will hire *for the company* rather than for a specific position. At telecommunications giant Ericsson,

Management Planning Director Anne-Christine Carlsson says, "The focus is exactly on strategic and critical competencies; so if we find talented people that we think can contribute to our business, we bring them in, irrespective of whether or not we have an open position." Similarly, at supplemental insurer AFLAC, Senior Vice President and Director of Human Resources Angela Hart says, "We take open applications; we are not position specific. You put in your application, and any job that becomes available we can bump against your file and your skills to see if you qualify." And at Microsoft, Chris Williams asserts, "One of the things we've encouraged our people to do is to hire for Microsoft, not for their business or their problem." Such practices clearly call for flexibility as a desired skill, and that is exactly why, explains Henrik Gürtler, flexibility is the first item in Novo Nordisk's human resource policy and one of the qualities most sought.

At some of the best companies a highly desired competency, especially in an increasingly competitive world, is the ability to deliver results. Thus they seek job candidates with past successes, usually in the areas of interest to the company but sometimes in any kind of activity, not just business. Jim Moore, director of Workforce Planning and Development at Sun Microsystems, says, "We are looking for demonstrated success in a field that is of particular interest to us." At Compuware, Denise Knobblock, executive vice president for Human Resources and Administration, follows a similar practice: "We actively search for individuals who are successful in their current careers." John Hofmeister, director of Human Resources at Shell, explains that achievement is one of the three major qualities the company has focused on in recruiting in the past decade, and the president of Royal Dutch/Shell, M. A. van den Bergh, declares that "Shell People are by nature achievers."[46] One of the "five individual capacities" by which Ericsson identifies and assesses job candidates is "result orientation." And one of the three principal qualities sought by Singapore Airlines is business sense and, as Wu Yoong Lynn, senior manager Human Resource Planning, succinctly expressed it, "track record."

George Binder, former chairman and CEO of Amgen, the world's largest biotechnology firm, believes the net must be cast even wider: "We want to see somebody who has been successful before," he told *Industry Week*, "and that success can be in whatever they chose to do. If they played violin, we want to know if they were a really good violin player. If they played football, were they on the starting team or did they sit on the bench?"[47]

Finally, for a number of the best companies, the soft skills sought are related to their businesses and corporate cultures. High-technology companies, like those in pharmaceuticals and information technology, search for people who show initiative and who can work independently, persistently, and patiently. David Kaye, associate director of Corporate Communications at Amgen, put it this way: "If you've come from a company where you have a very defined job and your boss tells you what to do and you follow the ten steps and check them off, you are not going to succeed here. We look for people who figure out how to get the work done their own way."

At Microsoft, Chris Williams spoke at length of searching for people who were not "vertical," meaning with great depth in one field. "Instead, we want someone who has been doing this and that and the other thing, who is open to exploring new ideas and new changes, who is a good thinker, a good learner, a good problem solver." Similarly, Microsoft's Web site states, "We encourage our people to speak out, take risks and challenge conventional wisdom." But qualities of persistence and patience are equally important. Williams also points out that the most honored achievement at Microsoft is "to ship a piece of software" (recognized, as described in Chapter Two, by the presentation of a plaque to every member of the development team, in a culture not prone to individual performance awards) and, as a recent *Fortune* profile of the company revealed, "The reality of software development . . . is that a substantial portion of the work involves days of boredom punctuated by hours of tedium."[48]

For those best companies whose employees are regularly involved in face-to-face relations with customers, people skills are most desired.

"Retailing is, above all else, a people business," says Coleman Peterson, executive vice president of Wal-Mart's People Division, and Kevin Harper correspondingly notes that one of "the three basic beliefs" underlying the company's recruiting and hiring policies is customer service. Starbucks, Sharon Elliott says, has a foundation of "critical skills" that underlies all its human resource processes, and central among these are people skills. At MBNA, one of the world's largest issuers of credit cards, "Getting the right customers . . . and keeping them" is a veritable mantra, on the walls and over every door in the company's Wilmington headquarters. Putting this into practice means that MBNA, as Ken Pizer, senior executive vice president, emphasizes, "must be a company of people who like people."

Searching for Candidates

In the search for job candidates, companies look both internally, to their current workforces, and externally, to traditional resources such as the media, colleges and universities, job fairs and affinity group organizations, and executive search firms and employment agencies. In addition, in the last few years a totally new medium for recruiting has exploded to widespread use—the Internet.

Internal Sources. Finding job candidates internally, through employee referrals or through transferring or promoting existing employees, has several important advantages. It saves time, and it saves money. Also it is more likely to result in candidates who are compatible with the company's culture, and—when current employees are transferred or promoted—it involves people who already know the company and how it operates and who in turn are known quantities to the company. In addition, independent research provides evidence that people hired through employee referrals have longer tenures with the organization than those recruited from other sources.[49]

Several of the best companies make wide and successful use of employee referrals. Dennis Liberson, executive vice president for

Human Resources at major credit card provider Capital One, told me that its largest (up to 45 percent of new hires) and best source of recruits worldwide is referrals, and according to *Fortune* he has found that "candidates recruited through the company's internal referral program were stronger applicants who wound up having longer tenure at the company."[50] At leading independent software vendor BMC, Human Resources Senior Vice President Johnnie Horn finds that "employee referrals have been a powerful resource in attracting talent. In fact, over the past two years we have increased our employee referral participation worldwide." And Diana Root, BMC director of Human Resources, notes that a large percentage of the company's hires come directly from employee referrals. The first page of MBNA's *Guide to Employment and Benefits* tells employees, "We encourage you to refer friends and associates you think may be qualified for employment at MBNA," and at Microsoft, where Chris Williams believes that "when you get good people, they attract other good people," almost 40 percent of employees are recruited through internal referrals.

Most of the best U.S. companies that use employee referrals pay substantial bonuses for them, though none of the best companies outside the United States do. Capital One awards up to $2,500 for each applicant hired. BMC pays a $3,000 bonus for exempt-level referrals and $750 for nonexempts. At MBNA, $250 is typical, with up to $1,000 to $1,500 given for technical positions. Compuware, in addition to a finder's fee of $1,000 to nonmanagement staff for any referral resulting in a professional level hire, recently introduced a targeted program that pays employees $10,000 for successfully bringing in sales and technical personnel. Others paying bonuses include Intel, which offers a standard bonus and also a bonus for more competitive jobs that can run higher, "definitely into four figures," says Tony Fox," and Amgen, which pays $1,000 and a t-shirt ("it's a great t-shirt," senior director of Human Resources Ilana Meskin assured me).

At Microsoft, however, the bonus is only a nominal one, a $50 gift certificate at the company store. Chris Williams explains: "In order for it to be most effective to get the best and the brightest, [the bonus] would have to be very large. Our concern is that employees would get fixated on the reward. Giving someone a new Porsche for bringing you a new employee may not be the correct motivating factor."

Some of the best companies also follow a practice of promoting from within. At Amgen, Ilana Meskin states, "We fill 25 percent of our jobs internally, so there is healthy career mobility on a regular basis." CDW, the leading U.S. direct marketer of computer products, promotes "almost exclusively from within," according to Vice President of Coworker Services Art Friedson. At Cisco, says Barbara Beck, "60 percent of the people in management positions we want to be able to promote from within; but 40 percent of the managers we want to bring from the outside, because we want fresh ideas and we don't believe we have them all in-house."

External Sources.   In searching outside their organizations for job candidates, the best companies use a wide variety of sources, but most of these companies recognize the necessity of looking for people who are representative of both the evolving labor market and future customers.

Media advertising is still an important external means of bringing in job candidates at some of the best companies. MBNA's Ken Pizer says, "I still call responses to targeted ads and referrals the principal source." Even though internal associate referrals are Capital One's single largest source, it also does "a lot of paid media—both newspapers and radio." But, says Dennis Liberson, the company is not a big classified advertiser: "We've found that, typically, the only people who read classified ads are those people looking for work, often because they don't have jobs. Those people are not the most attractive candidates for Capital One."[51]

In the high-tech field, where the need for skilled knowledge workers is especially great, classified ads have even less value. When Cisco was growing rapidly in a very competitive job market, a survey of employees in competing companies—put together by an outside contractor—revealed that these employees did not pay attention to want ads. What they said, Barbara Beck told me, was, "We have better things to do than read the want ads. We're not looking for jobs. People are calling us." Cisco's response was to find out what they did read, what got their attention, and in particular, what would cause them to leave their companies and go elsewhere. The answer was that they change jobs if friends they respected told them of a better place to work. This led to a campaign, "with banners in all the locations frequented by the people Cisco most wanted, which said simply, 'If you have friends at Cisco, call them. If you don't, we'll give you one.' We guaranteed them that within twenty-four hours they would get a call back, not from the human resources department, but from someone in their field, someone who would tell them what it was like to work here, someone who would answer any questions they had. And the response we got from that was phenomenal."

In a somewhat similar fashion, several of the best high-tech companies have turned to new hires and their own personnel to augment their recruiting efforts. BMC's Johnnie Horn says, "We have reduced substantially the use of contingency agency relationships . . . we have hired professional recruiters . . . we are even rotating line people through HR to help source specialized skill sets." Microsoft, Chris Williams explains, "has several hundred people who do nothing but recruit because an important part of our charter is to grow and recruit well."

For most of the best companies, colleges and universities are still major sources for job candidates. CDW has twenty-one campuses it visits every year exclusively to find candidates for sales positions. Harley-Davidson, says Tim Savino, director of Organizational Development and Training, is "going more directly to colleges and universities, doing a lot more recruiting there than we did five years ago." To fill its regular openings for scientists, Genentech maintains numerous relationships with specific universities and research institutes. Similarly, Sun Microsystems targets selected schools and, according to Jim Moore, has "ramped up college hires to a little over 400 from less than 100 three or four years ago." Intel, according to its Web site, "maintains a comprehensive college intern program that works as a feeder for recent college recruitment," and in 1998, approximately 15.4 percent of its worldwide hires and 45 percent of U.S. hires were part of Intel's Recent College Graduate program. In Japan the role of universities is even more pervasive. Mitsuo Kinoshita of Toyota explains that the customary practice is for professors at Japanese universities to make recommendations to companies about their students. "Because of this, the students do not have difficulty joining companies." The drawback is that students' "choice of companies is limited by the recommendations."

For almost all the best companies, recruiting is becoming more global. Wendy Yarno of Merck says, "As talent gets more and more scarce, you just have to look more and more places to find it," and she points out that as Merck expands into other countries, it wants "to predominately staff the local organization with people from those geographies." At MBNA, Terri Murphy, formerly in HR and now director of Marketing, believes that one of the practices that has made the company successful is its sensitivity to other cultures and its willingness "to hire in local markets." Sun Microsystems, says Jim Moore, "has mostly in-country managers," and at Intel, Tony Fox told me, "We certainly think that for any country in which we have a facility we should be leveraging the population there." Microsoft, with 31 percent of its employees located outside the United States and over 4,000 new job openings each year, "does recruiting trips around the world," said Chris Williams, mentioning a recruiting group that had just returned from a visit to Belarus in the former Soviet Union.

In the United States, where minorities are a steadily increasing percentage of both the customer base and the workforce, many of the best companies are actively searching among minority groups for job candidates. Intel, according to its Web site, "has formally sanctioned employee groups that have been formed by volunteers to provide networking, integration, development and outreach activities. This includes African Americans; Asians; Indians; Christians; Muslims; gay, lesbian, bisexual or transgender employees; women and others," and Tony Fox reports that these employee groups play an important role in recruiting. AFLAC, whose workforce is 36 percent minorities (non-Caucasian), actively recruits from minority ranks by attending job fairs and working with affinity groups. Judy Heyboer, former senior vice president for Human Resources at Genentech, which has 38 percent minority employment, describes the company's very active involvement with minority job fairs and minority organizations, and Merck has long had fellowship programs for minority students.

Harley-Davidson wants "to get people inside to look out," says Brenda Brimage, "so we've expanded our recruiting efforts to include a broader range of colleges and organizations of different interest or race or focus, such as black engineering groups and women engineering groups. We're doing things we have never done before. We want to be as inclusive as possible so that we can put butts on those seats."

Finally, all the U.S. best companies, especially those in high-tech fields, and the European ones, but not yet the Asian ones, have important initiatives directly targeting women. Sun Microsystems is particularly focused on women at the executive level. "We do target to hire women," Jim Moore says. "We do target interest groups that are particularly attractive to women. But it's a challenge for a technology-driven company because the percentage of women graduating from the technology schools is not very high. The woman issue for us is tougher than almost any of the others."

When Microsoft discovered it was not finding the numbers of women it wanted in the colleges where it was recruiting and asked why, the colleges replied that the women were not in the pipeline. So Microsoft decided it had to go back further. To do so, the company funded programs with the YWCA and a number of other groups to try to get—and keep—women interested in math and computer science at much earlier ages. Similarly, the Intel Web site announces that that company makes "special investments for women and people of color in science, engineering and technology." In 1998 alone, Intel contributed more than $101 million to such educational programs.

Ericsson is domiciled in Sweden, where the national legislature is 45 percent women, by far the highest percentage in the fifteen-nation European Union, and the company is a leader of activities around the world to promote female leadership throughout society, not just in business. Programs exist in every part of Ericsson for the recruitment, development, and advancement of women, particularly through their participation in the Ericsson Management Institute. So serious is this commitment that three company presidents ago the rule was established that every class of instruction in the institute, no matter how small, had to have at least two women, otherwise the president would not come to address it. Figure 3.1 shows the percentage of minorities and women employed at the U.S. best companies.

The Internet. According to Nua, a Web publishing service, as of August 2001, 513.41 million people worldwide had Internet access. Of these an estimated 180.68 million were in the United States and Canada (approximately 60 percent of all North Americans, up from 6.7 percent in 1995), 154.63 million in Europe, and 143.99 million in the Asia-Pacific region, with nearly a third of these last in Japan alone.[52] It is also clear that these numbers are rising very rapidly. For example, one on-line research service, Strategy Analytics, forecasts that by 2005, an astonishing 91 percent of U.S. homes will be on-line.[53] Given such numbers, on-line services of all kinds are being created and are growing rapidly. Among the fastest growing are on-line recruiting services.

Most of these services—often called *job boards*—post jobs, take résumés, and assist in matching the two. Several are comprehensive in scope, covering all types of jobs in all locations; others cover particular fields, like finance or the media, or particular geographical areas, like New York City or California's Silicon Valley. One—6FigureJobs.com—is presumably only for applicants not willing to settle for compensation of less than $100,000! The advantages for job seekers are considerable: the cost of listing is about 5 percent of

FIGURE 3.1. Minorities and Women Employed
in U.S. Best Companies.

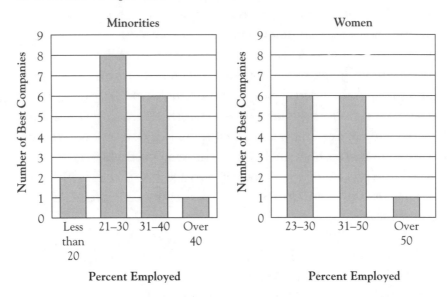

Sources: S. Branch, "The 100 Best Companies to Work For in America," *Fortune*, 1999, *139*(1), 118–144; R. Levering and M. Moskowitz, "The 100 Best Companies to Work For," *Fortune*, 2000, *141*(1), 82–110; R. Levering and M. Moskowitz, "The 100 Best Companies to Work For," *Fortune*, 2001, *143*(1), 148–169.

the cost of placing a classified ad in a major newspaper for thirty days, the range can be global, and the response—usually electronic—is often much faster. With these advantages, the use of these services is widespread and growing. The Bureau of Labor Statistics reports that with 6,000 Internet job sites in operation, more than twice as many people now look for work on-line as use private employment agencies;[54] and a recent poll of 300 U.S. companies by kforce.com, a Web-based staffing concern, showed that on-line recruiting accounted for one out of every eight hires in 1999.[55]

Many of the best companies make use of these on-line recruiting services. Most also have or are adding Web site pages that list available jobs, accept résumés, and include steadily increasing capabilities to facilitate the recruiting and hiring process. As might be expected, the companies furthest along in this activity are IT firms. Not only are their businesses often principal developers and service providers for the Internet, but the employees they want are those who are already familiar with the Internet and most able and most comfortable using it. Intel's Tony Fox says: "The Internet has changed our whole approach to staffing quite radically. We've actually seen more and more of our applicants coming through it. So we've really had to shift our practices to make sure that we are easily accessible via the Internet." Chris Williams of Microsoft says: "We get 60-plus percent of our résumés over the Internet. We do a great deal of advertising on it because we've found that's the way we've gotten many of the people we want to hire. They are not in the job market, they are not actively searching for jobs, they are just trolling the Internet."

Cisco, which makes much of the equipment that powers the Internet, has been one of the companies furthest along in using it for recruiting. When it found itself in heavy competition for high performers, it used informal surveys to learn which Web sites the people it wanted to recruit liked to visit, and then created links between its Web site and these other sites, such as the site of Scott Adams, creator of the long-suffering cartoon character Dilbert. Those people who ventured further into Cisco's list of available jobs and began selecting jobs were then given the option of clicking on a button labeled "profiler" to see a profile of the kinds of individuals who could be successful in the jobs the site visitors had put in their shopping carts. If still interested in the jobs, they were asked a series of questions, first, about their capabilities and, second, about their behavior, such as how they worked in a team. In the course of this profiling, says Barbara Beck, "We infuse our culture, we make it interesting, we make it fun. We know that most people fill these out during their work hours, so there is a little button on the left side that says, 'Uh oh, my boss is coming,' and when you click on it the screen changes to something like, 'The top ten gifts to buy my boss for Christmas.'" This self-screening profiler was a success: "We hired one person out of every four who submitted profiles, as compared to the 20,000 résumés we were putting into our résumé tracking system each month."

A number of companies outside the information technology field are also making use of the Internet for recruiting or are planning to do so very soon. At Merck, Wendy Yarno told me in early 2000, "We are just at the point where we are putting in the capabilities for people to submit their résumés to our database, along with the capabilities of managers to search that database for the talent they are looking for." Sharon Elliott at Starbucks sees the Internet as "a highly competitive tool . . . because, when you've got the right screening processes, you can reach many more people, much more quickly." MBNA has linked its HR database to the Internet, enabling it to receive, acknowledge, and store the résumés it receives. Capital One, which has successfully used a telephone voice-response system to acquire 40 to 45 percent of its applicants, has done a validation study for a similar instrument for the Internet to acquire applicants for professional jobs.

Internet use is especially high in the Scandinavian countries, and all the best companies there are employing it for recruiting. Anne-Christine Carlsson of Ericsson finds it particularly useful for "the young technical guys we are interested in; this is their way of life today." For Nokia, domiciled in Finland, which has one of the highest per capita rates of Internet use in the world, Internet recruiting "seems already to be improving the previous practice we had," according to Juhani Hokkanen; and at Novo Nordisk in nearby Denmark, where the Sunday newspapers have long been the traditional place to find job advertisements, Henrik Gürtler says, "We need to be on the Internet because the majority of the new students at the business schools and universities are getting used to going on it and they're not reading the Sunday newspapers."

In all the best companies in Asia, Internet recruiting is also growing rapidly. Acer Associated Vice President Terry Lu told me that the company had used the Internet earlier just to advertise jobs, but in the last six months it had begun to take applications for open positions over the Internet, and Taiwan Semiconductor Manufacturing Company (TSMC) Vice President for Human Resources S. H. Lee explained that in 2000, the year the company started "e-recruiting," more than 75 percent of incoming résumés arrived electronically. Singapore Airlines has been both advertising jobs and taking applications for them over the Internet. In Japan, where widespread use of the Internet is a factor transforming the way the Japanese live, reducing the traditional emphasis on personal relationships, Toyota is actively recruiting and hiring on the Web. Among the Internet's many benefits, noted Mitsuo Kinoshita with a smile, is that receiving job information electronically means more room for Japanese students, whose traditionally small living quarters used to become crammed with company pamphlets.

Almost all the executives with whom I spoke felt that Internet recruiting was faster and more efficient than other means of finding job candidates. Applications are easier to trace and retrieve, qualifications can be quickly searched using keywords, candidates can be compared more easily, and prescreening allows companies to accelerate and focus the entire process; and these advantages will likely grow in the future. Most of the executives also believe that Internet recruiting is reducing costs, for example in travel, for both companies and job applicants. But several point out that saving money is not the most important consideration. S. H. Lee says, "Lower cost is not the reason for e-recruiting. You use it because you can reach out to global talent, and you get far better effectiveness and efficiency with electronic processing capability." Wendy Yarno also says, "I don't see it as a tool to save money; I see it as another avenue to find talent." And Chris Williams echoes her words, but with his own emphasis: "The Internet isn't about saving. It's about reaching people who otherwise wouldn't be in the job market."

Even though the number actually being hired through Internet recruiting is still rather modest—in the range of 10 to 15 percent of all hires in several of the best companies—it is rising rapidly. The inherent advantages of the process and the steady increase of people on-line throughout the world mean that Internet recruiting will become more widespread and more sophisticated and soon will be the principal means of recruiting for most organizations. Nevertheless, the best company executives felt that it was not and probably never would be sufficient unto itself. To select appropriately from those recruited, it is still necessary to meet job candidates face to face.

Selecting Among Those Recruited

Selecting among job candidates who have been recruited usually involves testing and interviewing. At the best companies, use of the former is selective and use of the latter is universal.

Testing

Preemployment tests are generally of two kinds: (1) ability tests and aptitude tests, which measure the skills already learned and the capability to learn or acquire a new skill, and (2) psychological or personality tests (also called psychometric tests), which attempt to measure behavioral qualities such as sociability, flexibility, creativity, self-confidence, and leadership.

Both kinds of tests are widely used, though the American Management Association's 2000 survey of workplace testing finds a new divergence in their use among the 2,133 member and client companies from which the AMA received responses. From 1998 to 2000, the percentage of respondents doing job skills testing increased slightly, from 57.9 to 60.0, whereas the percentage making psychological measurements decreased dramatically, from 52.3 to 33.0. The AMA speculates that this decrease may represent either a labor market so tight that companies felt less need for psychological tests to help them select among otherwise equal candidates or a disenchantment with their use.[56]

Nevertheless, several of the best companies do conduct preemployment tests, usually of the psychological kind and usually as an adjunct to interviewing job candidates. Among the most comprehensive testers is Ingram Micro, the world's leading wholesale distributor of computer products. According to David Finley, senior vice president for Worldwide Human Resources and an organizational psychologist himself, "A half day of testing is part of [Ingram's] selection process for the most senior level of people." One example of successful testing is Ingram's concurrent validity testing, in which the existing workforce is queried in order to develop valid criteria for performance and performers, which can then be used to predict the likely performance of other groups, such as job candidates. Concludes Finley, "While a combination of interview and test information clearly enables the best selection decisions, given the choice between only having test information or having someone just do an interview, I'll take the test information every time."

At Capital One, says *U.S. Banker*, managers have "a fanatical belief in the power of testing, measurement, logic and analysis."[57] Nowhere is this better seen than in the company's hiring processes. Selection among job candidates to staff its important call centers, for example, is a multistage process that begins with seventeen questions on an automated telephone voice-response system, which candidates answer by pushing the appropriate buttons on the telephone keypad. "We have done a selective study on these questions," says Dennis Liberson; "they predict work orientation, who is going to be employed, and who won't be suitable for the call center environment. [The voice response system] is just like an interview, except it's much more predictable." The results, says *Workforce* magazine, are "stunning. Overall cost-per-hire dropped 45 percent, while the pass rate increased by 30 percent."[58] Now, concludes *U.S. Banker*, "the company sees [its hiring process with these candidates] as a good predictor of their job performance, that these employees have higher productivity and show more initiative than peers at other companies."[59]

Other U.S. best companies conduct a variety of preemployment screening systems and tests. Wal-Mart has a toll-free applicant prescreening system (TAPS), and Cisco's Web-site profiler serves as a kind of automated preemployment test. AFLAC uses assessment tests at the administrative and clerical levels and the professional level as well, and Harley-Davidson gives a basic comprehension test to applicants for many of its positions.

The best companies outside the United States make wider use of preemployment testing. Ericsson assesses management candidates against five individual capacities it believes are indicators of overall capacity and potential. Novo Nordisk makes psychological tools like the Myers-Briggs Type Indicator available for the hiring process, though their use is left up to local personnel departments. Toyota, a much sought-after employer of entry-level managers, uses tests to help determine such qualities as creativity and teamwork capability among its many managerial applicants. For the same purpose, it also engages candidates in structured debates and asks them for brief oral or written presentations on specific themes. TSMC is developing various tools including psychometric tests to supplement interviewing, and Singapore Airlines has an outside contractor administer psychological tests during the employee selection process.

Many of the best companies, however, eschew testing of job candidates, especially psychological testing. Executives at MBNA, Merck, Intel, Sun, Amgen, and Compuware all said no when asked if their companies used psychological or psychometric testing. When *Fortune* asked Microsoft's director of Recruiting, David Pritchard, whether psychological testing was of interest to him, his answer was unequivocal: "It doesn't really interest me much. In the end, you end up with a bunch of people who answer the questions correctly, and that's not always what you want. How can a multiple-choice test tell whether someone is creative or not?"[60]

For these companies, as well as for most of the other best companies, the principal means of selecting among those recruited is interviewing.

Interviewing

Although there are many types of interviews, there is general agreement among professionals that the most effective is the *structured interview*. As Claudio Fernández-Aráoz, a partner at the executive search firm of Egon Zehnder International, recently summed up the current view: "Since World War I, extensive research has been conducted on the efficacy of various evaluation methods, including different forms of interviews, reference checks, personality tests, and even graphology and astrology. Without a doubt, the research has shown that structured interviews are the most reliable of all popular techniques for predicting performance."[61]

The key element of a structured interview is a list of well-prepared questions, created in advance of the interview and designed to reveal a candidate's competencies in such areas as skills, general abilities, and relevant knowledge. Usually, each applicant is asked the same set of questions, and the replies are scored or otherwise evaluated so that a record of the interview exists and comparisons among candidates can be made. Structured interviews or variants of them are widely used by the best companies.

Starbucks uses a "structured interviewing process" that Sharon Elliott describes as "designed not only around the criteria necessary for success in a particular job, but more importantly, also designed to elicit the degree to which an individual has had experience with each of the items that comprise the criteria." Cisco also uses a structured interview process that is both thoroughly planned and yet sufficiently flexible to take advantage of the different positions and perspectives of interviewers of the same candidate. "When a manager fills out a requisition," Barbara Beck explains, "we ask that person to list on the interview sheet, which is all automated, the competencies the candidate should have to be successful in the position, and to identify who needs to be on the team of interviewers and what each member of the team should be focusing on." The advantage of this is that "everyone doesn't ask the same question. You don't get a narrow brush of someone's capabilities. You have six people asking very deep questions in the areas that are important for this person to be successful."

A widely used form of the structured interview is the behavioral interview, in which candidates are asked about their behaviors in certain work situations during their previous work or in hypothetical situations or both. The goal is to determine whether and to what degree a candidate possesses the attributes desired for the company in general and for a particular job.

At Amgen, says Ilana Meskin, "We use fairly rigorous behavioral interviewing to get our best guess at how people will actually behave." The process is carefully planned and deliberately extended. "Typically, the people who are interviewing a candidate have a series of advance discussions about what is to be asked to determine, in depth, whether the candidate has the particular capabilities desired." The interviewing alone at Amgen can take as long as a day and a half, because, as David Kaye points out, "Once you pass muster with some of the key interfaces during the interview process, you're hired. There's no six-month learning period. That's all done. The whole indoctrination period is done in the interview process, and you start on day one and you go to work."

Intel has a set of values that according to Tony Fox, "we really try to operationalize. So, as we go through the hiring process we do behavioral interviewing that looks for people to give us examples of customer orientation results, discipline, and other things that are fundamental values for Intel." Groups vary in scoring the results of these interviews but that has advantages, such as forcing a dialogue when the numbers differ, and "we're a very numbers oriented company." Harley-Davidson also has particular values it wants to maintain, and believing, in the words of Flip Weber, retired director of Human Resources Staffing, that "past behavior is a predictor of future behavior," it does behavioral interviewing when hiring both salaried and hourly staff. For the latter, many of whom are employed on production floors, the company asks lots of questions related to team behavior.

Capital One uses "a strict behavioral interview approach" that Dennis Liberson has described as "based on the premise that the best indicator of future performance is a demonstrated behavior in a previous role. We may ask a potential employee to give us an example of an interaction with a customer where the customer wasn't satisfied with his or her answer. The candidate would then take us through a real-life situation. We look for the existence of past behavior to predict future behavior."[62]

For some of the best companies, behavioral interviewing is a means of determining whether candidates are strong in attributes central to a company's culture or mission. Merck's annual report states, "Our emphasis on leadership sets us apart from other companies and gives us a competitive edge in all aspects of our business;" so in interviews, Wendy Yarno explains, "we want to make sure we're hiring people who have the right leadership beliefs and behaviors." Compuware emphasizes employee empowerment, and the "core" of what it looks for in employees in the interview process, says Denise Knobblock, "is do they feel secure with themselves and do they feel confident in how they're relating themselves to you." At MBNA, with its strong mission of customer service, Terri Murphy explains that "the last interview is with a senior manager of the company, and the whole point of that interview is not to check qualifications or the candidate's aptitude for the job but whether [the candidate is] a good person who likes people."

Microsoft doesn't have a "crisp set of questions," says Chris Williams, "but there is an interviewing style we like to use." This style seeks to draw out evidence of the qualities the company is looking for. For example, applicants might be asked about such apparently non-job-related matters as manhole covers: Why are they round? (So they will not fall through the manholes.) How many are there in the city of Seattle? (There are lots of approaches to answering this one, such as determining the number of miles of streets and the average number of manholes per mile.) "The point," Williams explains, "is to try to ask you a question that has very broad implications and to see how you go about trying to answer that question. What we're trying to do is figure out if you know how to think, if you can think well on your feet, if you can think outside the box."

Several of the best companies also involve nontraditional participants in the interview process. Capital One, recognizing that there is a skill to recruiting, attempts to find and use people in the company who are good at recruiting and have a passion for it. At MBNA, a candidate has not only an interview with his or her potential manager but also extensive interviews with two persons who will be peers in the job. Intel also includes job peers in its interviewing teams and sometimes partners or customers as well. Amgen, which views its extended hiring process as a surrogate for a probationary period, is even more inclusive, conducting what it calls a "consensus" style of interviewing. To the traditional interview team, it adds people with whom the candidate may interface on the job, including representatives of totally different business groups, and in the case of a managerial candidate, even people who will be direct reports.

Finally, although most of the best companies wait until all interviewers have seen a candidate before the interviewers and others exchange views on his or her qualifications and qualities, one employs a unique "rolling" approach to the interview process. In this approach, an HR manager of the company explains: "After every interview, wherever it is done, the person who does the interview writes a message to the rest of the people involved saying, this is how I think the candidate did, these are some areas I think we should explore more." Those who are still to see the candidate will read these messages first and thus be able to pursue any matters needing clarification, presumably resolving any doubts and, at the least, ensuring that no one will be saying later, "I wish I had asked that." Table 3.1 summarizes the testing and interviewing practices of the best companies.

In the end though, what matters most is the success of an organization's recruiting and selecting practices.

Evaluating Recruiting and Selecting Practices

To "close the loop" on the recruiting process, argues Jeffrey Pfeffer, it is necessary to assess both its results and its performance.[63] One of the simplest and most obvious ways of doing so is by monitoring

TABLE 3.1. Testing and Interviewing Practices at the Best Companies.

Practice	Used	Not Used
Preemployment testing	56%	44%
Psychometric testing	40	60
Behavioral interviewing	36	64
Nontraditional interview participants	32	68

employee turnover. A number of the best companies also use several other means of evaluation.

Monitoring Employee Turnover

To evaluate the success of recruitment and selection efforts, companies usually monitor voluntary turnover, in which employees leave companies of their own volition. Such turnover occurs for many reasons, including career opportunities or better compensation elsewhere, dissatisfaction with management, a move to a more favorable place to live, family issues, and of course retirement. But whatever the reason, it is a fair presumption that better recruitment and selection will lower voluntary turnover and the costs associated with it; hence it is a reasonable measure of the success of these practices.

It must be remembered, however, that turnover rates may vary for a number of exogenous reasons over which management has little control. For example, organizations with older workforces usually have lower voluntary turnover rates than those with younger employees, whereas organizations in which skill requirements are low for most employees, as in retailing and routine assembly work, generally have higher rates than those with more skilled workforces. Furthermore, turnover rates vary with level and type of position. In a recent survey of 206 medium to large U.S. companies, the William M. Mercer human resource consulting firm found that technology workers and administrative staff had the highest turnover rates, whereas management and professional employees had the lowest.[64] Thus any comparison of turnover rates must take account of the nature of a company's business and the composition of its employee population.

As might be expected, economic growth and low unemployment rates in the prosperous years of the late 1990s in the United States have tightened U.S. labor markets, increased employee mobility, and raised voluntary turnover rates. The 2000 retention practices survey of the Society for Human Resources Management (SHRM), employing a random sample 473 HR professionals from the SHRM membership, found that 41 percent of the respondents said the number of voluntary resignations at their organizations had increased during the previous three years, 40 percent said they had remained stable, and 13 percent said they had decreased. Three years before, the 1997 SHRM retention survey found that 50 percent of respondents had experienced no change in the number of voluntary resignations over the previous five-year period, and 35 percent had noted an increase. In actual percentage rates, the 2000 survey found that the average voluntary turnover rate among all respondents was 17 percent, and that it increased in proportion to the number of employees in a company. In organizations with 1,001 to 5,000 employees, the rate averaged 21 percent, and when there were more than 5,000, the rate averaged 26 percent.[65]

Using 26 percent as a benchmark for the U.S. best companies (all but one with over 5,000 employees), it is clear that they have done very well in terms of voluntary turnover rates. Table 3.2 shows these rates for the years 1997, 1998, and 1999 for the fifteen of the seventeen that have appeared on *Fortune*'s annual "100 Best Companies to Work For" list at least two of the last three years. More than half have seen their turnover rates actually decline during this period or stay about the same, and all except retailers CDW (the only company with less than 5,000 employees) and Wal-Mart Stores (in an industry where average turnover rates are normally high)— had rates of 15 percent or less in 1999. As for Wal-Mart, its recently launched program to increase retention in its worldwide million-plus workforce (especially by reorganizing its orientation process to place

TABLE 3.2. Voluntary Turnover for Fifteen Best Companies.

Company	1997	1998	1999
AFLAC	11%	8%	11%
Amgen	9	6	5
BMC Software	12	14	*
Capital One	20	13	11
CDW Computer Centers	24	29	18
Cisco Systems	6	5	6
Genentech	14	12	9
Harley-Davidson	3	*	3
Intel	7	10	6
MBNA	9	NA	15
Merck	6	8	6
Microsoft	NA	7	10
Starbucks	16	19	*
Sun Microsystems	13	11	6
Wal-Mart Stores	26	*	28

Note: These companies were selected because they appeared on *Fortune*'s "100 Best Companies to Work For" list for at least two of the last three years.

* Not on the *Fortune* list for these years.

Source: S. Branch, "The 100 Best Companies to Work For in America," *Fortune*, 1999, *139*(1), 118–144; R. Levering and M. Moskowitz, "The 100 Best Companies to Work For," *Fortune*, 2000, *141*(1), 82–110; R. Levering and M. Moskowitz, "The 100 Best Companies to Work For," *Fortune*, 2001, *143*(1), 148–168.

more emphasis on relationship building and less on technology) has already won it considerable praise.[66]

Some of these companies set turnover or turnover-related goals. Compuware's turnover goal in late 1999 was 14 percent, for example. CDW and Starbucks also set specific targets, and Merck, as it develops more formal human resource plans, intends to establish measures for goals like turnover. Sun Microsystems chooses a somewhat different tack and sets retention goals, one for personnel overall and one for the top 5 percent of the company. And some companies, like

MBNA, choose not to set turnover goals. "Not everyone is going to work out here," explains Terri Murphy, "and we don't want to motivate [managers] to hold on to every single person. So we intentionally took turnover out as a company-wide goal."

Turnover rates at the best companies outside the United States are also low, as examples in both Europe and Asia indicate. John Hofmeister said that historically Shell has had a very low attrition rate, "less than 1 percent at the management level and at the technical level as well." He noted that recently the overall rate had risen somewhat, perhaps to 2 or 3 percent, but that it was still very low because of the "strong engagement and commitment process at Shell." At TSMC, S. H. Lee says, "We have been very lucky to have very low attrition, averaging about 3 or 4 percent for indirect levels—what you in the United States call 'exempts'—and about 8 to 9 percent for direct levels."

Other Means of Evaluation

Ingram Micro's David Finley believes that "turnover percentage is a very spurious number," and so the company places greater confidence in tenure as a measure of the success of recruiting and hiring practices. "If you take median days or weeks or months, or whatever period is appropriate for an organization," says Finley, "and measure that, you have a much more stable indicator than turnover percentage."

In a different use of time spent on the job, several companies use probationary periods to provide a fixed number of months in which to monitor the performance of new hires and acquire feedback helpful in evaluating the processes used to hire them. Intel has a six-month probationary period for exempt positions and a nine-month period for nonexempts. Singapore Airlines has both a one-year probationary period and a three-month internship, also depending on the position. At Toyota, however, in accordance with Japanese practice, there is no probationary period. "Once newcomers join us in April," Mitsuo Kinoshita says, "even though after that we find them not fully qualified, it is against our way of thinking for us to dismiss them or fire them." Clearly, the pressure on Toyota, as on other Japanese firms, is to get it right the first time.

Like many organizations, most of the best companies conduct exit interviews with departing employees, not only to evaluate internal conditions and practices but also to guide future recruiting and hiring. At MBNA, exiting employees rate fifteen different indicators, covering all aspects of their association with the company from the time they were recruited and hired to the time they leave. The results, summarized and arrayed in a variety of functional and demographic categories, are then distributed to everyone on the company's Senior Operating Committee. In order to refine the exit interview process further, some companies, like BMC, also conduct focus groups with departing employees.

The most comprehensive evaluations are done by those companies that attempt to examine hires of a particular year or from a particular group, tracking their performance and associating it with the practices in place at the time they were recruited and selected. At Cisco, Barbara Beck, who calls herself "a metrics-driven person," has gone back to the hires of particular years to examine the subsequent annualized turnover of each year's group. Capital One, as noted earlier, also applies considerable quantitative rigor to all its human resource practices. Using the large amount of data collected annually from its comprehensive associate survey process, it has not only reduced attrition but also learned that its highest performing people are those who come through its referral process.

Sun Microsystems evaluates its recruiting process from the standpoint of "time to fill" a position and "perceived quality of candidates," and also analyzes the retention rates of particular groups, like college hires. Even more comprehensive is the big study it recently completed, called *Sun Art*, short for *Sun Attraction and Retention*. The study interviewed current employees, people who had left, and people who were thinking about leaving, seeking to understand both what attracted them to Sun and what motivated their decisions to depart or to consider departing. From these interviewees, Jim Moore explains, "we identified the features of the company they valued most and then went out and benchmarked them against our 'people competitors,' the six companies that attract people away from us. We then put the results in a little two-by-two matrix, showing where we were at parity, where we were at a competitive disadvantage, and where we had a competitive advantage." The goals then are "to turn competitive disadvantage at least to parity, and parity to competitive advantage; and where we were well above average, to trade that off for something rated more highly."

Attentive to changing workforce composition and changing worker attitudes as well as to the skills and competencies required by the changing nature of work, the best companies have used the practices described in this chapter to recruit and hire the employees they need. How then do they compensate them to obtain their high performance and keep them?

4

Compensation and Benefits

It is not possible to imagine an offer of employment that does not state a salary and possibly other terms of compensation as well as descriptions of the various benefits available with the employment. So when candidates for jobs consider offers or negotiate over them, they are seeking a compensation package with a monetary value they regard as a fair exchange for their labor. There may be other reasons why they choose to accept or reject employment, but for most, compensation is important. Money matters.

However, even though money plays a central role in decisions to accept employment, its role in obtaining best performance and in retaining employees is less clear. Though still important, it may not always be essential. In this chapter I look first at the complex relationship between compensation, performance, and retention, as revealed in the attitudes of employees and in the research of leading business writers, academics, and consulting firms. Then I review the compensation and benefits practices of the best companies, concluding with a brief description of several companies' efforts to evaluate these practices.

Compensation, Performance, and Retention

Numerous polls and surveys have asked employees about the importance of compensation in choosing a job and about its role in persuading them to perform better for their employers and to stay with them. Business writers and academics have also tackled the subject. Some have tried to draw conclusions from the little empirical research done linking compensation to actual performance and retention figures; others have sought insights from the research and theories of behavioral psychologists and sociologists. What emerges are a number of hypotheses and suggestions that may supply some guidance for employers but also require further investigation.

Employee Attitudes

It is clear that workers throughout the world consider compensation one of the major factors in what constitutes a good job, though not necessarily the most important one. Gemini Consulting's 1998 survey of more than 10,000 workers from thirteen industrialized nations across four major geographical areas (Europe, Japan, Russia, and the United States) finds that workers consistently identify the same five key attributes of a good job. One of these five is "good pay."[1] Similarly, the survey of 1,800 U.S. workers in the *1999 Workforce Commitment Index* of Aon Consulting's America@Work/United States @Work series identifies "benefits and compensation" as one of five "company commitment driver categories."[2] The *Work Trends Fall 1998 Survey* of the John J. Heldrich Center of Workforce Development, employing 1,001 telephone interviews with adult members of the U.S. workforce in the forty-eight contiguous states, also finds that compensation is highly regarded. In a list of sixteen job factors, "total annual income" ranks third, with 33 percent saying it is "extremely important" and 51 percent saying it is "very important." Only "ability to balance work and family" and "health and medical coverage" rank higher.[3]

However, when dealing with the factors that drive performance, surveys of employee attitudes show that the role of compensation is far from certain. In 1994, a study of 663 performance-reward plans, sponsored by the American Compensation Association (ACA) and conducted by the Consortium for Alternative Reward Strategies Research, did find that such plans "can provide an organizational tool to improve performance through people, often with attractive and calculable returns."[4] But six years later, *WorldatWork's Rewards of Work 2000* study reports that direct financial rewards are tied for third (selected by 54 percent of respondents) among five kinds of rewards considered very or extremely important for performance motivation. First, at 69 percent, is work content.[5]

Other surveys of employee attitudes also cast doubt on the linkage between compensation and performance. The *1996 Towers Perrin Workplace Index* study points out that as companies "focus the employment relationship on performance rather than tenure and loyalty, they also raise the expectations of their employees." Noting that these expectations imply that companies will share the fruits of their success, a research leader of the study, Steve Bookbinder, concludes, "What the data suggest is that real sharing hasn't fully materialized."[6] The 1997 version of the same study, as *Workforce* reports, "indicates that employees feel there's a strong decline in how their employers are holding up their part of the pay-for-performance bargain."[7]

Finally, survey questions on the importance of compensation in remaining in one's job bring forth positive though also tentative responses. The *2000 Randstad North American Employee Review*, reporting the results of a study of 6,000 North American workers, finds "59 percent of employees consider 'competitive industry wages' as an important consideration in staying with their current job if a new job were offered."[8] The second annual BridgeGate *Employee Retention Survey*, which surveyed 667 working Americans, asked which factor would keep them in their present jobs. Cited most often (46 percent of the time) was "a raise." Just as important though were several nonmonetary issues, which together were also cited 46 percent of the time.[9] The recent *WorkUSA 2000* survey of the attitudes of 7,500 workers by Watson Wyatt Worldwide presents the same not-so-strong, not-so-weak view of the importance of compensation to retention. Of the seven key factors the survey identifies as driving employee commitment, "competitiveness of rewards" ties for third with "job security."[10]

Research Findings

In recent years, management theorists, consultants, and academics who study compensation have reached different conclusions and made different recommendations concerning its role in improving performance and aiding retention. One of the most comprehensive arguments against the use of financial rewards, including corporate incentive plans, was made by a leading writer on the subject, Alfie Kohn, in his 1993 book, *Punished by Rewards: The Trouble with Gold Stars, Incentive Plans, A's, Praise, and Other Bribes*, later excerpted in a widely noted article in the *Harvard Business Review*. In a sweeping analysis, Kohn contends that it is not poor design that causes incentive programs to fail but rather the inadequacy of the fundamental psychological assumptions that underlie them. As a result, he says, "rewards typically undermine the very processes they are intended to enhance," and he condemns them with a broad six-point indictment: (1) they do not motivate, (2) they punish, (3) they rupture relationships, (4) they ignore reasons, (5) they discourage risk-taking, and (6) they undermine interest.[11]

Kohn's views elicited a number of rebuttals and a spate of journal articles in defense of financial rewards. Defenders, though acknowledging some of the detrimental effects of such incentives, nevertheless felt that they made both intuitive and practical sense. For example, one human resource manager wrote: "Incentives are neither all good nor all bad. Although not the right answer in all cases, they can be highly effective motivational tools." Several defenders cited the importance of financial rewards in reinforcing desired behavior.[12] Two management professors specializing in compensation systems argued that "behaviors that are rewarded are repeated, behaviors that are punished are eliminated. When certain behaviors are followed by money, then, they are more likely to be repeated."[13] Others wrote of the successes of their own firms in using financial rewards to improve performance.

Among those who found some value in the use of incentives, a common theme was the importance of tying them to corporate strategies and goals. "The focus should be on business objectives, not tasks," wrote Jerry McAdams, director of the Consortium for Alternative Reward Strategies Research.[14] A sophisticated variation on this theme, which retains but reorients the role of money as a motivator, is offered by leading compensation authority Edward E. Lawler III in *Rewarding Excellence: Pay Strategies for the New Economy*. Lawler argues that new technologies and major social and political changes have created a major revolution in the way organizations are managed and that these two fundamental changes have increased the importance of employees' knowledge and skills and thus resulted in a transfer of power from employers to employees. In terms of compensation, this means that pay rewards should be given not to jobs fitting specific descriptions but to individuals who have acquired the knowledge and skills companies need to achieve their business objectives and that this individual focus is what the most desirable employees are and will be demanding.[15]

For Lawler, money still matters: "The lesson in all this is clear. If organizations want to attract high performers and be high performers, they have to be willing to reward excellent performers highly."[16] His view is consistent with recent company practice, which, as research and business writers indicate, has steadily enlarged the role of compensation both in rewarding performance, past and anticipated, and in retaining high performers.

Performance.   Paying for performance is not a new idea. Piece rate pay has been around at least since the early twentieth century, when Frederick Taylor began applying scientific management to tasks. Commissions have long been a major part of the compensation of salespeople, and merit pay and bonuses are well-established methods of rewarding good performance. But the widespread use of *pay for performance*, often referred to as *variable* or *incentive pay*, and its implementation in increasingly discrete and sophisticated forms are more recent phenomena. In the United States, it was especially spurred by the recession of the early 1980s, when companies sought to cut fixed costs by freezing salaries and linking a larger portion of compensation to profits. In mid-1985, under the headline "Companies Turn to Incentives: Pay Linked to Performance," a *New York Times* article stated: "In industries ranging from financial services and telecommunications to food processing and high technology, more and more companies are pushing incentive pay farther and farther down their white collar ranks in a bid to tie compensation more closely to individual and divisional performance." The article also cited a study by the Hay Group, a human resources consulting firm, reporting that more than 100 of 400 firms surveyed either had begun to spread incentives to lower levels in their organizations or planned to do so. Their goal was "to make the fixed salary a smaller and smaller part of total compensation."[17]

Since then the practice has spread rapidly and widely. In a 1996 survey sponsored by Wirthlin Worldwide and O. C. Tanner, 78 percent of CEOs and 58 percent of human resource vice presidents said their companies had rewards programs recognizing performance or productivity.[18] Four years later, reporting on a survey of 800 U.S. firms, Hewitt Associates, also a human resources consulting firm, found that nearly 80 percent were using performance-based pay for some groups of employees, compared with only 47 percent in 1990.[19] European companies, for whose senior executives fixed pay is still a higher percentage of total compensation than is found in U.S. firms, are also rapidly increasing their variable pay.[20]

Types of variable pay have proliferated. They include profit sharing, in which all or certain groups of employees share a percentage of company profits; gain sharing, in which part of pay is tied to the achievement of certain goals by specified groups or units in a firm; incentives offered to small groups or teams; and incentives offered to individuals. Closely related types of pay that also seek to improve performance are skill-based pay, rewarding employees' acquisition of new skills, and competency-based pay, rewarding the development of competencies—often knowledge related—that create value for companies.

All these kinds of pay for performance are usually given in the form of cash. But also growing in use and importance for rewarding employees and for creating greater feelings of ownership and thus aiding retention are the issuance (or the sale at a discount) of shares of stock and the granting of stock options. Although a growing number of companies are making shares of stock and options to buy stock available to more and more employees, this form of compensation is still most extensively practiced for senior executives and tied to improvement in overall financial objectives over which they presumably have significant control. It is for members of this group that the growth of variable pay, both in absolute amounts and as a percentage of their total compensation, has been greatest. According to one commentator, "performance-based pay now accounts for more than half of all compensation for top executives and directors."[21] Some of this variable pay is in long-term incentives and other lump-sum cash payments, but a substantial portion is in stock options alone—more than 50 percent of total compensation for CEOs and about 30 percent of senior operating managers' pay—with both portions growing rapidly.[22] Watson Wyatt's *Executive Pay in 2001: The Land of Opportunity*, incorporating results from 13,115 executives at 1,545 companies, reports that executives at U.S. companies saw an average increase in total cash compensation in 2000 of 7.8 percent over the prior year, and an average increase in stock option grant value to CEOs of nearly 25 percent, to almost $4 million from $3.2 million in 1999.[23]

The critical question is, is this working? Is increased pay for performance producing better performance in the companies that are practicing it? The answer is that the results are mixed. In one specific area of variable pay, employee stock ownership plans (ESOPs), there is evidence of a positive correlation between the existence of such plans and improved performance. In a 1986 study of forty-five companies with ESOPs, covering the five years before and the five years after they instituted their plans, two researchers compared each company with at least five similar firms, looking at a total of 238 companies. They found that on average, sales and employment increased 5 percent faster in the ESOP than in the non-ESOP firms in the five years following the installation of the plan and that 73 percent of the ESOP companies significantly improved their performance during this period.[24] More recently, a quantitative study done at Northwestern University's Kellogg Graduate School of Management of the financial performance of 382 companies two years before and four years after adopting an ESOP finds that these companies' return on assets is 2.7 percent higher than that of their industry peers for each year in the four-year postadoption period.[25]

However, for more comprehensive incentive plans the results are less clear. In a study of innovative reward programs in Fortune 1000 companies in the late 1980s and early 1990s, three experienced researchers found that "no reward practice was reported to be 'unsuccessful' or 'very unsuccessful' by more than 11% of the firms using it. A clear majority of firms reported each practice to be 'successful' or 'very successful.' . . . However, many firms reported that they were undecided about the effectiveness of each innovation (20% or more in most cases)."[26] More recently, two other researchers reported on a longitudinal investigation of multiple organizations that found a linkage between pay and subsequent organizational performance. "However," they commented, "this relationship does not always reveal itself and at other times it has been both positive and negative in nature," leading them to conclude: "Recent reviews of the compensation literature highlight that our ability to offer firm conclusions as to the motivational and attitudinal effects of merit pay is limited and in need of more detailed investigation."[27]

Corroborating this conclusion, a report of the fifth annual Watson Wyatt *Strategic Rewards* survey, covering 410 employers and released in December 2000, concludes: "Only 24 percent regard rewards as a means of engaging people to improve business performance. Rewards, generally, are not seen as a source of competitive advantage, nor do most employers regularly measure the effectiveness of their reward plans."[28]

Finally there is the question of the results of incentive pay for top executives, especially CEOs. For top executives in general, there is continuing uncertainty. "The concept of pay for performance has gained wide acceptance," writes Alfred Rappaport of the Kellogg School, "but the link between incentive pay and superior performance is still too weak."[29] This seems especially true of stock options, which rise and fall at the same rate for both below- and above-average performers. "Stock option grants have come to dominate the pay of top executives," writes Brian J. Hall, another leading compensation authority, "but while they have made many people wealthy, their impact on business in general remains controversial."[30] However, in the special case of CEOs, Watson Wyatt's 2001 *CEO Pay Study*, which examined compensation levels at more than 1,300 large public companies, as reported in fiscal year 2000 proxy statements, concludes: "CEOs with higher pay opportunity, as measured by their total direct compensation over five years, had total returns that outperformed those of CEOs with lower pay opportunity."[31] This is consistent with past findings. Yet, as the *Wall Street Journal* has pointed out, CEOs tend to do well no matter what happens in their firms: "Pay for performance? Forget it. These days, CEOs are assured of getting rich—however the company does."[32]

Retention. In her 1998 study *Strategies for Retaining Critical Talent*, which surveyed 114 U.S. and European companies, Helen Axel finds that compensation remains the top retention incentive, especially among the U.S. companies surveyed. Eighty-nine percent of the 114 report using this incentive in the three years prior to the survey, and 36 percent (including some of the previous users) have it under consideration. Coming in second as a retention incentive is advancement opportunities, with 60 percent having used it and 25 percent having it under consideration.[33]

Similarly, Peter Cappelli of the Wharton School in Philadelphia and director of the school's Center for Human Resources writes:

"The most popular retention mechanism today is compensation. Most companies try to lock in their most valuable employees with 'golden handcuffs,' pay packages weighted heavily toward unvested options or other forms of deferred compensation." But Cappelli also points out a major shortcoming—these forms of compensation are easy for outsiders to match. Golden handcuffs are routinely bought out with signing bonuses, or "golden hellos," and such incentives thus "end up becoming just another element of compensation, contributing more to wage inflation than to long-term retention."[34]

Research by consulting firm McKinsey & Company shows that new employees are more than twice as likely as veteran employees to make tenure decisions based on total compensation,[35] and psychological research shows that one of the most important reasons for voluntary turnover is a desire to earn more money.[36] It is also clear that top-performing companies pay more than lower-performing companies, and that all companies have been steadily increasing pay packages, especially to top executives.[37] But although companies are evidently paying more, in more creative ways, to keep people, there is scant evidence that more people are staying because they are getting more money. In one recent survey of more than 600 human resource professionals by the outplacement and career services firm Lee Hecht Harrison, 55 percent report that they have taken steps to reduce turnover at the professional and executive levels, mostly by raising pay and increasing incentive compensation. However, only 10 percent report that turnover rates have fallen.[38]

Given the uncertain influence of financial rewards on performance and retention, how have the twenty-five best companies managed their compensation practices to motivate and retain their high performers?

Providing Compensation

Compensation today is generally of three kinds. The basic component is almost always salary or wages. This base pay is appropriate to the position for which it is paid and adjusted for the skill level and the experience of the person occupying the position. A second kind of compensation grew in use during the twentieth century and is now offered by nearly all for-profit firms and even by some nonprofit organizations. Usually paid in the form of a bonus and often representing a sharing of company profits, it reflects the firm's financial success and is often paid differentially to groups or individuals, according to the degree their past performance is considered responsible for that success. The third kind of compensation for employees is more recent. Employees receive a portion of the firm's equity in the form of shares of stock or—especially in the United States—the granting of options to purchase stock at fixed preferred prices. This third kind of compensation is also intended to reward performance, but even more it is designed to promote feelings of ownership, thus presumably encouraging still greater efforts to succeed and instilling a desire to remain.

Base Pay

In determining levels of base pay, the best companies have several objectives. The most important, in a global business environment characterized by strong demand for talented experienced employees, is to be competitive. This usually means at least meeting and often surpassing pay levels not only in one's own industry but also in other industries competing for the same talent. In fact a firm's closest competitor for human resources often is not its closest industrial competitor. In addition, the best companies are attentive to the levels of compensation appropriate to the different regions and countries where facilities are located or where workers originate. At the same time, some are developing truly global cadres of managers, whose pay scales are more consonant with those of similar managers in other companies than they are with typical rates of pay in either the firm's headquarters country or in its overseas locations.

Implementation of these objectives usually means surveying the competition and establishing benchmarks based on the compensation practices of leading companies, activities often done with the assistance of consulting or executive search firms. For most of the best companies, such surveying has resulted in pay levels well above the going average (usually around the seventy-fifth percentile), especially for senior managers and persons with important specialties. MBNA, for example, sets the seventy-fifth percentile as its target for both base pay and total compensation for its officers, but it uses the fiftieth percentile as the target for lower-level customer contact positions.

Some of the best companies seek leadership in compensation. Art Friedson, CDW's vice president of Coworker Services, says, "It's important for us to be a leader. You're going to work harder at CDW than you work anywhere else, and you're going to make more money here than you're going to make anywhere else." Dennis Liberson, executive vice president for Human Resources at Capital One, says, "We want to differentiate ourselves through our benefits and compensation programs";[39] and Fortune magazine reports that "Merck pays top dollar, and its benefits are extraordinary."[40] At Taiwan Semiconductor Manufacturing Company (TSMC), the tenth of its ten "business principles" states, in part, "Our goal is to provide salary and benefit packages that are above the industry average," and S. H. Lee, vice president for Human Resources, told me, "I would say we are actually one of the best-paying companies in the world in terms of total compensation."

However, many of the new economy best companies follow a different competitive approach, setting lower targets for base pay and leaving more compensation "at risk" through performance-based bonuses and variable pay, thus creating a total compensation package with the potential to outstrip the competition. Intel pays "close to or sometimes slightly below market in terms of base pay," says Tony Fox, manager of Intel University, "because we think that our overall compensation, with our bonus and stock programs, actually puts us ahead of market." Similarly, Microsoft has always given a substantial portion of its compensation in stock options and only recently (in mid-1999) upped its base compensation from the fiftieth to the sixty-fifth percentile for its industry.

All the best companies evaluate their employees periodically and adjust their base pay accordingly. Most do so annually, but some practice interesting variations. Wal-Mart evaluates new hires within ninety days and gives them a pay increase dependent on their evaluations; subsequent reviews are annual and also have pay increases tied to them. Novo Nordisk conducts an annual performance interview, typically in the first quarter; then, as Henrik Gürtler, corporate executive vice president, explains, there is a mid-year "talk with your boss where you make sure the targets are still the same, and if they are not, what they are." Harley-Davidson's "performance effectiveness process" involves quarterly discussions between employee and supervisor and an annual review documented in writing. BMC has an annual review process and quarterly "focal point" salary increases, and Acer performs half-year evaluations of employees and gives annual salary increases. At Sun Microsystems, says Jim Moore, director of Workforce Planning and Development, there are "annual salary increases with a distribution based on performance" and "a mandatory distribution of performance ratings," meaning that a percentage of employees will be at the bottom each year and will receive little or no pay increase.

Although employee evaluations are traditionally performed by supervisors, more and more of the best companies are adding other participants and steadily moving toward what are known as *360-degree evaluations*. In reviews of this kind, performed principally to gather information to guide development, the participants include not only supervisors but also peers, team members, subordinates, sometimes even customers—in other words, the full spectrum of 360 degrees. *Wall Street Journal* columnist Carol Hymowitz reports that despite the process's shortcomings, a recent survey of 232 companies by consulting firm William H. Mercer found that more than 65 percent are using such reviews, up from about 40 percent in Mercer's 1995 study.[41] Four of the best companies in a variety of industries— Amgen, Capital One, Intel, and Starbucks—do 360-degree evaluations at all organizational levels. Three others, Harley-Davidson, Microsoft, and Sun Microsystems, use these evaluations at senior levels for development reasons, usually for performance improvement. Merck has been using them for five years, Cisco does so "systematically," and Genentech has just started.

Finally, in some of the best companies, particularly those outside the United States, the annual review process is often very comprehensive, reaching well beyond adjustments in basic pay and also engaging employees in goal setting and long-term career planning. One U.S. company that undertakes a comprehensive annual performance appraisal process is AFLAC. As the company's senior vice president of Human Resources, Angela Hart, explains, "We break it down into two components: the first is measuring how well the employee did the last year; the second is the development piece, and it is a wonderful tool to indicate opportunities for development and to do career planning for the individual." Among the European companies, Nokia uses what Juhani Hokkanen, senior vice president for Human Resources, calls "a kind of performance map," incorporating the company's annual targets, to assist managers in agreeing with their team members on concrete measures. The annual review determines the extent to which these measures have been achieved. In Japan, Toyota carries out its annual reviews in April of each year, simultaneously with all the country's major companies. Each individual writes a mission statement that is certified by the appropriate supervisor. A year later, in a process of mutual communication involving employee and supervisor, the individual's performance is evaluated against the mission statement, and a new mission statement is then written for review the following April.

Among the best companies, TSMC conducts the most comprehensive annual reviews. They are rooted in TSMC's Performance, Management, and Development process, the goal of which, explains S. H. Lee, is to maximize the employee's performance and potential: "How do we define performance? We look at both the what [accomplishment against goals] and the how [soft elements, like skills, attitudes, behaviors, team work]." These reviews, usually conducted in January, include "cross team" participation, meaning that managers from adjacent teams participate. The reviews "thus provide opportunities for feedback and review on each employee's performance and individual development plan, with the resulting ratings then directly tied to both salary review and profit sharing."

Cash Bonus Pay

All twenty-five best companies pay cash bonuses. All of them do so in recognition of past performance, hoping to influence future performance, and some attempt to explicitly target retention. At most of the companies, bonuses reflect a combination of company and individual performance. Six companies, however, reward mainly company performance, and four focus principally on individual performance. In addition, many of the companies in each of these three categories pay *spot* bonuses, rewarding instances of notable one-time performance. They may also offer other one-time bonuses, such as sign-on bonuses and bonuses for the acquisition of particular skills or competencies. In most of the companies, all employees are eligible to earn these bonuses, which, except for those that are spot, or one-time, are a percentage of the recipient's annual base pay. For lower-level employees, the bonus is usually in the range of 10 percent or less; at senior levels it can go to 100 percent or even more. At these higher levels in firms rewarding both corporate and individual performance, the portion of the bonus based on the company's performance is usually much larger than the portion for individual performance.

The following sections describe the practices of several best companies in each of the three performance-based pay categories: company and individual, predominantly company, and predominantly individual. Figure 4.1 summarizes their use by all the best companies.

Company and Individual. Amgen's cash bonus system is typical of many best company systems that are based on both corporate and individual performance. First, an overall bonus pool is calculated. The amount depends on how the company did financially the previous

FIGURE 4.1. Performance Basis of Cash Bonuses in the Best Companies.

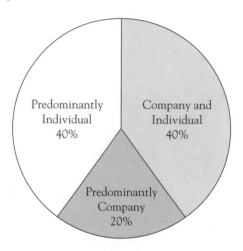

Predominantly
Individual
40%

Company and
Individual
40%

Predominantly
Company
20%

year and is expressed as a percentage of the firm's total salary bill. This percentage is then translated into a percentage of each eligible employee's base salary. The resulting figure also reflects the employee's level in the organization. The actual amount received by the employee, explains David Kaye, associate director of Corporate Communications, is "based on the individual's grade performance for the year and could be 100 percent of that figure or 75 percent or 110 percent, or even higher."

MBNA's *Guide to Employment and Benefits* explains that the company strives "to make [its various] incentive programs available to all people to reward achievements that exceed individual and group standards for quality and Customer satisfaction." To carry out this goal, says Senior Executive Vice President Ken Pizer, MBNA has literally hundreds of different monthly incentive plans for employees and also annual plans for corporate officers. These plans can result in bonuses ranging from 10 to 12 percent of base salary at the lower end, for nonexempt employees manning banks of phones, for example, to as much as 100 percent of base salary at the highest levels. For lower-level direct customer contact employees, performance may be measured in terms of calls per hour or customer sat-isfaction feedback, and at the higher levels it is calculated on meet-ing corporate objectives.

In its "Culture Audit" prepared for submission for *Fortune* magazine's 2000 list of the 100 best companies to work for, CDW states, "Fully 85 percent of our coworkers receive monthly or quar-terly bonuses tied to the productivity of themselves and their de-partments." Some of these bonuses are based on the productivity of individual workers, which in many cases can be very precisely measured—warehouse workers electronically scan the boxes they pack, for example, resulting in a exact record. Nonexempts (about 40 percent of the workforce) also receive a 5 percent bonus on quarterly earnings. This is given in the form of one-year deferred compensation and is meant to be a retention incentive. At the oth-er end of the company hierarchy, says Art Friedson, "managers and supervisors share in a year-end bonus, based on profitability, that comes right out of the pockets of the company's three founders." Finally, everyone is rewarded when major corporate milestones are reached. In 1996, as the company neared sales of $1 billion, then CEO Michael Krasny promised that when the goal was achieved, $1 million of this money would be shared among all employees, "not by job level but according to their number of months partici-pating." A few years later, with sales approaching $3 billion, $5 million in incremental bonuses was promised and also granted.

Nokia was giving annual bonuses but has recently shifted to semiannual ones. The amounts are based on both performance of the company and performance of the individual. In the case of the former the bonus is tied to the value of the company's stock and is extended to every person in the organization. However, Juhani Hokkanen explained, these sums are usually fairly modest, coming "on top of any other bonuses we have," such as those for individual performance. The latter, especially for individuals at higher levels, are awarded through a management incentive system with set tar-gets against which results are measured and amounts accordingly calculated.

Twice-a-year cash bonuses based on both company and individual performance are also the practice at best companies in Asia. Toyota provides cash bonuses in the summer and winter. The average total amount, which lately has been roughly equivalent to six months of an employee's salary, depends on the performance of the company; the exact amount is based on evaluations of individual performance. Acer gives an annual cash bonus and also a festival bonus at the time of the New Year's festival. The festival bonus can equal up to two months of salary, and the annual bonus—based on a combination of company, business unit, and individual performance—can equal from 20 to 50 percent of salary. Singapore Airlines also offers two cash bonuses. One, tied to individual performance, is an annual wage supplement equivalent to one month's salary; the other, tied to company profitability, is known as a "profit sharing bonus" and historically has amounted to the equivalent of one-quarter to one-third of annual salary.

Predominantly Company. AFLAC's cash bonus program, available to all employees, is based on two corporate targets: specific levels of profitability and persistence of policies on company books. The usual monetary goal for bonuses is 4 percent of employee salary. However, in recent years both corporate targets have been exceeded, resulting in bonuses of 6 percent of annual salary for all employees. A recently added component, acknowledging the greater responsibility of managers and supervisors, allows them to earn an additional amount. As a further convenience, AFLAC has a bonus deferral plan that permits its employees to defer up to 100 percent of their bonuses to their 401(k) plans.

In the past, Harley-Davidson had plant and site-specific bonus programs, but it found them cumbersome. So it now has a program that is based on performance of the company as a whole and is inclusive of everyone, even hourly employees. In the words of Brenda Brimage, director of Diversity: "There is a set formula. If the company succeeds and you have done your share, you automatically succeed. When all is said and done, this incents every site to support every other site." Seventy percent of the corporate target is financial performance, and most of the rest is achievement of quality measures. The bonus target is 5 percent of annual salary; but as at AFLAC, lately it has been running much higher, up to as much as 8 or 9 percent.

Intel has two bonus programs based on corporate performance. One, the Employee Cash Bonus Program, is a profit-sharing arrangement in which everyone in the company, in twice-a-year payouts, receives a share of the profit of the company as whole. Payment is calculated in number of days of pay, and in recent years, according to Tony Fox, it has made a significant contribution to employee remuneration. The other program, the Employee Bonus Program, awards bonuses based on the financial performance of the company overall and on the performance of each employee's business group. Each employee has a target based on his or her grade level and scope of impact. The amount received reflects the relationship between that target and actual business results. Internal Intel documents say that "over the past ten years the employee bonus program has been a key component of Intel's total compensation package."

Predominantly Individual. Everyone at Capital One receives bonuses, "all of them are performance based, and they are predominantly individual based." Dennis Liberson also explains that bonuses for teams, departments, and groups are "less than we used to do," and that although some bonuses may have a "team orientation, because we are a very collaborative culture," most are oriented toward individual competency and results. They are equivalent to anywhere from 9 to 70 percent of annual salary, with call center employees at the lower end and the executive group at the higher end.

Microsoft gives bonuses once a year, at the time of its annual reviews. Bonuses focus largely on individual performance, and amounts range from 0 to 15 percent of the amount of annual salary, with a company-wide budget that varies from year to year. "They are given to more than three-quarters of the population," former

Vice President of Human Resources Chris Williams says, "as a reward for immediate past performance, for how well the work you did recently impacted the company." Novo Nordisk also focuses its bonuses on individual performance. "It's possible to reach out for what corresponds to three months of cash bonus," says Henrik Gürtler, "linked back to the personal goals and business goals you have." Bonuses are very much valued, even though company "investigations show that the line management, particularly in Denmark, seems to have all sorts of trouble allocating their bonus pools." Despite this finding, Gürtler adds, "We are not ready to give everything as fixed pay because that was where we came from ten years ago, where everything was just a function of how long you had been in the company."

Many of the best companies also give one-time, or spot, cash bonuses for individual performance:

- Merck has a variety of spot awards for specific achievements in performance, ranging from a few hundred to a few thousand dollars, and sometimes even higher.

- Cisco "boasts . . . on-the-spot bonuses of up to $2,000 for exceptional performance."[42]

- AFLAC uses "spot awards" to reward specific individuals who come up with concepts that save the company significant amounts of money.

- Sun Microsystems has a program that allows a manager to "go on-line and . . . submit an employee for a spot bonus of from $200 to $5,000 for some extraordinary level of service."

- Ericsson gives spot bonuses of as much as $5,000 and higher for specific jobs that are particularly well done.

- TSMC's Quarterly Incentive Fund is available to vice presidents for discretionary spot recognition of individuals or teams "for exceptional performance or behavior, or for team building efforts."

Stock and Stock Options

Compensation through the issuance and assisted purchase of shares of stock and through the granting of stock options has grown rapidly. In the United States in 1974, 200,000 workers had equity in their companies; by 1999, the number had risen to 10 million.[43] Sanford C. Bernstein & Company, surveying 2,000 companies from 1992 to 1997, found that during that period the value of stock options and grants grew from $8.9 billion to $45.6 billion,[44] and by 2000, WorldatWork could report that 56.1 percent of the more than 2,800 for-profit respondents to its 2000–01 Total Salary Increase Budget Survey made use of some type of stock program for compensation purposes.[45] Outside the United States, similar programs have been instituted. In the United Kingdom, recent legislative changes have made employee stock ownership plans more attractive, and several hundred UK companies now have them; in Japan, 90 percent of publicly traded firms have mechanisms for employees to buy company stock; and in Russia, most enterprises with over 200 employees have been sold primarily to their workforces, with average ownership by nonmanagement employees ranging from 55 to 65 percent.[46]

The goal of these stock programs is to instill in employees feelings of ownership that will result in higher performance and lower turnover. If employees have a portion of their net worth in their companies, the reasoning goes, they will have a strong incentive to do their best to make those companies grow and prosper, thereby increasing that net worth. And if employees see their net worth growing, they will have an incentive to remain, an incentive their companies will likely reinforce with restrictions on the sale of stock issued to them and on the exercise of options granted to buy more stock. For executives, who have greater opportunity to affect corporate results, the portion of their compensation that is stock based and hence at risk will usually rise as the executives rise in their companies.

To attain the goal of a degree of employee ownership, most of the best companies provide programs for all or selected employees to acquire shares of stock, and many grant options to purchase stock at favorable prices.

Stock Purchases and Stock Awards.   All but a few of the best companies have plans that enable their employees to purchase their stock. In the United States, employee stock purchase plans (ESSPs) usually enable employees to purchase their companies' stock with no brokerage commissions and at a 15 percent discount. Under current accounting rules, this discount is not considered compensatory and thus is not a corporate expense—the employer's objectives are construed to be either to raise additional equity capital or expand ownership among employees as a means of enhancing loyalty to the enterprise.

ESSPs are available to all eligible employees, and purchases under these plans are usually made through payroll deductions of taxable compensation within specified limits. The total number of shares in the plans and the duration of each plan are generally subject to shareholder approval, a potential check on stock dilution. Among the plans of the best companies there are a number of minor variations. At Sun Microsystems and Starbucks, the share price for employees is the market price at either the beginning or end of the purchase quarter, whichever is lower; at Cisco, Intel, and Compuware, the employee price is the lower of the first day price or last day price in a six-month period. Wal-Mart, in lieu of a discount, adds to employee purchases 15 percent of the purchase amount, up to a limit of $1,800. At several of the best companies ESSPs have become very popular. At Capital One, 44 percent of employees participate, and at BMC, more than 50 percent do.

Among best companies outside the United States, Shell offers stock purchase plans in those countries where the plans are legal, and Toyota has created a stockholding association. Mitsuo Kinoshita, managing director and member of the board, explains that

Toyota employees joining the association receive "some advantages or incentives for them to acquire stocks easily."

Although awards of shares of stock—usually with restrictions on their sale or transfer—are sometimes made to relatively high-level executives as part of long-term incentive programs, the most advantageous way for U.S. companies to make broad-based awards is through employee stock ownership plans (ESOPs). Typically, ESOPs operate through trusts that accept tax-advantaged company contributions and use them to accumulate company stock, which is then allocated to accounts for individual participants. Among the U.S. best companies, for example, Compuware has an ESOP it operates in conjunction with its 401(k) Salary Reduction Arrangement, the purpose of which is "to reward eligible employees for long and loyal service by providing them with retirement benefits." All salaried Compuware employees, exempt and nonexempt, including all part-timers who average twenty hours a week or more, are eligible to participate in the ESOP. Allocations are made at the end of each fiscal year, based on the company's performance and proportional to each eligible employee's base pay.[47] In operation over twenty years, the plan has been a huge success. According to Ron Watson, director of Human Resources, "Depending on the value of our stock on any particular day, we could have a hundred or so millionaires walking around this organization because of the ESOP."

Several of the best companies outside the United States also award shares of stock or issue instruments of corporate ownership on very favorable terms. Shell occasionally makes use of restricted stock grants, and during 1997, Ericsson implemented one of the largest international issues of convertible debentures (bonds that can be converted into common stock) to employees that any company has ever arranged. In all, over 40,000 employees in forty-six countries participated in the issue, which had a value of 6 billion Swedish kronor (approximately US$615 million). Nokia awards stock based on corporate and individual performance, a system Juhani Hokkanen describes as "very much related to the retention of people," and Novo Nordisk makes stock grants that Henrik Gürtler characterizes as "not excessive, more on the order of one month's pay." These are not based on performance, he explains; instead, "according to where you are in the system, you get so many shares of company stock." Furthermore, in Denmark shares cannot be sold until five years after they are granted, thus aiding employee retention.

In Taiwan, where legal and accounting constraints make the granting of stock options difficult, awards of shares of stock are much more widely used. At Acer, according to Terry Lu, associated vice president, stock grants are based on four criteria: the level of the person in the company, the person's performance, the contribution the person is making to the company, and the company's future development. "If targets are achieved, dividends are issued to employees as shares of stock, and these can be considerable, ranging from one to one and a half times one's salary." Similarly, at TSMC profit sharing is given out as a company stock grant and can be "a very big part of compensation, equal to multiyear base salary," S. H. Lee explains. "Everybody participates, with the award tied directly to company profitability and individual performance for the year." First, a certain percentage of net income after tax is set aside as the budget for the whole company. When this total is distributed, each employee is allotted a budgeted amount of stock according to a formula with many elements—such as job level and salary level. This amount is then adjusted up or down based on individual performance.

Stock Options. The idea of stock options was conceived in the 1930s but was not put into practice until thirty years later, in the 1960s, and only after thirty more years, in the 1990s, did it burst into widespread use. The National Center for Employee Ownership estimates that in 2000, between 7 million and 10 million employees in the United States were receiving stock options, a dramatic increase from the 1 million employees eligible to receive them in the early 1990s.[48] And the number continues to accelerate rapidly. In a survey of 1,352 companies released in January 2000, Watson Wyatt

Worldwide found that nearly 19 percent of employees were eligible for stock option grants in 1999, up from 12 percent in 1998.[49] The Bureau of Labor Statistics (BLS), in its *Pilot Survey on the Incidence of Stock Options in Private Industry in 1999*, found that 22.1 percent of publicly held companies and 2.4 percent of private establishments offered stock options.[50]

In the United States, stock options have considerable advantages and also some important disadvantages for both companies and employees. Companies use stock options because, as with other forms of equity compensation, they see them creating bonds of ownership, with the anticipated benefits of higher performance and lower attrition. In addition, because options have no cash value they are not expensed, as other forms of compensation are, an outcome that can have positive implications for stated corporate earnings. Moreover, when employees exercise *nonqualified* stock options (the more common of the two types of option plans), companies obtain deductions equal to the employees' gains, even though the companies have spent nothing to grant them, and these deductions can reduce taxes. On average, the total cost to a company of using stock options is about a third that of awarding full shares, thus giving options hefty leverage.[51]

However, even though options can reduce a company's compensation expense and thus improve earnings, the reverse can happen in a falling stock market. To retain valued employees, existing options may have to be repriced, making current stockholders unhappy and incurring new compensation costs if the options become valuable again. And to attract desirable new employees in a declining market, companies may be required to extend job offers with a larger proportion of the compensation in cash, further increasing costs. In addition, if large numbers of options are granted, large numbers may eventually be exercised, a dilution that can reduce earnings per share and lower shareholder value. Finally, even when the value of a company's stock rises over a long period, the firm may still experience a talent drain when option holders cash in. Some may retire early, free to pursue philanthropic goals, lifelong hobbies, or simply lie on the beach. Others may look for still greener pastures, eager to put their talents and their newfound wealth to use in innovative start-up ventures.

Stock options also have significant advantages and disadvantages for employees. The greatest advantage occurs when stock prices rise and employees exercise their options to buy. These may be "cashless" transactions in which the purchaser, usually through a broker, simultaneously acquires and disposes of the stock and receives the difference between the option exercise price and the stock's market value on the day of the exercise. Alternatively, the employee may purchase the stock at the exercise price and retain it. In either case, if the option is in a *nonqualified* (or *nonstatutory*) stock option (NSO) plan, the employee incurs a tax liability at the time of exercise at the rate for ordinary income. If the option is part of an *incentive* (or *statutory*) stock option (ISO) plan—which is more restrictive, for employees only, and somewhat less advantageous to the company—the tax treatment is more favorable. The employee is taxed not at the time of the exercise but when the stock is sold and then at the more favorable rate for capital gains, provided the sale comes at least two years after the option is granted or one year after it is exercised, whichever period is longer. It is such option grants in Silicon Valley and elsewhere that have created "instant millionaires," allowing people to amass wealth far faster than they could through base pay and cash bonuses.

However, the downside risks for employees are considerable, for options can create not only millionaires but also negative net worth. An employee awarded a share of stock may see it fall, but only as far as zero and then only if the company goes out of business, but an employee who exercises options may actually incur debt. When the price of a share falls below a stock option's exercise price, an unexercised option is worthless, or *underwater,* to use the popular terminology, and the loss is purely a paper one. Consider what happens though if an employee exercises options to purchase shares that subsequently decline below their exercise price. If the options were part of an NSO, the employee has already incurred a tax li-

ability on the difference between the exercise price and the purchase price at the time of exercise, maybe even at the highest marginal tax rate of 39.6 percent. Later the employee may have to sell
the shares at the lower price, perhaps to cover the tax liability,
resulting in a total loss of the amount used to buy the shares plus the
tax paid. This could happen particularly in the case of an ISO
(which could also trigger an alternative minimum tax liability), if
the employee, seeking to maximize gain, holds the stock for the
required period, hoping the price will rise and the eventual sale of
the stock will incur the lower capital gains tax. Or it could happen
if an employee must hold onto stock, even when the price is falling,
because of a *lockup* period imposed on company insiders.

A simple illustration demonstrates the kind of net loss that can
occur. Assume that Jane Smith, a senior executive at ABC Enterprises with a marginal tax rate of 39.6 percent, is granted options to
purchase 1,000 shares of ABC stock in an NSO plan with an exercise price of $100 per share. ABC does well, its share price rises to
$200, and Smith borrows $100,000 to exercise the option and purchase the 1,000 shares, recognizing an immediate tax liability of
$39,600. But instead of continuing to rise, the stock starts falling.
Smith, however, locked up as a company insider, cannot sell for a
year. When she is able to sell, she does so at $10 a share, losing most
of her $100,000 investment and incurring borrowing costs plus the
$39,600 in taxes. Clearly, she would have been much better off not
exercising the options.

Twenty-three of the twenty-five best companies grant stock
options. The exceptions are the two firms in Taiwan. Those with
stock option plans exhibit important variations in the employees to
whom the options are granted, on what basis they are granted, and
when employees are vested and can exercise them. Until recently,
most companies granting options offered them primarily to senior
executives, most often the employees they wanted to motivate and
usually the ones with the means to exercise the options. Even as
late as 1999, the BLS reported that the overall percentage of U.S.
publicly held company employees receiving stock option grants was

5.3, while the percentage of executives was 19.6. The overall percentage of private industry employees receiving such options was even lower, 1.7 percent.[52] However, a number of major firms, including thirteen of the seventeen U.S. best companies, have now extended their stock option plans to make nearly all of their employees eligible to receive them, making the plans *broad-based*. Starbucks was a pioneer in taking this step, making the first grants in its Bean Stock program, on October 1, 1991, to over 700 of its partners (employees). Today, the number eligible exceeds 30,000, including part-timers working at least twenty hours per week. At CDW every coworker (employee) receives stock options each year, and Merck has twice made worldwide grants to all its employees.

As might be expected, it is at the fast-growth, new economy, high-technology companies that broad-based stock option plans have really taken off. At BMC, Johnnie Horn, senior vice president for Human Resources, told me "everyone is eligible," and the number receiving them is "past 50 percent." At Microsoft, long a leader in options programs, "virtually every employee is eligible to receive stock options at the annual performance review," according to Chris Williams. Cisco "gives stock options to all employees when they are hired," explains Barbara Beck, the former senior vice president for Human Resources, "and then every year they are eligible to receive additional options. We grant additional options to about 90 percent of the population." Tony Fox says that Intel's options program is "open to all employees." At Sun Microsystems, everyone is also eligible, but the number of employees actually receiving them is greater in the upper ranks. "At the director level and above, almost everybody gets stock options," Jim Moore reports. "Below that, it's more targeted to our retention plans and to our top performers."

Some of the U.S. best companies, particularly those of the old economy type, have more narrowly based stock option programs. Harley-Davidson, Wal-Mart, and MBNA have plans primarily for their executives, and Ingram Micro, which made a broad-based grant of options when it went public in the mid-1990s, has backed off that policy because, explains David Finley, "the competitive practice is now from the director level up." Stock option programs of best companies outside the United States also tend to be more narrowly based, though several are now broadening. At Novo Nordisk options are offered to the top 350 in the company. Shell makes stock options available for its top 1,000 employees, and has recently extended them to an additional 5,000 staff. Nokia is also expanding, "including more and more people," says Juhani Hokka-nen, "like key performers, and especially those people who are very difficult to recruit"; and in 2000, Nokia rival Ericsson increased those covered from 2,000 to 7,000. Singapore Airlines recently became the second major company in its country to introduce a stock option plan for all employees, now numbering over 28,000. Toyota is also a pioneer, in the summer of 1997 becoming one of the first Japanese companies to grant stock options. Currently, however, they are available only to senior executives, and because Japanese law limits the value of stock that can receive more favorable capital gains tax rates when it is sold, the number granted is small.[53]

The basis on which stock options are granted also varies among the best companies. The total amount available, the *pool* as it is sometimes called, is usually a function of how well the company is doing, rising or falling with its corporate fortunes. Some companies then simply apportion this amount, determining the exact number of options for each employee according to position or salary. Starbucks's U.S. Total Pay Summary, appropriately titled "Your Special Blend," states, "Stock options may be awarded each year based on: Starbucks success and profitability for the fiscal year, the exercise price, and a partner's [employee's] fiscal year base earnings."[54] Similarly, at CDW every coworker receives stock options based on salary and level in the organization. Henrik Gürtler explains that at Novo Nordisk the granting of options "is based solely on financial performance. If bottom line growth is living up to the target for the year, then everybody gets stock options." Likewise, Ericsson's annual report says of the size of stock options for key persons, "The amount allocated will depend not only on the individual's salary but on how well Ericsson fulfills the commercial objectives set for the year in question."[55]

A variation of this form of allocation is found at Ingram Micro, which first determines the percentage of total compensation for an employee (at the level of director and above) that it wants to deliver in stock options. Also factored into this process are data collected on competitors. From the percentage, the number of options to be granted is calculated according to the Black-Scholes method (the most commonly used stock option valuation model). Another variation is practiced at Sun Microsystems, which bases its stock option allocations more explicitly on business needs. "Every department gets a different allocation of shares based on its business needs," explains Jim Moore. "So if in fact chip designers are really at a premium and we're really trying hard to retain our chip designers, then we'll throw a lot of stock options into our chip company." Once departmental allocations are made, individual allocations within departments are based on each person's potential, and how much Sun wants to keep that person.

Other companies base their allocations of stock options largely on individual performance. Wal-Mart and Intel use employee performance, evaluated at the time of annual review, to determine the number of options granted. BMC bases its distribution of options on two individual factors: the current performance of the person and the contributions expected of the person going forward. At Merck, according to Wendy Yarno, senior vice president for Human Resources, "in addition to annual grants, senior managers have the ability to grant quarterly stock options for strategic contributions," and at Amgen, where annual option grants are based on both the person's level and performance, managers can also make instant spot grants for outstanding achievement.

Finally, vesting periods, which determine when employees can exercise the stock options they have been granted, are usually designed to promote retention. In a recent survey of over 600 organizations by William M. Mercer, 80 percent were found to use *installment* vesting, allowing grantees to exercise a set percentage of their options each year over a fixed number of years, and 20 percent were found to employ more restrictive *cliff* vesting, which prohibits any exercise until the end of a multiyear period.[56] Among the twenty-three of the twenty-five best companies granting stock options, roughly similar percentages apply. Sixteen use installment vesting, with five years being the favored period, thus allowing 20 percent of the options to be exercised each year. Three of the sixteen use shorter periods— Ingram Micro and Ericsson use three years, and Harley-Davidson uses four years, while stock options at Wal-Mart and CDW vest over seven years. The six companies that have cliff vesting of options, therefore maximizing the options' usefulness for retention, use various periods: two years at Singapore Airlines; three at AFLAC, Shell, and Novo Nordisk; five at Merck; and two to five at Intel, depending on the employee's position. In a method unique among the best companies, Capital One's options vest not at the end of a specific time period but when the company's stock hits certain market prices, thus increasing employees' risk but presumably spurring higher performance. Figure 4.2 summarizes eligibility, grant basis, and vesting in the twenty-three best companies granting stock options.

Often just as important for retention as vested stock options, and sometimes even more, are corporate benefit plans. Because of their clear monetary value, benefits are often considered indirect financial compensation.

Benefits

Employees value benefits. In the list of sixteen job factors in the Heldrich Center's *Work Trends Fall 1998 Survey*, 85 percent of the respondents rank "health and medical coverage" as "extremely important" or "very important," second only to "ability to balance work and family."[57] Aon Consulting's *1999 Workforce Commitment Index* reports that 73.5 percent of the workers in its survey group rate their organizations' benefit programs from "important" to "critical" in keeping them from looking for a job elsewhere.[58] Confirming the importance of benefits for retention, the *2000 Randstad North American Employee Review*, surveying 6,000 workers, finds "health insurance/benefits" cited most often (by 70 percent of respondents) in a list of nine items considered important to staying in one's current job if another were

FIGURE 4.2. Stock Option Practices in
Twenty-Three Best Companies.

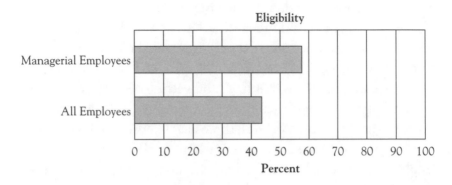

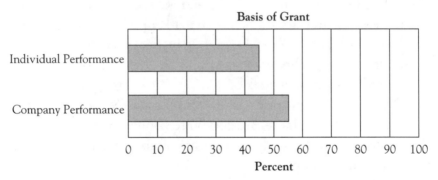

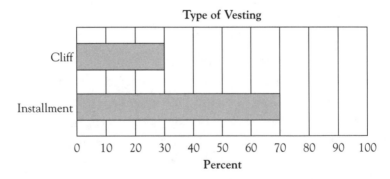

offered.[59] Similarly, the 2000 BridgeGate employee retention survey reports "improved benefits" to be the second leading retention factor among 667 working Americans.[60]

Company-provided employee benefits have traditionally been more important in the United States than elsewhere. Many countries, especially in Europe, have long furnished health care and retirement income as part of tax-supported, public programs. In the United States, salaries and wages accounted for almost all compensation in the private sector until the onset of World War II. The war, however, brought wage and price controls, and employers were encouraged to offer other forms of compensation, such as insurance, paid vacations, and pensions—all originally known as *fringe* benefits. After the war, the growing strength of unions led to the continuation of many of these benefits, both as bargaining chips in labor negotiations and to avoid further unionization.

Today, participation in company-provided employee benefit plans in the United States is widespread, and these benefits constitute a substantial portion of employee compensation. The BLS *Employee Benefits Survey* reports the following percentages of employee participation in selected programs in medium and large private establishments: 76 percent in medical care insurance, 95 percent in paid vacations, and 79 percent in retirement plans of all kinds.[61] Taken together, it has been estimated that these and other corporate-sponsored programs constitute 28 percent of total compensation costs.[62] But as U.S. corporations, increasingly competing with companies outside the United States that do not have to provide similar levels of benefits, now look to trim benefit costs, the peak may have been reached in such expenses. In December 1997, Brookings Institution economist Robert D. Reischauer told participants at an Employee Benefit Research Institute policy forum that "over the next few decades, we're going to see a continuation of the slow but steady reduction in the importance of employer-provided benefits."[63] Bearing out this forecast, the *New York Times* recently reported that "the aggregate level of employee benefits has actually fallen over the last five years, as companies have pared health and retirement plans."[64]

Of late, U.S. employees have become increasingly critical of company-provided benefits—perhaps in part in response to this paring, perhaps because of perceived inadequacies in these programs, or perhaps in part simply due to the common tendency to rank satisfaction below importance for many programs. In the Heldrich Center survey that ranks health and medical coverage second in importance among sixteen job factors, satisfaction with such coverage ranks twelfth, and satisfaction with retirement and pension plans, rated seventh in importance, ranks fifteenth.[65] In a 1999 Gallup poll asking about satisfaction with fifteen job characteristics, "health insurance benefits your employer offers" comes in fourteenth and "retirement plan your employer offers" ranks last.[66] Corroborating these findings, the Hudson Institute and Walker Information 1999 *Employee Relationship Report* concludes, "Only one in two employees (52%) believes that their company provides family friendly benefits."[67]

Thus companies, especially U.S. companies, face the dual challenge of offering benefits programs that are truly responsive to employee needs while containing program costs. How have the best companies met this dual challenge in the three major benefit areas of health care and insurance, time off and vacations, and retirement and savings?

Health Care and Insurance

Steadily rising health care costs have made medical benefits both the most valuable to employees and the most targeted for cost reduction by employers. As a result, companies have been introducing major changes and considerable innovation in this benefit area. One of the most dramatic changes has been the rapid decline of traditional indemnity plans and the increase of preferred provider organizations (PPOs), groups of hospitals and physicians that contract to provide comprehensive medical services at prearranged prices, and health maintenance organizations (HMOs), companies and nonprofits that deliver comprehensive health care on a prepayment rather than a fee-for-service basis. A BLS survey finds that the percentage of full-time employees participating in indemnity plans fell from 67 in 1991 to 27 in 1997, and during the same period the percentage in PPOs rose from 16 to 40 and in HMOs from 17 to 33.[68] More recent evidence shows that growing dissatisfaction with HMOs has slowed their rise and is prompting still further innovations in the delivery of health care benefits.[69]

Other changes include the extension of benefits to persons not traditionally covered, such as part-time employees and dependent domestic partners of both the opposite and the same sex; the increasing use of flexible, or *cafeteria*, benefits plans that allow employees to select the combination of benefits they prefer from among a range of benefits offered by the employer; the implementation of new programs such as wellness promotion, long-term care insurance, and adoption assistance; the availability of on-site clinics and other medical facilities; and the growing use of information technology to log employee benefit use and—through company intranets— to communicate information about programs and receive and record requests and options chosen.

As might be expected, among the best companies the pharmaceutical and biotechnology firms offer the most comprehensive and generous medical benefits, and insurers the widest insurance coverage. *Fortune* says Merck "offers virtually every benefit known to humankind."[70] Although Wendy Yarno modestly calls this "an exaggeration," Merck is very generous with its medical benefits, including among them infertility assistance, long-term care insurance, and a wide range of preventive services including child immunizations. At Amgen the employees' *Welcome to Amgen* pamphlet describes a considerable array of medical, dental, and vision care benefits, and David Kaye points out the "wide latitude of physician choice in our medical insurance program," and emphasizes the generous prescription drug program, with a copayment of only $5 for up to a thirty-day supply of medication. Genentech offers health care insurance without a premium and provides adoption assistance, health seminars, and long-term disability insurance. AFLAC, along with generous medical benefits and an on-site acute-care clinic, also pays for part of its employees' life insurance and offers them its cancer policy at no charge.

Several of the best companies outside the pharmaceutical and biotech industries also offer very generous health care benefits. Compuware pays the full premium for medical and dental family coverage at no cost to its employees, and it funds 50 percent of vision care coverage, all through FlexCare, a plan that offers employees the opportunity to customize benefits, change coverage levels, create tax-free reimbursement accounts, and purchase additional specified insurance. Capital One, which seeks to differentiate itself through its benefits and compensation programs, provides for preventive care, including physical exams. In the mid-1990s, according to Dennis Liberson, having presciently determined "that all HMOs would do was cause . . . employee problems," the company decided to "do everything through a POS [point-of-service] plan."

MBNA uses a managed care plan—the first corporation in Delaware to do so—but it also continues its very generous indemnity plan. To encourage use of the former rather than the latter, says Ken Pizer, it created "incentives rather than disincentives to use the network," including having no copayments and "getting virtually every physician in the community to participate." MBNA also keeps track of complaints about its benefits program, provides up to $20,000 in financial support for an adoption, and has a prescription drug plan that covers even—after much careful consideration—expensive Viagra.

Other innovative medical benefits practices at best companies include the eligibility of part-timers for benefits at Starbucks, Wal-Mart, and CDW; the extension of benefits to same-sex partner dependents by Sun Microsystems, Intel, and Microsoft; and the maximization of choices through flexible benefit plans at Ingram Micro and Nokia. Among the best companies using information technology to improve benefit delivery, the most advanced appears to be Microsoft. In the words of Chris Williams: "One of the things we've seen in other companies is that in order to get payment for a doctor visit or whatever, there are lots of hoops and hurdles you have to jump through. So we're continuously trying to find ways to do most of these things electronically, on our internal Web. You don't have to fill out paperwork; you don't have to wait six months for somebody to respond. We want employees back at their desks, doing their work, not worrying about how come this doctor's claim didn't get paid."

Vacations and Time Off

The BLS finds that 95 percent of all full-time employees in medium and large U.S. private establishments receive paid vacation benefits and that nine out of ten receive paid holidays. In addition, it reports that unpaid family leave was available to 93 percent of full-time employees in 1997, up from 84 percent in 1995, reflecting the continued implementation of the Family and Medical Leave Act of 1993.[71] Among the best companies, most offer the usual two to four weeks of paid vacation based on number of years of service. Some, however, are more generous to those with shorter tenure. Amgen and Capital One each provide fifteen days for first-year employees; BMC provides fifteen days after the first year of service, twenty-five after ten years. To help employees reach their time-off destinations, Singapore Airlines also provides free annual travel. In addition, two of the best companies offer sabbaticals—longer periods of paid time off in addition to annual paid vacations. Genentech gives em ployees six weeks every six years, and Intel eight weeks every seven years.

An increasing number of companies are offering paid time off *banks*, which lump vacation, sick, and personal days together so that employees can use these days as they wish, or are providing paid time off for a variety of medical and family reasons. Cisco gives employees twenty days of paid time off for vacations, illness, and personal business; this time off is earned on a daily basis and accrued at twenty days per year beginning from date of hire. Genentech permits unlimited paid sick days, some of which can be used to care for an ill child. It also offers paid maternity and adoption leave, as does Microsoft, where new birth mothers are eligible for eight weeks of paid maternity leave and, along with new fathers, up to four weeks of parental leave. Finally, MBNA offers each newlywed staff member an extra week of paid vacation.

Retirement and Savings Plans

Four-fifths of full-time employees in medium and large U.S. private companies participated in one or more employer-sponsored retirement plans in 1997, according to the BLS.[72] But this benefit area too continues to experience considerable change and innovation.

The major development has been a shift away from *defined benefit* plans—in which the benefit at retirement is known in advance; is calculated on a formula involving salary, age, and years worked; and is usually funded entirely by the employer—toward *defined contribution* plans—in which the benefit at retirement is unknown in advance although the portion funded by the employer is specified. From 1991 to 1997, the percentage of full-time employees in medium and large U.S. establishments participating in defined benefit plans fell from 59 to 50, and the number in defined contribution plans rose from 48 to 57. The fastest growing of the latter have been *401(k) plans,* in which employee participants determine each year how much of their pretax salary they wish to contribute, an amount that is usually matched up to some predetermined level by the employer. From 1991 to 1997, the percentage participating in these plans grew from 44 to 55.[73] In very large firms the change has been even more dramatic. The *New York Times* recently reported that "just 1 percent of large American employers still offer defined benefit pensions as their workers' sole sustenance in retirement, while more than a third have replaced those vehicles with 401(k)'s and other programs that transfer most risk and responsibility to employees."[74]

All the U.S. best companies provide retirement and savings benefits through defined contribution plans, usually 401(k)s. Employees are generally given a variety of investment options, often including company stock, for their own contributions, in which they are vested immediately. Most employers match these contributions at fifty cents on the dollar up to 6 percent of the employer's annual contribution, sometimes adding a share of company profits. These employer contributions vest after an employee has five years of service. A few best companies, however, are more generous.

MBNA automatically contributes an amount equal to 1 percent of base pay, then matches voluntary employee contributions up to 6 percent of base pay at a rate of 50 cents on the dollar, with immediate 100 percent vesting of all amounts. Amgen matches 100 percent of the first 5 percent that participating employees save, and also contributes 3 percent of pay each pay period to the accounts of nonparticipating employees. Capital One also contributes 3 percent to nonparticipating employees, matches 50 percent of the first 6 percent of participants' contributions, and—for participants only—adds a "performance contribution" based on 3 percent of pay and contingent on the company's achieving financial targets. Company contributions are fully vested after just two years. Finally, BMC matches employee contributions dollar for dollar up to $4,000, and typically adds another $1,000 if corporate goals are met.

How then do the best companies evaluate the effectiveness of their compensation and benefits practices in obtaining high performance and retaining high performers?

Evaluating Compensation and Benefits Practices

Senior executives in the best companies do believe—for a variety of reasons—that there is a connection between compensation and benefits and performance and retention. They design programs based on this belief, and they seek evidence that their programs are having the desired results. However, discovering such evidence is difficult. Sometimes there are confirming findings, but more often, continued belief rests on anecdotal evidence or simply on faith.

Belief in the Connection

At Ingram Micro, David Finley points out that "there's a lot of research that says people behave according to where the rewards are; so we make sure our reward systems are in line with the objectives we're really trying to achieve." At TSMC, where all employees receive stock as their share of the company's success, S. H. Lee stresses the importance of ownership: "Every employee is a shareholder, don't forget that," he told me, "and people are very very dedicated to the company because of their strong sense of ownership." Similarly, John Connors, chief financial officer at Microsoft, has said, "We very much continue to believe strongly in the direct linkage to our employees being shareholders and creating long-term shareholder value."[75]

Some best companies believe compensation and benefits are very important in recruiting. At MBNA, Ken Pizer says, "We think our pay and benefits are among our largest assets in achieving our recruiting goals." Juhani Hokkanen of Nokia says that stock options are useful "especially for those people who are very difficult to recruit and whose importance for the development of the company is essential." And Diana Root, BMC director of Human Resources, maintains that "the compensation and the benefits here at BMC are a key factor in our ability to attract, hire, and retain the talent we want."

Belief in the importance of compensation for performance is also strong at a number of the best companies. On its Web site, AFLAC states, "We believe employees who have an ownership interest will perform better. At AFLAC, we are inspiring excellence through ownership." At Compuware, where all salaried employees are eligible to participate in the company ESOP, Denise Knobblock, executive vice president for Human Resources and Administration, explains, "Our philosophy is that you have an investment in the company and that you will manage your day-to-day transactions and your business as if you were the owner of the company because you are part owner." Pär-Anders Pehrson, vice president for Leadership and Culture at Ericsson, raises the belief to an article of faith: "You need to have some sort of religious belief," he says, "that the need to recognize individual performance in money terms makes a difference." And he asks, rhetorically, "What would have been the result if the company had not provided any incentive schemes?"

Belief is also strong in the value of compensation and benefits for retaining desired employees. The *Wall Street Journal* recently reported that "Microsoft Corp., vying to retain top talent, has quietly instituted a series of new employee rewards that include bigger-than-usual stock-option grants and extra vacation time."[76] Ericsson's Pär-Anders Pehrson says, "I strongly believe that the whole compensation package has to be competitive so as to not have people leaving due to pay," and the company's Web site reflects that same belief, stating that "the options program . . . serves as an encouragement to key persons to stay with Ericsson and as a challenge to do an even better job in each person's area of responsibility." Nokia also views stock options as a retention device; and at one of the best companies that clamps the golden handcuffs of cliff vesting on its stock options, a senior executive admits that "the employees don't like it, but a lot of people believe it actually contributes to our retention factor."

Seeking Evidence

Because a truly scientific evaluation of the effectiveness of specific compensation and benefits practices on performance and retention would require the collection and analysis of huge amounts of data and probably the use of control groups, it is simply not a viable option. So the best companies use a variety of surrogates, however imperfect and incomplete they may be, to gather evidence.

In one of the most common evaluation techniques, companies compare what they are doing with what the competition is doing.

They identify competitors in both their own and other industries, looking at companies that compete for talent in the same specialties and geographical areas. Wendy Yarno explains that Merck "annually benchmarks the marketplace in which its competition operates," especially for certain skill sets for which demand is high and more flexible compensation approaches may be necessary. At Intel, Tony Fox says, "Our philosophy is to look on a regular basis at our compensation mix and see how competitive we are." In determining such matters as the percentage of compensation to be delivered as stock options, David Finley of Ingram Micro readily admits that "it's all based on the competition rather than saying we've done some research and we find that a particular approach has produced better results."

Several of the best companies survey their employees. Ingram Micro asks employees about their satisfaction with various compensation measures and compares the results with data from other companies. Amgen conducts its climate survey every two years, asking about satisfaction with benefit programs. Sun Microsystems compiles its *Employee Quality Index*, says Jim Moore, by asking what employees "see as the barriers to their productivity, what's blocking them from performing as they'd like to perform." AFLAC administers intranet surveys about its compensation and benefits programs, and it supplements these surveys with focus groups, a methodology that BMC also uses and considers especially valuable, in the words of Johnnie Horn, "in finding out what really works."

Finally, some companies do precise studies of particular activities. Ingram Micro has carried out a detailed study of its telesales function to determine the effectiveness of the 153 different sales incentive programs it has for various parts of the business. CDW counts the boxes packed by each warehouse employee to determine bonuses, evaluating which of its bonus plan incentives works best. MBNA measures calls per hour at its calling centers for the same purpose. MBNA also looks at turnover and the reasons people leave and has been doing so regularly since 1991, finding this the best way to identify and attend to any emerging adverse trends. Genentech has conducted a specific evaluation of its cafeteria-style benefits program.

Results

In a few cases, results are measurable. MBNA feels confident that the evaluations it regularly makes of call center activities produce data that enable the company to optimize its bonus programs. It has also analyzed the results of the suggestions adopted through its Master-Piece Program, says Director of Marketing Terri Murphy, and determined that it got back three times what it paid out and that every year "there seems to be an idea that approaches a million dollars, either in efficiency or effectiveness." CDW also feels that the exact data it receives from the scanners its workers use in packing boxes in its warehouse enable it to fine-tune its bonus programs to optimum effect.

In other cases, employee data can reveal strong correlations. During the years Compuware's ESOP has been in operation, the company's retention figures have steadily improved. At Amgen, where the biennial climate survey has shown strong satisfaction with compensation and benefits plans over the last six years, Ilana Meskin, senior director of Human Resources, says that "the strongest correlation in terms of retention is certainly the stock option program. Turnover goes down to below 5 percent when the stock is high, and the inverse is true when the stock drops." Dennis Liberson at Capital One, which extensively collects, measures, and analyzes employee data, states that "stock purchase is a much better indicator of ownership than options." Behavioral characteristics that are highly correlated with participation in Capital One's stock purchase program are dramatically lower attrition, lower absenteeism, and increased sales activity.

In many cases, however, results of compensation practices at best companies are stated in general descriptive terms, suggesting that they reflect selective observation or anecdotal evidence rather than specific measurements based on reliable quantities of data. For example:

- BMC's evaluation of its compensation program has caused it to "sway more to basing it on company performance" than it has in the past.

- Novo Nordisk's investigations have concluded "we do not get much mileage out of our cash bonus system, excepting for the people at the top."

- Microsoft believes its stock option program "has been an incredibly powerful vehicle" but "has a negative side if the stock stays stable or goes down for a significant period of time."

- CDW's evaluation of its compensation plans reveals that its 5 percent quarterly bonus to nonexempts "does not make a big difference whether people choose to stay or go" but that the "stock options are hugely effective."

- Starbucks finds that although "cash is a motivator; it is never a long-term or exclusive aspect of retention."

- Wal-Mart has learned that "the usefulness of stock options gets better the longer an employee stays."

- Sun Microsystems concludes that its stock options are an important contribution to retention, that "golden handcuffs do work."

But at one major new technology best company, a senior HR executive confessed his frustration over stock option–based compensation when he admitted: "We've outsourced our compensation program to NASDAQ. We've given so many options that the swings in [this company] have as much to do with employees' perception of reality as with any of our salary or bonus plans."

Most companies believe that human resources are their most important resources, and for most, compensation and benefits programs for these resources are their largest business expense. On balance, however, it is clear that even among the best companies, evaluation of the effect of these programs on performance and retention is more selective than systematic. This is equally true of another critical practice area, one vital to high performance in the era of postindustrial intangible work and also one incurring major expense: education and training.

5

Education and Training

In his thoughtful book *Human Capital: What It Is and Why People Invest It*, Thomas O. Davenport opens his chapter on training with this question: "Which adds more to productivity: a 10 percent increase in worker education or a 10 percent increase in capital stock?" His answer: "Put your money on education." He then cites the findings of a 1994 survey designed by the National Center on the Educational Quality of the Workforce and administered by the U.S. Bureau of the Census inquiring about the employment, training, and hiring practices of approximately 3,000 establishments employing twenty or more workers. For all firms, a 10 percent increase in education was associated with an 8.6 percent increase in productivity, whereas a 10 percent increase in capital stock saw a productivity increase of only 3.4 percent. For nonmanufacturing establishments the results were even more dramatic. An increase of 10 percent in education equated with an 11 percent rise in productivity, and the same increase in capital stock meant only a 3.9 percent rise.[1]

Watson Wyatt Worldwide has discovered a similar association between education and performance. Its *Human Capital Index* research (with 405 publicly traded companies responding) finds the items "training is provided to employees for attaining higher-level positions" and "training programs are maintained even during less than favorable economic circumstances" among the "HR activities with the strongest links to financial success."[2] The Watson Wyatt

1998 study *Competencies and the Competitive Edge* (with responses from 1,020 North American organizations) finds that "nearly three-quarters (70 percent) of companies with above average financial performance say employee development is a building block of future success."[3] And the Watson Wyatt *1999 Communications Study* (in which a total of 913 organizations participated) finds that "high-performing organizations focus on communicating with and educating their employees."[4]

The commitment of employees to their employers, and hence the likelihood of their remaining with those employers, is also closely associated with opportunities for education and training on the job. Aon Consulting's 1999 America@Work study reveals that one of the "five most powerful drivers of workforce commitment" is "skills of coworkers keeping pace with the skill demands of the job."[5] In the *2000 Randstad North American Employee Review*, among the nine items employees would consider important in the decision to stay in their current job if another were offered, "on-site/internal training" ranks third, selected by 50 percent of respondents, and "outside training resources" is fourth with 45 percent.[6] Similarly, *WorldatWork's Rewards of Work 2000* study finds that among the five career variables predicting retention are "training and development opportunities."[7] Corroborating these findings, the *1995 Survey of Employer-Provided Training* of the Bureau of Labor Statistics (BLS) indicates that high-turnover establishments provide less formal training than do establishments with lower turnover.[8]

It is clear that employees accord high value to training and consider it important in determining whether they stay or move on; however, they do not feel that employers are doing a very good job of providing it. A two-year Towers Perrin study, completed in 1999 and involving 200 line and HR executives in North America and 300 in Europe, finds considerable difference between importance and fulfillment. Among U.S. respondents, 91 percent think the need for education is important, yet only 52 percent think current programs are meeting that need. Worldwide the figures are almost the same: 90 percent think the need is important; 59 percent think it is being met.[9] Similar results come from the Hudson Institute and Walker Information 1999 *Commitment in the Workplace Study*, which reports that only 44 percent of the nearly 2,300 full-time workers surveyed believe their companies care about developing employees for the long term.[10] And a job satisfaction survey conducted by The Conference Board in 2000 finds only 28.2 percent of approximately 3,500 respondents satisfied with their firms' educational and job training programs.[11]

In this chapter I first examine the changing role of education and training, which explains in part the gap between employee need and employer fulfillment. Then I review the practices of the best companies as they seek to create education and training programs that improve performance and retain high performers. Finally, I briefly discuss the efforts of these companies to evaluate their practices.

The Changing Role of Education and Training

In the historic shift to the postindustrial era, information has become society's principal transforming resource, succeeding human labor and energy, the primary resources in the preindustrial and industrial eras. The gathering and understanding of information and the creation of knowledge that flows from those activities require cerebral skills, and these skills have rapidly replaced manual skills as the principal requirements for today's jobs. Ten years ago, Charles Handy estimated that by the turn of the century 80 percent of all jobs in the United States would require cerebral rather than manual skills.[12] Today even that high figure appears to be an underestimate.

Cerebral skills are not only more essential today but also more valuable. Manual skills are usually learned once, and though they may need to be varied somewhat to operate new equipment and new processes, they are usually learned for life. The value they add is more or less fixed. But cerebral skills, by their nature, are constantly growing. Enriched by new information and enlarged by new knowledge, they increase in scope and variety. Manual skills add value; cerebral skills multiply it. It is the latter that have created knowledge workers and made today's employees their companies' most important assets.

All workers need education and training, but for the cerebral-skilled majority of today's workers, education and training are different in important ways from what their manual-skilled predecessors needed. What is required today is learning that is continuous, often informal, and widely shared.

Continuous Learning

When manual skills were predominant, most of the training for a job took place at the beginning of a worker's tenure; it was in effect another layer added to the formal education and training acquired in schools and institutes. Now that cerebral skills are predominant, the opposite is true. The worker comes to a job with an education that has given him or her the capability to acquire knowledge as it is needed. Most of the acquisition comes later, in the months and years after going to work. This means learning must be continuous throughout one's career.

Continuous learning is necessary for several reasons. One is simply the steady increase in information and knowledge. What was learned before beginning work or during orientation or in formal courses along the way is soon in need of upgrading. It has been estimated that information, particularly in technical fields, is doubling every five to seven years. If this is true, then in a sense, half of what students learn in a typical four-year science-based college curriculum could be obsolete by the time they graduate. A second important reason continuous learning is necessary is the ongoing demand for already knowledgeable individuals to acquire yet more skills and competencies. More and more companies are realizing the value-creating power of cross-training, and more and more managers are recognizing that opportunity and advancement require the "soft" skills and associated competencies of communications, interpersonal relations, and leadership. Finally, continuous learning is imperative because the global business environment is constantly evolving. In this environment, with its increasing number and variety of competitors, the need to perform has become a greater imperative than the need to know, but the latter remains the necessary prerequisite to the former.

Today, new means of education and training are dramatically facilitating continuous learning, and development of such techniques is likely to increase in the future. Classrooms and teaching laboratories are still important and will continue to be so. But they have been enormously supplemented and even replaced in some cases by passive and interactive computer training delivered by intranets within organizations and by the Internet around the world. In range and depth of subject matter (literally everything known), in variety of format (data, text, audio, and video), in speed of delivery (virtually instantaneous), and in size of audience (potentially everyone on the planet), *e-learning*, as it is coming to be called, promises to be nothing less than the greatest change in the history of education.

Companies that create programs to facilitate continuous learning among employees often identify themselves, explicitly or implicitly, as *learning organizations*. Among their number are several of the best companies. Intel's Web site proclaims that the company "encourages every employee to continue his or her professional development in skill areas that are of benefit to both the company and the employee," and Tony Fox, manager of Intel University, says, "the learning environment that's been provided here is so rich." *Fortune* has said of Intel that "training is relentless,"[13] and that "there's a culture of learning."[14] Wendy Yarno, Merck vice president for Human Resources, told me, "The culture of Merck is unique in that it encourages people to strive to learn, to always be pushing to know more; it's very much a learning organization and a striving organization." Similarly, Dennis Liberson, executive vice president for Human Resources at Capital One, explains that "a lot of [Capital One] culture is around learning." For example, one resource at Capital One is a People Learning Center, with Internet access and a coffee bar. Harley-Davidson speaks of "lifelong learning," and one of the items of "joint consensus" in its Partnership Agreement with its two main unions is "continuous skill improvement."

Continuous learning is also strong among the best companies outside the United States. The second of Shell's seven "people principles for working together" is, "We promote and take responsibility for continuous learning and personal growth." *The Nokia Way of Learning* states, "Learning is a continuous process and supports the widening of experiences across units, functions and countries." At Novo Nordisk, "continuous learning" is an integral part of *The Novo Nordisk Way of Management,* and at Taiwan Semiconductor Manufacturing Company (TSMC), the third of the five principles of its HR Department Social Contract states, "We are committed to continuous learning, individually as a team member, and collectively as a team."

Informal Training

In order for continuous learning to occur, it must be an everyday part of the job, not limited to formal training courses. By definition, therefore, most continuous learning takes place through informal training. The BLS defines *formal training* as "planned in advance" with "a structured format and a defined curriculum." It often occurs in a nonwork location, exposes all learners to the same material at the same pace, and is usually not immediately put into practice. *Informal training,* in contrast, is defined as "unstructured, unplanned and easily adapted to situations and individuals." It uses material and a pace adapted to the learner and almost always takes place in a work setting where it can be immediately applied.[15] Following a two-year study on the nature of the workplace, the Teaching Firm research team of the Educational Development Center concluded that "approximately 70% of the way employees learn their job is through informal learning."[16]

Both formal and informal training are widely used. In its *1995 Survey of Employer-Provided Training*, the BLS collected data from both employers and employees. The employer data show that nearly 93 percent of establishments with fifty or more employees provided or financed formal training for their employees in the twelve months preceding the survey. On the employee side, nearly 70 percent reported receiving formal training, and 96 percent said they received informal training.[17] Drawing on its 1994 *National Employer Survey*, the National Center on the Educational Quality of the Workforce (NCEQW) reports the incidence of formal and informal training in establishments with more than 1,000 employees as 99 and 98 percent, respectively.[18]

It is also clear that the provision of formal training is steadily increasing. The NCEQW 1994 survey found that at 57 percent of all reporting establishments (employers with twenty or more employees) formal training had increased since 1990, whereas at 42 percent it remained the same, and at only 2 percent had it decreased.[19] During almost the same period, the BLS found that 75.5 percent of firms of 500 or more employees reported increases in formal training, 18.9 had no change, and 5.9 had decreases.[20] The 1999 report from an annual overview of employer-sponsored training in the United States revealed that U.S. organizations with 100 or more employees would spend 3 percent more for formal training in the coming year than they did the year before and that since 1993 total training budgets had increased 24 percent.[21]

Although there are no comparable figures for informal training, it is highly likely that the steadily increasing introduction into workplaces of new equipment and processes—especially in information technology and telecommunications—is causing the incidence of informal training to rise at an even faster pace. BLS data reveal that during the six-month period from May to October 1995, employees spent thirteen hours in formal training and thirty-one hours in informal training, a ratio of 1 hour of formal training to every 2.39 of informal training.[22] Although there are no recent data to update these figures, Brian Hackett of The Conference Board, an experienced HR researcher and the author of several comprehensive reports on employee training, wrote in 1997 that "in three years, the ratio of classroom training to newer forms of training is expected to be half of what it is today."[23] If the BLS follows up soon with a new survey of employer-provided training, it may show us how much informal training has increased to meet the demands of continuous learning.

Several of the best companies acknowledge the importance of informal training. Toyota's comprehensive Three-Fold Education System, designed "to help employees develop their own capabilities," is depicted as a pyramid with "improved capabilities" at the peak resting on a three-part base of "on-the-job training," "formal education," and "informal education."[24] *The Nokia Way of Learning* states: "Deep learning occurs when training is combined with practice. Practical work is used as the learning situation and learning through assignments and projects is encouraged on the job and on development programs."[25] CDW has established stores at its corporate site in part to merchandise its products but mostly to provide training for nonstore salespeople. "They come back from what is mainly training on our systems and in sales skills," explains Art Friedson, vice president of Coworker Services, "and they hit the phones. The phones are really where their careers are."

Speaking of management development at Cisco, Barbara Beck, former senior vice president for Human Resources, says, "Most of the things managers learn they learn in different ways. Some of it they learn through training, but they also learn from mentors, they learn from watching other people at work. So there's a lot of management development by example here." In Capital One's six-month training program in team effectiveness, team meetings and coaching are important elements that occur in between the less frequently scheduled formal sessions.[26] Intel also makes wide use of mentoring. The original intention was "to focus on mentoring for women," Tony Fox explains, "but it has actually expanded to be an overall mentoring program that has been quite successful." In fact, in a recent survey to identify factors aiding managerial development at Intel, the most frequently cited items were coaching and mentoring relationships. In addition, Intel has "spent a lot of time on . . . putting together training around 'working with,' especially working with other centers in our global company. Not only does this help Intel employees understand others' differences, it also enables them to tap into those differences."

The most important adjunct to informal training is the computer. Microsoft, as might be expected, places a special emphasis on on-line education. "We have a huge number of programs," says Chris Williams, former vice president for Human Resources, "and you can do many things with them. In one corner of a screen you get a videotape of the person talking, in another the slides being presented, and in another the outline for the presentation. You can click your way through it in any sequence you want, and it remembers where you were so you can go back later to where you left off." CDW has 200 different computer modules for teaching oneself, and Merck, according to its Web site, uses the company's intranet "to provide a host of non-classroom-based development resources to employees around the globe." BMC also makes extensive use of the computer for its management training program Learning at BMC (L@B for short). "It's entertaining and interactive," says Director of Human Resources Diana Root, who points out that the way computers are used in this program not only accelerates the learning of skills but also facilitates interaction with colleagues. Johnnie Horn, senior vice president for Human Resources at BMC, agrees, but she adds, "Web sites are nice tools, but they are never going to replace face-to-face development."

Knowledge Management

Face-to-face development often involves sharing, and to be effective, continuous learning and informal training require information sharing. In recent years the sharing of information within organizations has blossomed into a large new management practice area, known generally as *knowledge management*.

Within organizations there are vast amounts of information, inexorably and rapidly increasing. Much of this information is *explicit*, existing in databases and documents of various kinds; even more is *tacit*, existing in the heads of employees. Depending on the organization, it may be information about research, products and services, the business environment, competitors, customers, or employees. Often this information is of great value to a company in the development of new products and services, in the improvement of existing ones, and in the expansion and exploitation of markets. It is also of great value in the training and development of employees. In the words of Jan Carlzon, former president of Scandinavian Airlines System: "An individual without information cannot take responsibility; an individual who is given information cannot help but take responsibility."[27]

Knowledge management is about identifying, collecting, organizing, disseminating, and using information and the knowledge developed from it, and doing so quickly and where it will have the desired results. Although good companies have always tried to do this, it is new technology, also growing rapidly, that is enlarging knowledge management in scope and depth far beyond what had ever been achieved before. It is e-mail, intranets, groupware, search engines, sophisticated database management, and other IT tools that have really launched the practice known as knowledge management.

According to a 2000 survey by The Conference Board of 200 senior executives at 158 global companies, 80 percent of these firms have knowledge management efforts under way. Six percent report using it enterprise-wide, and 60 percent expect to be doing so in five years.[28] Benefits claimed include increased innovation, improved efficiency, reduced cycle times, lower costs, and increased customer satisfaction. By identifying needed skills and competencies and helping deliver the training to develop them, information sharing through knowledge management has the potential to become a powerful adjunct to continuous formal and informal learning.

None of the best companies has a formal enterprise-wide knowl-edge management program. Some executives dismissed the practice as a "fad" or only the latest in an endlessly passing parade of man-agement "buzzwords." Others described it as an "abstract concept" or found themselves "not in agreement on what it is about." One even blurted out, "I hate knowledge management. I hate the term and everything that goes with it, the sterility and all that." Never-theless, he added that his company was one of the founders of the Society for Organizational Learning and had worked closely with Peter Senge, author of *The Fifth Dimension: The Art and Practice of the Learning Organization* (1990) and justifiably considered one of the leading authorities on knowledge sharing and management.

In fact, even though no best company has a formal enterprise-wide knowledge management program, several have well-developed ones in subsidiaries or major divisions, others have practices that are clear surrogates for such programs, and many of the rest are devel-oping such practices. Royal Dutch/Shell Group has been described as one of the multinationals "in the vanguard of the knowledge management revolution,"[29] in part because of the Shell Learning Center, established in 1994 in Houston, Texas, by the Shell Oil Company. Employing ten subject matter specialists who scour inter-nal and external literature for leading-edge practices and ideas, it focuses on knowledge in three general areas: business models; lead-ership; and engagement, or human interactions.[30] *The Nokia Way of Learning* states in part, "Everybody should learn from one another and competencies are spread by active networking across bound-aries within Nokia."[31] To facilitate this kind of learning, the Nokia Research Center uses Lotus TeamRoom technology (an electronic version of a project war room) to bring together, under the com-pany's Future Watch initiative, geographically dispersed individu-als and groups to scan the environment for important trends and changes.[32]

Compuware does not have a formal knowledge management program, but Denise Knobblock, executive vice president for Hu-man Resources and Administration, says, "We try to document all of our processes and procedures so that things are shared and when someone leaves they don't take everything with them, leaving us to redevelop something. Furthermore, it's the nature of our organization that we have to share knowledge in order to be effective in doing our jobs." Jim Moore, Sun Microsystems director of Workforce Development and Planning, explains that the company has no formal program to manage knowledge, but it does have "a culture of sharing. Nobody here really gets ahead by withholding knowledge; we definitely dislike people who do that." Microsoft has a form of expert network specifically for the purpose of identifying the competencies required by members of software development project teams and finding people with those competencies.[33]

At Ericsson, Pär-Anders Pehrson, vice president for Leadership and Culture, points out what numerous studies have identified as one of the major barriers to successful knowledge management: "Sharing is not what you do normally. What you don't know puts me in a better position because as long as you don't know, my market value is higher. When I tell you what I know, my market value declines." To overcome this, says Pehrson, "We try to foster a culture of sharing, a culture where we really reward people for sharing." At Novo Nordisk, Henrik Gürtler, corporate executive vice president, speaks of a corollary problem: "In a company culture like ours where everything is based on people contact, [sharing and exchanging better practices] simply doesn't pay off. People have difficulty putting better or best practices into the system because they are kind of saying to their colleagues and peers, 'look here, how good I am.'" But Novo Nordisk still strongly encourages the sharing of better practices, and it solves the problem by using its unique globetrotting facilitators. "They are responsible for the bulk of the better practices," explains Gürtler. "Databases are not really what you are looking for; the idea [of sharing practices] is good, but you need to do it at a person-to-person level."

Several of the best companies that do not yet have knowledge sharing or management programs are aware of these programs' possible value, are considering them, or are moving toward putting them into practice. At Genentech, Judy Heyboer, former senior vice president for Human Resources, told me, "We're conscious of it and conscious of the idea that we need to get to it, but haven't yet." Tony Fox explains that Intel has "a very effective internal Web site, called Circuit, where we post information so that anybody in the company basically can find out what is going on in terms of best practices, especially around integrating newly acquired companies. [In addition, a] number of our organizations are working on knowledge management efforts. One of our Intel Fellows—the most senior technical people in our company—is leading a cross-functional knowledge management consortium. So we have a lot of initiatives going on in that area."

What remains to be done is to link information and knowledge sharing with education and training, creating, in effect, *learning management*. In the words of one authority, this will mean going beyond traditional knowledge management parameters "by focusing on individual and organizational capabilities, and utilizing tools to explicitly link learning to performance metrics."[34] Several of the best companies are already well along in this direction. At Singapore Airlines, says Loh Meng See, senior vice president Human Resources, knowledge sharing and management are integral parts of training and development. The database of Microsoft's expert network for software development projects "currently provides a means of balancing employee educational and training objectives against current and projected job requirements."[35] And the knowledge management processes of the Shell Learning Center have already propelled its role beyond that of a traditional training activity. Its "two value propositions" are "to leverage the cutting-edge tools of learning to improve business performance and to provide a platform for the development of high-potential employees."[36]

Today, effective education and training must combine continuous learning, informal training, and shared information. As Robert Buckman, whose Buckman Laboratories Inc. has been one of the pioneers in knowledge management, accurately puts it, "It's not a project, it's a journey."[37]

Education and Training Programs

All the best companies believe strongly in the value of education and training, and each has a wide range of programs designed to provide employees with the knowledge and skills to carry out their work correctly, efficiently, and productively. Most of these programs relate in some manner to specific jobs employees hold or are preparing to hold. Some, however, simply aid employees in continuing their general education and adding to their overall qualifications. The first of the following two sections will deal with those that are directly job related; the other with programs that focus on general education.

Job-Related Programs

As discussed earlier, the incidence of informal training in organizations is more than twice that of formal training and is undoubtedly steadily increasing. Yet when companies discuss training programs, they almost always speak of those that are formal—with specific content, scheduled for set times, and of fixed duration. These formal programs may even instruct employees about the provision of informal training, but the instruction itself is still formal. In time and of necessity, companies will develop specific descriptions of their informal programs, but because they have not done so yet, the programs of the best companies briefly reviewed here are the formal ones. These programs that specifically seek to improve performance—and at the same time to indicate a commitment that encourages retention—focus on orientation, management development, training in interpersonal skills, and comprehensive competencies training.

Orientation. The 1994 NCEQW *National Employer Survey* found that third highest in a list of thirteen types of training was new worker orientation training, offered by 73.9 percent of the approximately 3,000 respondents.[38] A number of the best companies believe that a thorough, well-executed orientation program is not only critical to preparing workers for their new jobs in a new company but also, by demonstrating employer commitment to the success of new hires at the outset, fosters employee commitment to the organization.

At MBNA, orientation begins on the first day on the job with a history of the company, its commitments, and its expectations of new employees. Also explained are employee benefits and MBNA's generous MasterPiece Program, which rewards suggestions and other initiatives. Within ninety days, every employee goes through two days of "customer college," learning of the attentiveness to clients that has made MBNA a customer loyalty leader. Sun Microsystems has one orientation day, Thriving at Sun, that talks about the company and its business, and another, Surviving at Sun, that focuses on the employee's workstation and responsibilities. Cisco holds a "new manager orientation" for managers new to management or new to Cisco; it features CEO John Chambers speaking about what is unique about management at Cisco and what the company expects of its new managers. Starbucks considers its basic orientation program critical to conveying the qualities and culture that have made the company a market leader.

Among the most comprehensive of the orientation programs at the best companies is that conducted by BMC and referred to as the "assimilation process" by Diana Root. "We place a lot of emphasis on the first six to nine months of the assimilation process," says Root, "making sure that information is shared, employees understand the information, and they feel good about BMC."

Management Development. Training in management skills is valued and widely offered. In a survey of 315 senior executives at companies among the Business Week 1,000, The Conference Board asked the respondents to select the most important areas among eleven areas of training. Ranked third, with 60 percent, was supervisory skills, and fifth, with 32 percent, was management development.[39] In 1999, *Training* magazine reported that 85 percent of all companies surveyed for its "Industry Report" offered management skills/development training, 82 percent supervisory skills, and 78 percent executive development.[40] From the employee perspective the BLS finds that in 1995, 28.4 percent of employees in establishments of fifty or more received management training and 30.9 percent were trained in professional and technical skills.[41]

For many of the best companies, management training is so important that it is mandatory. MBNA has a required curriculum for all employees becoming managers. According to Terri Murphy, "It has five elements: managing the efforts of others, influencing through communication, creating an inclusive environment, hiring the right people, and MBNA's Leadership Institute. Done in house, it is facilitated by senior managers from all around the company." The Novo Nordisk Human Resources Policy states that each business unit "must ensure that relevant employees participate in the corporate training programs defined as mandatory by Novo Nordisk."[42] At Singapore Airlines, where the training philosophy is "to train everybody regardless of hierarchical level, sex, or age," Senior Manager of Human Resource Development Lam Seet Mui says that management training is compulsory and "tracked in our computer system." At Intel, which puts a high priority on education and training, with employees taking on average six to eight courses a year, management training is also mandatory. Explains Tony Cox, "When someone becomes a manager, we actually have requirements that they go through some fundamentals of management training around things like selection, performance feedback, and setting goals for the organization."

Some best companies, recognizing the key role supervisors play in both performance and retention, have made special efforts on their management development. At BMC, where Human Resources is concentrating on management and executive development, Diana Root states that "BMC puts its focus on new managers, giving them the tools to do their jobs on a day-to-day basis." Similarly, at CDW, which promotes almost exclusively from within and knows that the single biggest correlate to turnover is how people feel about their supervisors, management training for supervisors is an imperative.

Other companies stress management development because candidates for supervisory positions often come from nonmanagerial ranks. A recent press release from Wal-Mart explains that "with more than 68 percent of its managers having started as hourly associates, Wal-Mart depends on training and development to manage and propel its growth."[43] Microsoft has the same challenge but from a different perspective. "We tend to hire people who are technically very skilled," Chris Williams says, "and we tend to promote the technically most skilled. But they're not necessarily the best managers; so we try and work hard at creating management development." Sun Microsystems, which also often finds its new managers among its technical people, stresses the timing for management training. "My belief," explains Jim Moore, "is that you do [management training] after someone's been appointed to be a manager, because training someone beforehand is what I call 'cold storage training.' You can't tell how good somebody is going to be as a manager until you make them a manager." AFLAC, says Senior Vice President and Director of Human Resources Angela Hart, has still another reason for emphasizing training for new managers. The company heard "from employees in focus groups that additional training was needed for newly promoted managers. So now all managers have eight required classes, from supervising to diversity to team building."

A few of the best companies adjust their management training to their special needs or unique cultures. At Shell, Director of Human Resources John Hofmeister reports that in the past the company had moved somewhat away from management training but more recently had gotten back into it—hiring the former dean of a major business school to head the program—because it was felt to be an important company need. Toyota managing director and member of the board Mitsuo Kinoshita explains that his company has implemented a training program for young executives to enable them to understand and use the "Toyota Way" of management. Acer recently opened the Aspire Academy. "Its mission," states Stan Shih, chairman and CEO of the Acer Group, is "to cultivate and promote effective Asian ways of management in a globally competitive business environment."[44] And Judy Heyboer explains how Genentech's work ethic limits the length of most management training programs: "The attention span of this management team is maximum two days, [after that] they start getting on the phone or disappearing to 'do just one thing' or 'solve just one problem.'"

Training in Soft Skills. The so-called soft skills, including interpersonal skills for communications, leadership, and personal growth, are highly regarded and addressed by many corporate training programs. In The Conference Board's survey of executives of Business Week 1,000 companies, leadership development was selected by 92 percent of the respondents, ranking first in importance among the eleven areas of training.[45] Curiously, communications, which ranks second to last in importance in this 1997 survey, chosen by only 11 percent, is second highest in type of training offered, reported by 88 percent, in *Training* magazine's 1999 "Industry Report." Personal growth, the only other soft skill listed in the report, is second to last, offered by 67 percent of the respondents.[46] Looking at soft skills training in terms of overall employee training as reported in the BLS 1995 *Survey of Employer-Provided Training*, communications (lumped together with employee development and quality training) is the only soft skill in the BLS's combined list of eleven job skills and general skills. It is received by 40.2 percent of employees, ranking it second overall to occupational safety.[47]

Most of the best companies have training programs in the soft skills, and in several cases they are enlarging them. Harley-Davidson, says Tim Savino, director of Organizational Development and Training, is devoting "a lot of attention [to] transitioning to the partnership arrangement we have created with the labor unions, for the formation of natural work groups, and for learning the soft skills." Sun Microsystems' corporate university, explains Jim Moore, has "a curriculum . . . that runs the gamut from executive education and management development to individual skills, including personal effectiveness." Part of Intel's "relentless" training is a weeklong course off site that Tony Fox describes as a "detailed analysis of what it's really like to be a manager." It addresses such matters as, "How do you improve your coaching skills? What are the things you need to help you make ethical decisions when you're in a particularly sticky business situation?"

As might be expected from the high importance companies assign to it, leadership is a major part of many soft skills training programs. At Merck, leadership is a core concept of company culture and a central element in the corporate training program. At BMC, in what I was told is a proven and long-enduring training model, leadership is one of three basic areas, the others being process and skills. Cisco has a multiday program for managers, called Leadership in Action. Wal-Mart offers Leadership Foundations, a four-day class in basic skills and role playing. Ingram Micro's program for senior people, Leadership Reflections, is part of the company's ongoing "feedback effort" to model and implement leadership qualities. At TSMC, leadership development is singled out for special attention in a new soft skills curriculum that includes "interpersonal skills, communication skills, language skills, presentation skills, influencing skills, negotiation skills, and people management skills."

Competencies Training.   The most comprehensive corporate education and training programs involve training in competencies, particularly those that are knowledge related and essential to postindustrial intangible work. These training programs are generally developed after organizations realize that to perform most effectively and to achieve their strategic goals they require certain competencies. What usually follows is an inventory of the competencies the company holds, the ones it needs to add, and the steps it needs to take to acquire the latter, often through a combination of corporate acquisitions, new hires, and training.

Starbucks offers each employee an extensive training program that facilitates four competencies it considers critical to the company's success: thorough knowledge of coffee, product expertise, a commitment to customer service, and well-developed interpersonal skills. Ericsson Management Planning Director Anne-Christine Carlsson explains that the company uses its "competence management" process to "build the link between our strategic plans and the competencies we need, right down to the individual employee. Then through training we fill the gap, for the individual and thus for the company." Nokia identifies the "competency gap" between required future competencies (derived from its corporate vision and strategy) and current competencies, and seeks to close that gap through "resourcing, performance management, compensation management, and development and training." "Training is based on competency areas," says Juhani Hokkanen, Nokia senior vice president for Human Resources, and the development activities that help fill the gap include both training programs and learning by doing.

At Capital One, "everything that we do around development, for individuals and the company," explains Dennis Liberson, "is tied to our competency model and our performance management process." For individuals, this means using performance reviews to learn about strengths and weaknesses and then using training to overcome the weaknesses. For example, this might mean saying to a particular employee, "Here is your performance review, and you know you are a great analytical thinker, but you appear to need work on your influencing skills. So what we have for you is an influencing skills training program." In the same way, Liberson adds, "because our whole business model is about moving flexibly and being very agile, we may want to develop certain organizational competencies, such as managing change. Since this is a really important competency, we then create programs in it for all managers." In the end both individuals and the company gain, helping performance "enormously" and aiding retention as well.

General Education

There is fairly widespread understanding that assisting employees to increase their general education will make them more valuable to their employers in a number of ways as the employees acquire new skills and competencies, become better at learning, and experience the satisfaction of achieving goals such as the completion of courses and degree programs. Employers realize that ultimately these gains can improve performance and increase productivity. Employees also feel they benefit from such assistance, especially in gaining new qualifications and enhancing their employability. When the source of their education is their employer, their sense of commitment and loyalty to that employer is also likely to grow.

For all these reasons, employers are active in supporting the general education of their employees. The NCEQW 1994 *National Employer Survey* reports that 47.5 percent of responding establishments engage in tuition reimbursement,[48] and a recent Hewitt Associates survey finds that about three-quarters of large U.S. corporations offer aid to employees who take college courses.[49] On the employee side, the BLS finds that 17.1 percent of trained employees participated in courses paid for by employers at outside institutions.[50]

Most of the best companies offer support for employees' general education outside the organization if it is related to employees' work inside the organization. Microsoft provides support for outside courses, but "for things that are work related," cautions Chris Williams; "if you want to do basket weaving, you're going to have to do that on your own." At Harley-Davidson, where I heard several times that education is a "biggie," Tim Savino said that most people who are receiving assistance "are either doing something to enhance their current position or to prepare for another opportunity in the company." Merck also supports general education that gives employees new skills that might be used in a subsequent job. "For example," says Wendy Yarno, "you could be in marketing and getting a law degree." Intel assists employees in degree programs, explains Tony Fox, depending on "whether we believe that the degree is going to be beneficial to the employee and to Intel in the long term." Toyota sends employees to institutions both abroad and in Japan, "depending on the necessity or needs they have," says Mitsuo Kinoshita. However, Amgen "provides each of its workers with one course yearly in a completely unrelated discipline such as art history."[51]

At a number of best companies, the decision to support general education in an outside institution is recommended, or even made, by the employee's supervisor. So widespread and decentralized is the practice at Harley-Davidson, that higher-level managers "don't often see what's approved mostly by the supervisor." At Merck, "if your manager approves it, the company will pay for it," and at Intel also, "the decision is left up to the employee's manager; it's not something that's mandated by the company." At Acer, however, the opposite is the case. Terry Lu, associated vice president, says the company would provide support "only if the training had been assigned or mandated by Acer."

Best company support for general education usually means tuition reimbursement—often plus a stipend for books and other needed materials—and it comes in a variety of forms, sometimes with stipulations. AFLAC offers scholarships for its employees at local universities. Singapore Airlines subsidizes the first S$10,500 (approximately US$5,800) of tuition fees, and offers an interest-free loan for the next S$10,500. Intel provides 100 percent tuition reimbursement. Genentech does the same for all employees, though some there feel more structure may be required to ensure that business values are fully considered. Amgen provides 100 percent tuition reimbursement for two courses each semester. At BMC, tuition is reimbursed to a maximum of $5,000 per semester; however, a grade of C or better must be received. Compuware has a similar stipulation but with the company's own variation: 100 percent reimbursement for an A, 75 percent for a B, and 50 percent for a C.

Employees are expected to take most general education courses on their own time. However, MBNA grants unpaid leave for job-related outside education it supports, and Acer provides time off to pursue training it has assigned or mandated. Nokia, Juhani Hokkanen reports, "heavily" supports employees who are "upgrading the graduate level" of their education, providing time off and covering all material costs. Novo Nordisk also on occasion makes major commitments to employee MBA programs, investing two years of salary plus tuition costs and stipulating only that someone choosing not to remain with the company must repay a certain fraction. Capital One "allows people to go on two-year sabbaticals to get their MBAs; they just have to come back when they are done."

What remains to be seen is how the best companies evaluate their education and training practices, especially in improving performance and retaining high performers.

Evaluating Education and Training Practices

Peter Drucker once wrote, "Training may already cost as much as health care for employees—perhaps more."[52] Although the costs of training, especially for steadily increasing informal training, are very difficult to calculate, estimates by the BLS indicate that in the United States at least he is correct and that training costs may still be increasing as fast as health care costs. Yet, as is the case with evaluation of compensation and benefits, efforts by the best companies to evaluate the effect of their education and training practices on performance and retention have been persistent and creative but still modest.

Training and Performance

For a number of years the best-known method of evaluating training in organizations has been the Kirkpatrick model, based on the research of Donald Kirkpatrick.[53] The model is usually expressed in four levels, rising in comprehensiveness and complexity:

1. Reaction—employee reaction to training activity
2. Learning—understanding of subject taught

3. Behavior—application of what was taught

4. Results—impact of training on business results

Sometimes a fifth level is added, usually expressed as ROI (return on investment). It examines the monetary value of the results with respect to the cost of the training. Although often criticized as ill suited to newer methods and objectives of training and rarely fully implemented, the levels of the Kirkpatrick model and especially its initial reaction level are widely employed.[54] A number of the best companies use the first level, surveying employee reaction to training. At AFLAC a corporate training department evaluation form is given out after every training session, and evaluation results are considered when developing new curriculum materials. BMC's Diana Root says that "at the end of every training module, employees are expected to give feedback on what they learned that they did not know before the training, which gives us data on what worked well and what hasn't worked so well."

Some companies using first-level evaluations add items from other levels. At Sun Microsystems, Jim Moore says, "We do level-one 'smiles' test evaluation, and we've done some level-two end-of-course testing, but we're trying to do a lot more. We've gone back to new hire orientation, for example, to see if it produces more-satisfied employees than those who don't go through it. The answer is 'slightly more [satisfied],' but it's not a slam dunk." Amgen is constantly reevaluating its courses in the light of participant evaluations and, adds David Kaye, associate director of Corporate Communications, "if we recommend that an employee take a particular course, then during that employee's performance evaluation the next year we will attempt to determine if there's been improvement based on that course." Intel does initial evaluations of trainees at the end of training, then does follow-up evaluations to determine if trainees have applied their training on the job. "Sometimes," says Tony Fox, "we actually go so far as to get feedback from managers on whether they feel particular employees have been more effective because of the training they have received."

Other best companies attempt to focus their evaluations on the fourth level, business results. David Finley, Ingram Micro's senior vice president for Human Resources, says, "Training is an expensive issue; like medicine, it's too expensive to be giving to people indiscriminately." So Ingram Micro is striving to determine training objectives in terms of costs and expected payback to the company and working to evaluate results in terms of performance difference achieved. "There are various levels of evaluation," says Finley, "but the best one, of course, shows if [training] does make a profitable difference." Compuware can measure the effectiveness of the employee training for its Professional Services Organization by determining how many trained individuals are placed on accounts and how productive they are. At Singapore Airlines, Lam Seet Mui explains, "We evaluate our training after every program and this helps us to audit the value of that program to the company, and on an annual basis we do what we call a training review of all training programs." Sometimes the results of training can be indirect and unexpected but nonetheless valuable. Art Friedson of CDW says the company's three-day program at The Kellogg Graduate School of Management at Northwestern University "has been hugely successful both in its own right and also because we really get to know each other a lot better."

Best companies doing training in competencies are conducting more comprehensive and more complex evaluation. At Ericsson "in the old days," Pär-Anders Pehrson says, "we used to measure training like everybody else, in terms of student days in classrooms and what [employees] said at the end of the training; but now we're looking much more at the way the business is doing rather than asking employees how satisfied they are." Nokia does evaluations after every training module, and also evaluates the total outcome of training in terms of success in closing the gap identified between future and current competencies. At Capital One, Dennis Liberson speaks of his progress in evaluating the company's competencies training: "I have both independent and dependent variables that enable me to . . . track people's performance over time at a competency level to be able to figure out if our training is moving the needle. I also now have enough people that have done this [training] that I can go in and capture the results. Next I have to have someone actually crank in the numbers for the analysis."

It is clear then that evaluating the effect of education and training programs on performance is still very much a work in progress, even for the best companies.

Training and Retention

Recently the *New York Times* commented that "companies are not eager to train or groom people anymore: why invest in someone who might jump ship?"[55] In contrast, BLS survey findings, as discussed earlier, generally indicate an inverse relationship between training and turnover: the higher the amount of training, the lower the level of turnover. On one hand, this could be because training is likely to result in an increase in productivity, which might then be translated into wages and salaries, providing employees with incentives to remain. On the other hand, if turnover is already high, employers might be reluctant to invest in training, knowing that workers might have to be laid off or might quit before a return on the training investment can be realized. Thus, even though the BLS correlation is highly suggestive, it is not really possible to prove a cause-and-effect relationship between training and turnover.

Among the best companies, only Intel, whose management practices survey has found a positive correlation between turnover and management effectiveness, attempts anything that could be considered an evaluation of the effect of training on retention. So, to elicit current thinking as well as practice on this subject, I posed the following question in each of the interviews I conducted: "Are you concerned that if you train people with skills and competencies that improve their employability, they will leave for other jobs at other companies?" The answers are varied and interesting.

A number of the best companies, especially those in the high-tech new economy, readily acknowledge this concern. "There's always that risk," says Ilana Meskin, senior director of Human Resources at Amgen, "but I think you have to make your investment and create the environment that makes people want to stay." Intel feels likewise. Tony Fox also says, "There's always that risk," but adds, "We see training and continued education as keys to our future, as an investment to maintain our competitiveness." Judy Heyboer points out that some employees who earn MBAs funded by Genentech's tuition reimbursement plan do go to other companies because Genentech "can't adjust quickly enough to provide jobs that fit what they now want to do. But the in-house training," she emphasizes, "does not have that effect." At Sun Microsystems (where charismatic CEO Scott McNealy counts thirty-five CEOs of other companies who were once Sun employees), Jim Moore told me, "The worst fear would be we don't train them and they stay! So for sure we're going to train them and they're going to go elsewhere; fear of losing them would be no reason to keep them underdeveloped." Microsoft, however, feels no similar risk that employees trained by the company might leave. Chris Williams's response to my question was, "Oh, God, that never even dawned on me."

Some of the best companies feel that generous training is the main reason employees do remain. AFLAC's employees are staying, says Angela Hart, because "by training them, we are providing them an enriching and rewarding environment." Merck's Wendy Yarno points out that "if you ask [our employees] why they stay, it's because they always feel like they are learning. They always feel like they are being challenged." At Compuware, says Denise Knobblock, "Our philosophy is that if you make an investment in the employees, they are going to be more loyal to the organization that helped them to get where they are."

The corollary, that if you do not train employees they will surely leave, is also felt by some of the best companies. In answer to my question, Ken Pizer, executive senior vice president of MBNA, said emphatically, "If you *don't* educate them, they are going to go elsewhere." And at Capital One, Dennis Liberson's reply was: "No, quite the opposite. Our surveys said for a long time that one of the leading drivers of attrition was people feeling that they weren't being developed. Now we are viewed as very good development company and because of that it is no longer a driver of attrition. So I would argue the more you develop the more you retain."

Outside the United States, the feelings were largely the same, but the reasons went far beyond the welfare of individual companies. TSMC Vice President for Human Resources S. H. Lee said that losing trained people to other companies "is part of the risks we take; but we believe that even if it happens, that it is all worth it, that it will be part of our service to the society." At Singapore Airlines, Lam Seet Mui answered, "As long as they are in the Singapore labor market it's all right," and Loh Meng See added, "We have no fear. In the end they will be our allies anyway, part of our network."

At Novo Nordisk the sense of responsibility goes beyond home country borders. I read to Henrik Gürtler this statement from the company bible, *The Novo Nordisk Way of Management:* "An ongoing dialogue between management and employees shall ensure that personal training and development activities strengthen our company and secure the employability of our employees preferably within Novo Nordisk," and asked him to comment on the word "preferably." "This is our tribute to social responsibility," he said immediately and went on to explain that on occasion, due to the pace of change and the constant establishment of new businesses, the company might have to both begin and terminate particular business units. In doing so, it might "like to get people from the outside and send the best of Novo Nordisk to other companies. [So] from time to time the contract must be that if you can make a career in another company, in Denmark or outside, we would like to help you."

Here then is the ultimate linkage between training and retention. A company so committed to the employees in whom it invests is likely in return to earn their highest commitment.

6

General Principles and Key Themes

The practices of the twenty-five best companies discussed in the four central chapters of this book reflect the profound structural changes that have occurred in the past fifty years in the nature of work and the values workers hold.

Work in today's postindustrial era is less about what is tangible, more about what is intangible. It involves services more than products, and much of the content of both services and products is increasingly information, ever growing and ever changing. Jobs, especially in managerial and supervisory positions, are less about specific tasks and duties (as in traditional job descriptions) and more about fulfilling responsibilities and obtaining results. This puts a premium on innovation, flexibility, and speed—traits that require continuous learning and widespread sharing of information and knowledge.

An equally dramatic change has occurred in the values workers hold. During the industrial era workers were strongly materialistic. Anxious to achieve and maintain economic security, they gave highest priority to maximizing material gains. In the postindustrial era, through a combination of public policy programs and accumulated personal net worth, they have attained basic levels of security. Thus, with survival now more or less taken for granted, they are giving higher priority to nonmaterialistic values emphasizing quality of life and subjective well-being.

The best companies whose executives I interviewed have understood and responded to these major structural changes. Particularly in their work environments and training, they have sought to encourage the innovation and learning necessary for a world where work is increasingly intangible and intellectual. Particularly in their recruiting and compensation practices, they have realized the need to deal with a workforce whose values are increasingly postmaterialistic, more concerned with self-realization and self-actualization than material gain.

From the practices of these best companies it is possible to derive general principles suggesting courses of action that can improve performance and increase retention. Furthermore, it is also possible to discern a number of key themes that guide the implementation of these principles. Taken together, these principles and these themes can enable executives and managers at all levels to create and keep high performers.

General Principles

General principles emerge from the practices of the best companies in each of the four main areas discussed in this book—work content and the work environment, recruiting and hiring, compensation and benefits, and education and training. Several of these principles are universally found, others are exhibited by a number of the best companies, and some are only suggested by the directions in which a few of the companies are heading. In addition, several may seem counterintuitive or contrary to current advice. But all are consistent with the structural changes occurring in the nature of work and the values of workers.

Work Content and the Work Environment

The practices of the best companies recognize that employees need, above all, to believe that the work they do is important and that they are valued, as discussed in Chapter Two. The general principles that arise from these practices concern conveying the importance of work, engaging employees, recognizing employees, and valuing employees as *whole people*.

Convey the Importance of the Company's Work. Because subjective well-being has become an important value for employees, their belief in the importance of the work they are doing is critical. Companies need to respond, first, by determining what it is about their products or services that is important. Sometimes they are new and pathbreaking, literally changing the world. Sometimes they can save lives or lengthen them or make them more comfortable. Often they provide essentials of living or make daily activities safer, more convenient, or more efficient. Yet others may offer entertainment, making life more enjoyable.

Second, companies need to find ways to convey this importance to their employees. They might do it through regular communications, oral and written, from senior management down through company ranks. These communications can be reinforced in turn through exhibits, testimonials, and advertising. Most effective, because people remember stories better than facts and respond more empathetically to them, are tales of how the company's products and services have made important differences at critical times. In sum, a central part of a company's shared culture has to be the company's and the employees' pervasive belief in the importance of the work they do.

Engage Employees. Employees need to believe not only that the work they do is important but also that their own part of that work is important, that they are valued for what they do for their organizations. In order to obtain high performance in postindustrial, intangible work that demands innovation, flexibility, and speed, employers need to engage their employees. Engagement requires attention to several critical activities: communications, supervisory relationships, empowerment, and performance management.

- *Communications* involves informing employees, listening to them, and responding to what is heard. It is conducted with persons at all levels. The content offers information about the organization, such as plans, activities, and results, as well as information designed to create and build company culture. Communications activity also transmits information of personal importance to employees about job postings, benefit plans, education and training programs, and the like. The principal means used are print and electronic communications, especially rapidly proliferating intranets. However, many of the best companies believe that the most important means of communicating is still in-person exchanges. There is much talk today about the rapid growth of virtual offices and telecommuting employees. The advantages of these approaches are many and their growth will continue. But the changing nature of work, with its need for continuous learning, informal training, and shared knowledge, requires regular and perhaps even increased face-to-face communication. Such communication creates friendships and builds networks that nourish both employees and their companies.

- *Supervisory relationships* are vital to engaging employees. All of the best companies agree that supervisors play the most important role in driving performance and retaining good employees. It is widely observed that employees commit more readily and more certainly to other employees and to an organization's culture than to the organization itself. It is supervisors who are in daily contact with employees, and it is they who are in position to manage, coach, and mentor, conveying the culture, spirit, and pride of their organizations. Thus it is supervisors to whom management must pay the greatest attention—in selecting them, compensating them, engaging them, and training them. The converse is also true: bad supervisors can lower performance, destroy morale, and drive away good employees. When they are discovered, companies need to take action to reeducate them, to transfer them, or to remove them before more damage is done.

- *Empowerment* tells workers that they are valued. It is also the biggest spur to innovation and creativity. The flood of ideas and initiatives and insights that is released may at first appear overwhelming, and only a relatively small percentage may be put into practice; but the ideas that are used often have a major impact on products, services, or procedures. Furthermore, by allowing employees a measure of autonomy and opening itself to diverse employee input, an organization builds a culture that encourages ever-expanding input. Giving employees freedom, allowing them to take risks, and tolerating their mistakes engages them and builds their confidence. Confidence, in turn, increases contribution and anchors commitment.

- *Performance management*, properly used, can be the most comprehensive means of engaging employees. But to do so, it must do more than just set goals, monitor progress, and evaluate results. Performance management needs to be an opportunity to show workers how their input is tied to corporate strategic goals and to obtain input on those goals from those who have the frontline responsibility for achieving them. It needs to provide the means to evaluate employee inventories of skills and competencies and to set in motion the education and training that will add to skills and competencies and upgrade them. It can do even more, replacing once-a-year performance reviews with far more effective, ongoing interactive management. And in a still broader role, performance management can create career development plans that engage and retain employees and, in so doing, enrich the organization's most valuable resources.

Recognize Employees. Recognition is the most time-honored and widespread means of showing employees that they are valued. In all the best companies it is still considered useful and effective; however, the preferred forms of recognition are changing. At a time when corporate actions (downsizing and layoffs) and employee preferences (mobility and rapid advancement) have made longevity less important, time-of-service awards are declining. Conversely, the push for higher productivity and more sales in an increasingly competitive global business environment has raised the importance of awards for performance. But here, too, important changes are evident. In part because of the rising importance to employees of nonmaterialistic values, companies are tending to give more nonmonetary awards. In addition, employees' growing need to believe the work they do is valued, along with corporate interests in encouraging feelings of belonging, have led to more public presentations before peer groups and with the participation of senior management. At the same time, with the transition to work whose products and services are intangible, ongoing, and ever-changing, recognition of the role of supervisors in making awards has increased, as has the use of immediate, informal, and personal awards.

Value Employees as Whole People.   Because increasing subjective well-being and quality of life has become a higher value for employees than maximizing material gains, employers seeking to foster high performance and retain high performers have to respond accordingly. They need to understand what surveys have overwhelmingly and repeatedly shown: that workers value highly the lives they live outside their workplaces and that workers' top priority is finding an appropriate balance between work and home. In short, companies need to recognize and value their employees not just for the work they do but for the *whole people* they are. When companies do so, both employees and performance benefit. The policies and practices required involve flexibility in work hours and in workplaces, services that help employees handle personal problems, facilities that make time-consuming activities easier to accomplish, and celebrations of both group achievements and personal milestones.

- *Flexibility* in work hours is widely practiced, with the exact policies depending on the nature and needs of the business. Flexibility in workplaces is more controversial, especially working outside the workplace via telecommuting. Although the arguments in telecommuting's favor are undeniable, the evident downsides have resulted in limited and somewhat wary use among the best companies. Most still consider a substantial measure of personal interaction to be critical.

• *Services* that offer employees counseling and other help with finding solutions to problems they have outside their workplaces are usually provided through company-sponsored employee assistance programs. They range from on-site, walk-in centers to toll-free, call-in services to on-line assistance, available in more and more cases twenty-four hours a day, seven days a week. The object of these services is to provide convenient, qualified help for any nonwork problem—all the way from a missing pet to a death in the family—that potentially could make work life and personal life more difficult to balance.

• *Facilities* can relieve employees of demanding tasks that might otherwise make it very difficult if not impossible for them to work, and they can provide services that are both useful and time saving. The principal example is dependent care, initially for preschool children in day centers but now increasingly for elderly parents. Although most of the best companies provide child care, there is considerable difference of opinion over whether it should be on site, at contracted outside locations, or paid for using tax-free dollars. Looming on the horizon and approaching rapidly, is the potentially larger problem of elder care. Although most of the best companies are aware of this increasing employee need, few have acted so far. Companies are also increasingly making gyms and fitness centers available. In addition, a number of the best companies provide on-site convenience facilities, like dry cleaners, laundries, and film processing shops, all to help employees save time and presumably perform more efficiently.

• *Celebrations* may be company-wide, division-wide, or department-wide. Built around holidays, seasonal changes, or company anniversaries, they bring together employees and their families, thus balancing work and home life by briefly merging them. Many of the best companies also celebrate employees' personal milestones such as weddings, new children, and academic and athletic achievements, explicitly acknowledging the importance of their nonwork lives. All these celebrations are meant to show how companies value their employees. In return they hope to earn not only their gratitude but also their good performance and continued loyalty.

Recruiting and Hiring

The best companies, as discussed in Chapter Three, cite a number of reasons why recruiting and hiring are the most important practice areas for creating and keeping high performers. The value of a good hire will continue to multiply throughout an organization, whereas a bad hire will diminish value. Good people attract other good people. There is a strong correlation between good hires and good corporate results. Good hiring reduces the costs of turnover. And most important, recruiting and hiring well is becoming ever more critical as the labor supply changes and labor demand grows in an increasingly competitive global business environment.

Three general principles emerge to which organizations must be particularly attentive: look to new and changing sources of labor, search for new skills in new ways, and select with changing techniques.

Look to New and Changing Sources of Labor. Major changes now occurring in absolute population numbers, relative sizes of different age groups, and population composition have two important implications for recruiting and hiring. First, they indicate a changing mix of future customers and clients, who will be older in all developed nations and increasingly nonwhite in the United States and nonnative in the countries of Europe. This shift requires a parallel change in hiring so that companies can be responsive to and more effectively serve changing markets for their products and services. Second, they indicate a changing pool of potential workers, meaning that companies have to recruit for all positions from a labor supply with more minorities, more women, and more elderly than before.

At the same time, continuing tight labor demand, especially for more highly trained and skilled knowledge workers, means that to find the people they need, companies have to increase their efforts to educate and develop the groups that constitute a rising percentage of the future labor pool. Of added importance, and not well understood, is that the increased participation of women, the elderly, Hispanics, and Asians in the U.S. workforce is dampening job volatility and aiding retention because these groups have a tendency to greater loyalty and commitment to their employers.

Search for New Skills in New Ways. Companies need to identify people with the capabilities and qualities required for their business plans and who fit their cultures and modes of operation. Increasingly, the skills and competencies sought will be those appropriate to the changing nature of work, emphasizing openness, flexibility, and creativity. Especially, the best companies feel, they need the soft behavioral skills of communications, interpersonal relations, and leadership. For many, it is more important to find these skills than technical skills; their view is that they should hire for attitude, knowing they can train for technical skills. The best companies also realize the importance of *hiring for the company* and *hiring continuously*, bringing on good people who fit the company culture whenever they are found rather than waiting for specific vacancies to appear.

In the search for job candidates, many of the best companies find their best sources are internal. They may have current employees who know the company well and are also well known to the company who could be good candidates for openings. Alternatively, a current employee may refer a candidate from outside. If the outside candidate is hired, the referring employee is often rewarded with a bonus. Many companies also feel that a steady stream of outsiders is necessary, bringing in new ideas, new perspectives, and new contacts, especially from minority groups and from elsewhere in the world. Companies also now have a new, rapidly evolving source for outsiders that promises to make recruiting faster, wider reaching, more efficient, and less costly—the exploding worldwide Internet. The Internet can locate job candidates in two principal ways. First, on-line recruiting services can post an organization's jobs and take résumés and then help match the two. Second, and more important, companies' Web sites can list available positions and accept résumés. Increasingly, the best companies are adding features such as testing, profiling, and preliminary screening to their on-line recruiting, quickly reducing large numbers of job seekers to the few on whom they want to focus.

Select with Changing Techniques. Preemployment tests are used widely by a number of the best companies, several of which continue to believe in the value of psychological tests. Some now automate their preemployment testing, using telephone voice response systems or Web sites. However, many still decline to do testing, especially psychological testing. For most best companies, including those who continue to use tests, the principal means of selecting among recruits is in-person interviewing, with general agreement that the most effective type is the structured interview. Many also use a popular variant, the behavioral interview, and several add distinct features to their interviewing methods, such as the participation of non-traditional interviewers. For a few of the best companies, selecting is detailed and extended. Their goal is to create a process so thorough that it makes a probationary period unnecessary and reduces both voluntary and nonvoluntary turnover.

Compensation and Benefits

Compensation, including benefits with monetary value, is not the most important driver of performance and retention, but it still plays a significant role, as discussed in Chapter Four. When linked to business strategies and when attentive to changes in both the nature of work and what workers value, it can have a positive influence, especially in forging stronger links between employees and their employers. The general principles seen in the practices of the best companies concern base pay, performance pay, retention pay, and benefits.

Make Base Pay Competitive and Equitable. All the best companies take care to be competitive—with other companies in their industries, with other companies in their geographical locations, and with other companies in other industries looking for the same talent. They also seek to be equitable, paying at comparable levels for comparable qualifications and experience, with full regard to the amount and composition of pay appropriate to different countries and regions. For most, this usually means setting base pay at the seventy-fifth percentile of the pay range found among competitors, particularly for senior managers and those with the most important specialties. Many of the high-tech best companies, however, follow a somewhat different competitive approach. They set lower targets for base pay and put a greater amount at risk in incentive pay. This serves two purposes. First, it more clearly and deliberately aligns compensation with strategic goals of innovation and creativity; second, it creates total compensation packages with the potential to outstrip those of the competition.

Although traditional annual evaluations, often with accompanying pay adjustments, are still most common, many of the best companies have instituted variations that consider performance in relation to a company's strategic goals and are more attentive to employees' attitudes. One of the fastest-growing variations is the 360-degree evaluation, employed principally to aid development and going beyond immediate supervisors to include peers, team members, subordinates, and sometimes even customers. It is also important that pay be equitable within an organization and that compensation processes such as assigning pay grades and administering pay be transparent and fair.

Pay for Performance. When companies do well, usually through the efforts of their employees, those employees want to share in the results. Most of the best companies seek to comply, but *line of sight* (a clear and timely connection between the efforts of particular employees and corporate results) is often hard to establish. Some firms reward all employees—usually with a share of profits or earnings in the form of a cash bonus—believing all to be responsible in some fashion for favorable results; others try to identify and reward the efforts of individuals; some do both.

Many now believe that rewarding all in the company—or all in a particular group or division clearly responsible for specific results—is more equitable than rewarding individuals in that it constitutes a clearer sharing of what all have made possible through their work together. Rewarding all also has the added advantage of strengthening feelings of employee engagement and hence ownership. Some companies increasingly seek to reward nonfinancial goals—often aligned to specific business strategies—such as developing new products and services, increasing market share, improving quality, enhancing customer satisfaction, and meeting safety and environmental targets. When it comes to rewarding individuals, several of the best companies now reward less for immediate results and more for attaining the skills and competencies that can mean later larger results.

Pay for Retention. The principal means of using compensation for retention is to offer employees company stock, in the form of shares or of options to buy shares at fixed preferential prices. Stock provides employees literal ownership, presumably encouraging them to take greater interest in the success of the organization they partly own and to continue their services with that organization. For senior executives, who have greater responsibility for company success than other employees do, the percentage of total compensation in stock (that is, at risk) usually rises as the executive rises in the organization. Many of the best companies see this as a means of aligning executive compensation with corporate goals. Executives in high-tech, new economy companies, which are dependent on constant innovation, may be inclined to be more entrepreneurial in order to keep stock prices rising; executives in more traditional, old economy companies may be more conservative in order to protect shareholder value.

- *Shares* of stock are acquired by employees from their employers either through purchase, usually at a 15 percent discount, or outright award. Outright awards may occur under the terms of an ESOP (employee stock ownership plan) or to reward particular achievements, such as notable performance of some kind. Awards of stock, especially to more senior managers, are usually accompanied by restrictions on the sale or transfer of the stock, thus creating *golden handcuffs* that aid retention.
- *Options* to purchase shares of stock are a form of compensation that has grown very rapidly during the past decade, especially in the United States. Originally mainly for senior executives, the granting of stock options has gone deeper and deeper into many of the best companies, serving both as an element of general compensation and as a reward for performance. By establishing vesting periods that prevent employees from exercising options immediately, employers can use options to encourage retention.

Among the best companies there is increasing discussion, heightened by the stock market declines of late 2000 and early 2001, of the efficacy of awards of shares of stock as compared to the granting of options to purchase shares for the purpose of advancing corporate goals such as encouraging retention. Holding shares of stock does appear to create feelings of ownership among employees, and there are data indicating shareholder returns are higher in companies with higher levels of employee stock ownership. On the down side, the share value of stocks can fall, though some argue that falling share prices can serve as a necessary wake-up call to employee owners to redouble their efforts on the company's behalf. Share values, of course, cannot fall below zero, thus limiting losses for employee stockholders.

Stock options also have advantages, especially for employers, who do not have to expense them when they are granted and can take them as deductions when they are exercised, a welcome boost to earnings statements either way. Employees too can benefit from stock options, especially if they cash them out in a rising market. But when markets are falling, companies that offer packages of cash and stock options may have to offer more cash than before to recruit those they want. They may also incur costs from having to reprice options, from dilution of share value through option *overhang,* and at any time, from the loss of key personnel who exercise their options and leave. For employees, the downsides can be even greater. Employees receive no advantage when the market is stable, and when the market is falling, a previous exercise of an option can actually create net losses. Furthermore, unlike shares of stock, options pay no dividends.

On balance, sentiment among the best companies appears to be moving in the direction of restricted stock awards as a more effective means than stock options of creating ownership, encouraging retention, and serving related corporate goals. Offering employees opportunities to purchase stock at a discount can be an even stronger incentive because purchase of this stock represents a tangible commitment by employees, a potentially far stronger bond than the acceptance of a corporate handout. As for trying to increase retention with stock options, it leaves a major part of compensation, itself a major lever of human resource management, at the whim of markets largely out of company control, hardly an action indicative of good business practice or responsibility. Even the argument that compensating with stock options aids corporate income statements rests, in the United States anyway, on the fragile reed of the rulings of the Financial Accounting Standards Board (FASB), an organization in self-confessed turmoil over how to account for stock-based compensation.[1]

Reassure Employees with Benefits. Employees rank benefits highly. First, benefits help relieve two major employee concerns: incurring costly, possibly even catastrophic, medical expenses and having an adequate income during postwork years. Second, responding to the higher value now given to subjective well-being, benefits provide time off, enabling employees to enjoy their nonwork lives more fully and balance work and home more easily.

Rising costs, however, especially for medical care, have brought radical changes in most corporate benefits programs. The response of most of the best companies has been to redouble their efforts to clearly and comprehensively communicate benefits program information to their employees. Benefit communication has long been recognized as a simple but very effective means of reinforcing employee commitment.[2] Studies show that companies that ably communicate benefits information have lower turnover rates.[3] Sweeping changes in many benefits programs now make such communications more important than ever. Fortunately, the need corresponds with the development of means to respond to it. New computer systems with capacious databases and sophisticated interactive programs can now deliver information about benefits, display comparative options, answer questions, receive requests for appointments, and track individual usage.

Many of the best companies also realize that through program design and administration they can reinforce behavioral patterns that are in line with their business strategies and corporate cultures. Flexible medical benefits programs permitting employees to select preferred options, time-off banks allowing workers to allocate how they use their days off, and 401(k) savings plans with investment choices are all consistent with the flexible, initiative-seeking, risk-taking behavior desired by high-tech, new economy firms. In addition, defined contribution retirement plans, far more portable than most defined benefit plans, better suit a mobile, advancement-oriented workforce.

Education and Training

Education and training, discussed in Chapter Five, are important to employers because they can improve performance, increase productivity, and contribute to better corporate results. Education and training are also important to employees. They can enhance employees' qualifications, and their employability as well, by adding and upgrading skills and competencies. Employers and employees each want education and training; both need them.

Five general principles that are responsive to ongoing postindustrial era changes in the nature of work can be derived from the education and training practices of the best companies: make learning continuous, make training informal, share information, meet changing needs with appropriate job-related programs, and promote general education.

Make Learning Continuous. When manual skills were predominant, learning was mostly a one-time event, occurring during the first weeks and months of one's job. Today, with cerebral skills predominant, learning must be continuous. Several of the best companies, aware of the need for continuous learning, are becoming *learning organizations*, encouraging employees— even requiring them in some cases—to pursue ongoing education and training using all available sources and especially company intranets and the ever-expanding resources of the global Internet.

Make Training Informal. Informal training, with its advantages of material and pace adapted to learners and a location usually in the work setting, is the natural adjunct to continuous learning. Today it appears to be replacing formal, structured classroom training as the principal form of corporate learning. A number of the best companies acknowledge the importance of informal training and are making wide and growing use of it. Essential to its continued development are increased coaching and mentoring, especially by supervisors. Computers are also likely to play the largest role in providing informal training, owing to their ability to change pace to suit the learner, repeat instruction as desired, and operate interactively.

Share Information. Continuous learning and informal training require the sharing of information, not only the explicit information in databases but also the tacit information in people's heads. Out of the realized need to share information, the practice of knowledge management has quickly grown to identify, collect, organize, disseminate, and use information and the knowledge developed from it. Although none of the best companies has a formal knowledge management program, a number have such programs in their subsidiaries, are using knowledge management practices, or are beginning to develop more structured programs themselves. A few are even moving beyond them, linking information and knowledge sharing with education and training to create learning management.

Meet Changing Needs with Appropriate Job-Related Programs. The best companies seek to improve performance and at the same time encourage retention with orientation programs, management development, education in soft skills, and competencies training. Orientation programs are considered especially important in demonstrating employer commitment so convincingly that it will be reciprocated with employee commitment. In management development, a number of the best companies focus on supervisors, mindful of the key role they play in both performance and retention. Other best companies are particularly attentive to the development of managers who have come from nonmanagerial ranks, individuals expert in other fields or moving up from lower-level line jobs. Especially important for the best companies is training in such soft skills as communications, interpersonal relations, and leadership. Even more important is the increase in comprehensive competencies training. Several of the best companies carefully identify the competencies required by their strategic plans, inventory what competencies they currently have, and create training programs to fill the gaps.

Promote General Education. Most of the best companies recognize the direct and indirect benefits of general education for their employees, and most understand that these benefits will give them more able workers and are likely to lead to improved performance and increased productivity. So they contribute widely and generously to the general education of their employees, usually by offering tuition reimbursement but also often by covering other costs and providing time off.

Ultimately, education and training are yet another means of engaging employees and investing in them. It is logical to believe, and usually true, that companies will be strengthened by the new skills and competencies they provide to their employees. It is also the case, as all the best companies testify, that enriching employees educationally earns their greater loyalty and commitment. For these companies, investment in employee capital clearly produces dividends for company capital.

Key Themes

A number of key themes appear throughout the practices of the best companies. They reflect especially the changing values of workers and the changed nature of postindustrial work, and they provide guidance for implementing the general principles discussed above.

Practices Should Be Aligned with Strategy. It has been said so often that practices should be aligned with strategy that it has become a cliché and often little more than that. However, a number of the best companies have carefully asked and answered these questions: Who are we? What do we do? What do we want to do? And they have reviewed all their practices to be certain that these practices are aligned with what they want to do. Thus, on the one hand, entrepreneurial firms may have recruiting policies, compensation plans, and training programs that emphasize employee choice and are consistent with strategic goals of flexibility, innovation, and risk taking. Less entrepreneurial firms, on the other hand, may have practices that lean toward asset preservation, job protection, and entitlement. And in between, there are infinite variations. What is important is to have practices that support strategy, not practices that are neutral or, worse yet, pulling in other directions.

Culture Is Critical.   All the best companies have strong cultures. These cultures are usually built around a few key ideas or ways of operating, rarely more than two or three. Often they can be summed up with simple words, like open communication, family-oriented, fun-loving, ethical, or customer-driven, and usually they are fully elaborated in a range of supporting practices and customs. Culture is the coin of the realm in any company, and it is very valuable. It gives employees identification and direction, and it is a source of pride that make association with the company special and desirable. However, it has to be created and then continually re-created, and this can be done in many ways, though probably none better than the regular retelling of simple stories of past achievement.

Paying Attention to the Competition Is Vital.   The best benchmark for a company is always at least one level above its toughest competitor, and it can know this benchmark only by paying careful attention to what competitors are doing. In all the practice areas discussed here, the best companies constantly track and survey the activities of their competitors, not just those in their industries but also those in their immediate geographical areas, and in the case of many best companies, those all over the world. Any company's highest performer is always another company's highest target, and the best defense against losing high performers is giving them what the other company does not. In the wise words of Jeffrey Pfeffer, "[A company's] differentiation, if it is to emerge from the firm's human assets, must come from assets unique to the organization that are not continually thrown on the market to work for the competition."[4]

Face-to-Face Relations Are Necessary.   Much is made today of virtual offices and telecommuting employees, and more of both are expected tomorrow. But work is a social activity, and contemporary postindustrial work even more so, because the qualities it needs from employees—free association, flexibility, creativity—are always greater in a group working together than in the sum of the efforts of its individual members. In all the practice areas discussed, and especially in recruiting, communications, performance management, and training, executives of the best companies emphasize the importance of in-person contact. In fact, according to the testimony of many of these executives, the very technology that has made work away from the office more common has made work in the office more necessary. High performance requires it; commitment is much more difficult without it.

Listening Is the Most Important Part of Communicating. Management writers often say, "You can never communicate too much." What they should say is, "You can never listen too much." Listening is the greatest compliment a supervisor can pay an employee. It says that what is being spoken has value and therefore the speaker has value too. To paraphrase the often-quoted Yogi Berra, *you can hear a lot by listening,* and what can be heard runs an invaluable gamut from hopes to suggestions to needs to concerns. Listening not only shows respect for employees, it includes them, and inclusion is the first step to both high performance and retention.

Engaging Employees Is Essential. Paradoxically, the most effective means of improving performance and reducing attrition is the least expensive, virtually cost free. Engaging employees—especially through participation, freedom, and trust—is the most comprehensive response to the ascendant postindustrial values of self-realization and self-actualization. When supervisors from CEOs down engage employees, they affirm both the importance of the employees' work and the value of employees' individual contributions. Performance data of the best companies show that in all the practice areas discussed earlier, objectives are more easily met when employees are engaged and more likely to fall short when they are not.

Investing in Employees Is Required. Companies make many investments—in research, in technology, in new equipment, in product and service development, in marketing, in bricks and mortar. Yet the investment with the highest potential payoff, investment in people, often ranks low in corporate priorities. Not in the best companies, however. They recognize that investing in employees through training, compensation, benefits, and facilities not only has a positive effect on performance but also builds loyalty and commitment, enhancing retention. They know that it is an investment whose return continues to grow and that in response to companies' investing in them, employees will more readily invest their human capital in their companies.

Evaluating Practices Is the Way to Learn How They Are Working. Few of the best companies evaluate the practices discussed here. In truth, it is difficult to do. Many factors affect the results of different recruiting policies or varying forms of compensation and training. Focusing on one practice and holding others constant, in what might approximate a scientific evaluation, is usually impossible. Yet it is possible to associate annual inputs of new hires with the recruiting practices that were in place when they were hired, then track their performance over time and calculate their attrition rates. In addition, correlations between practices and results can be researched and found, and although not positive indicators of cause and effect, they can be suggestive and can lead to improved practices. Several of the best companies are advancing on the evaluation frontier, and aided by the ever-growing capabilities of information technology, they are learning valuable lessons. In the future those joining them in such learning will also number themselves among the best companies.

Commitment Begets Commitment. There will always be turnover. Employees leave companies for many reasons, and many of them have nothing to do with how they were treated by superiors or fellow workers or how they were affected by company policies. But a number leave because of a work environment that is not encouraging, supervisors who are not attentive, compensation practices that are inappropriate or not fairly followed, or training that is not received. At the core of these reasons, surveys and interviews indicate, is employees' feeling that their companies were indifferent to them, that they did not care enough to commit to them and the work they did. Companies that do care, that engage their employees and invest in them, that are committed to them and their work, will still lose some, but they will retain many more, and these will be their high performers.

Afterword

Since September 11, 2001, the simple act of going to work has taken on a broader and deeper meaning. Never before have most of us thought of going to work as a matter of putting ourselves at risk. But now we must, whether we are flight attendants or bond traders in tall buildings or secretaries opening envelopes. Never before have we thought of going to work as a matter of national strategy. But now it is. As I write, flags are displayed across the United States, often with mottoes like "America: Open for Business." President Bush, describing those lost with the phrase "last seen on duty," has made work both an imperative and a patriotic act.

This broader and deeper meaning reinforces one of the important conclusions of this book, that to find and keep high performers companies need to convey to both candidates and current employees the meaningfulness of the work they do and the value of the contribution they make. To perform well when risks are higher, employees need to know that what they do, whatever it might be, matters, and who they are, both at work and away from work, is very important. The best companies have always known this. The events of September 11 make it even more urgent, and only those who understand will become tomorrow's best companies.

Appendix A:
Companies Interviewed

In the following list, all dollar amounts are U.S. dollars, in millions. Fiscal years (FY) end in December, except where otherwise indicated.

- Acer Incorporated, Taipei, Taiwan

2000 sales: $4,764
2000 net income: $205
1999 employees: 33,912

- AFLAC Incorporated, Columbus, Georgia

2000 sales: $9,720
2000 net income: $687
2000 employees: 5,015

- Amgen Inc., Thousand Oaks, California

2000 sales: $3,448
2000 net income: $1,139
2000 employees: 7,300

- BMC Software, Inc., Houston, Texas (FY: March)

2001 sales: $1,504
2001 net income: $42
2001 employees: 7,730

- Capital One Financial Corporation, Falls Church, Virginia

2000 sales: $5,424
2000 net income: $470
2000 employees: 19,247

- CDW Computer Centers, Inc., Vernon Hills, Illinois

2000 sales: $3,843
2000 net income: $162
2000 employees: 2,700

- Cisco Systems, Inc., San Jose, California (FY: July)

2001 sales: $22,293
2001 net income: $(1,014)
2000 employees: 34,000

- Compuware Corporation, Farmington Hills, Michigan (FY: March)

2001 sales: $2,010
2001 net income: $119
2001 employees: 13,220

- Genentech, Inc., South San Francisco, California

2000 sales: 1,646
2000 net income: ($16)
2000 employees: 5,000

- Harley-Davidson, Inc., Milwaukee, Wisconsin

2000 sales: 2,906
2000 net income: 348
2000 employees: 7,700

- Ingram Micro Inc., Santa Ana, California

2000 sales: $30,715
2000 net income: $226
2000 employees: 16,500

- Intel Corporation, Santa Clara, California

2000 sales: $33,726
2000 net income: $10,535
2000 employees: 86,100

- LM Ericsson

2000 sales: $29,026
2000 net income: $2,230
2000 employees: 105,129

- MBNA Corporation, Wilmington, Delaware

2000 sales: $7,869
2000 net income: $1,313
2000 employees: 25,000

- Merck & Co., Inc., Whitehouse Station, New Jersey

2000 sales: $40,363
2000 net income: $6,821
2000 employees: 69,300

- Microsoft Corporation, Redmond, Washington
  (FY: June)

2001 sales: $25,296
2001 net income: $7,346
2000 employees: 39,100

- Nokia Corporation, Espoo, Finland

2000 sales: $26,992
2000 net income: $3,499
2000 employees: 60,000

- Novo Nordisk A/S, Bagsvaerd, Denmark

2000 sales: $2,595
2000 net income: $385
2000 employees: 13,752

- Royal Dutch/Shell Group, London and The Hague

2000 sales: $149,146
2000 net income: $12,719
2000 employees: 90,000

- Singapore Airlines, Singapore (FY: March)

2001 sales: $5,510
2001 net income: $858
2001 employees: 27,254

- Starbucks Corporation, Seattle, Washington (FY: September)

2000 sales: $2,169
2000 net income: $95
2000 employees: 47,000

- Sun Microsystems, Inc., Palo Alto, California (FY: June)

2001 sales: $18,250
2001 net income: $927
2000 employees: 38,900

- Taiwan Semiconductor Manufacturing Co., Ltd., Hsin-Chu, Taiwan

2000 sales: $5,019
2000 net income: $1,966
2000 employees: 14,000

- Toyota Motor Corporation, Toyota City, Japan (FY: March)

2001 sales: $106,952
2001 net income: $3,755
2000 employees: 214,631

- Wal-Mart Stores, Inc., Bentonville, Arkansas (FY: January)

2001 sales: $191,329
2001 net income: $6,295
2001 employees: 1,244,000

Appendix B:
Population Projections

FIGURE B.1. Working-Age Population (20–64), Actual and Projected, in the United States, Germany, and Japan, 1950–2050.

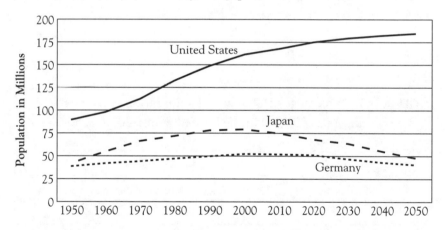

Sources: Population Division of the Department of Economic and Social Affairs of the United Nations Secretariat, *The World at Six Billion* (ESA/P/WP154), [www.popin.org/6billion], Oct. 12, 1999; U.S. Census Bureau, *Statistical Abstract of the United States, 1999* (Washington, D.C.: U.S. Government Printing Office, 1999); U.S. Census Bureau, *International Data Base*, table 094, "Midyear Population, by Age and Sex" [www.census.gov], accessed Dec. 10, 2000; National Institute of Population and Social Security Research, *Population Projections for Japan* (Tokyo: National Institute of Population and Social Security Research, Jan. 1997); Federal Statistical Office, "Population in Germany Will Decline by More Than 10 Million from Presently 82 Million by 2050 (Press Release), (Weisbaden, Germany, July 19, 2000).

FIGURE B.2. Population Cohorts as Percentage of Total Population in More Developed Countries, 2000–2050.

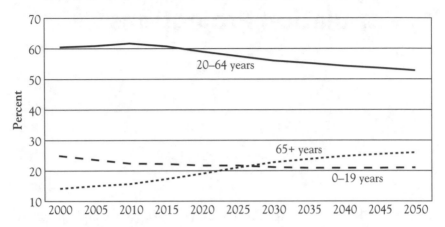

Source: U.S. Census Bureau, *International Data Base*, table 094, "Midyear Population, by Age and Sex," [www.census.gov], accessed Dec. 10, 2000.

FIGURE B.3. Percentage of Change in Composition of Groups in Prime Working Years (20–64) in the United States, 2000–2050.

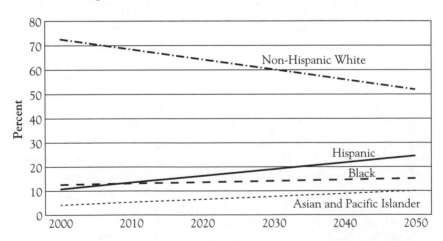

Source: Calculated from U.S. Census Bureau, *Projections of the Total Resident Population by 5-Year Age Groups, Race, and Hispanic Origin, with Special Age Categories: Middle Series* (NP-T4-A, C, E, F, G), [www.census.gov], accessed Dec. 14, 2000.

Notes

Chapter One

1. E. L. Axelrod, H. Handfield-Jones, and T. A. Welsh, "The War for Talent: Part Two," *The McKinsey Quarterly*, 2001, no. 2, [www.mckinseyquarterly.com], accessed May 2001.

2. Watson Wyatt Worldwide, "*WorkUSA 2000* Survey Finds Only Half of U.S. Workers Are Committed to Employers" (Press Release), [www.watsonwyatt.com/homepage/us], Jan. 11, 2000.

3. In particular, see J. Pfeffer, *The Human Equation: Building Profits by Putting People First* (Boston: Harvard Business School Press, 1998), especially chap. 2.

4. M. Berman, *The CEO Challenge: Top Marketplace and Management Issues 2001* (Research Report 1286-01-RR), (New York: The Conference Board, 2001), p. 32.

5. B. Hackett, *The Value of Training in the Era of Intellectual Capital* (Research Report 1199-97-RR), (New York: The Conference Board, 1997), p. 25.

6. S. Branch, "The 100 Best Companies to Work For in America," *Fortune*, 1999, *139*(1), 118–144.

7. "Shareholder Scorecard," *Wall Street Journal*, Feb. 25, 1999, pp. R14–R15, R17.

8. N. Byrnes, "The Best Performers," *Business Week*, Mar. 29, 1999, pp. 98–108.

9. E. Brown, "America's Most Admired Companies," *Fortune*, 1999, *139*(4), 68–73.

10. L. Grant, "Happy Workers, High Returns," *Fortune*, 1998, *137*(1), 81.

11. R. Levering and M. Moskowitz, "The 100 Best Companies to Work For," *Fortune*, 2000, *141*(1), 82–110; "The 100 Best Companies to Work For," *Fortune*, 2001, *143*(1), 148–168.

12. G. Hasek, "The World's 100 Best Managed Companies," *Industry Week*, Aug. 17, 1998, pp. 78–79.

13. J. Leung, "Asia's Most Admired Companies," *Asian Business*, May 5, 1999, pp. 24–32.

14. T. Jackson, "World's Most Respected Companies," *Financial Times*, Nov. 30, 1998, p. 3.

15. R. Inglehart, *The Silent Revolution: Changing Values and Political Styles in Advanced Industrial Society* (Princeton, N.J.: Princeton University Press, 1977); *Modernization and Postmodernization: Cultural, Economic and Political Change in 43 Societies* (Princeton, N.J.: Princeton University Press, 1997). For a summary, see R. Inglehart, "Globalization and Postmodern Values," *Washington Quarterly*, 2000, *23*(1), 215–228.

16. R. Inglehart, "Modernization, Cultural Change and the Persistence of Traditional Values," *American Sociological Review*, 65(1), 26.

17. P. F. Drucker, *Management Challenges for the 21st Century* (New York: HarperBusiness, 1999), chap. 4.

18. C. Handy, "Trust and the Virtual Organization," *Harvard Business Review*, 1995, *73*(3), 48.

Chapter Two

1. Roper Center for Public Opinion Research [at the University of Connecticut], "New York Times Poll," Public Opinion Online, [www.ropercenter.uconn.edu], July 19, 2000.

2. Families and Work Institute, "Executive Summary," *1997 National Study of the Changing Workforce* (New York: Families and Work Institute, 1997), p. 12.

3. "Workers Everywhere Want the Same Thing," *Workforce*, 1998, 3(6), 8.

4. J. Fitz-enz, "The Really Big Question," [www.workforceonline.com], accessed July 22, 2000.

5. J. Pfeffer, *The Human Equation: Building Profits by Putting People First* (Boston: Harvard Business School Press, 1998), p. 297.

6. "FC-Roper Starch Survey: Expectations," *Fast Company*, Nov. 1999, p. 214.

7. D. Grote, "The Secrets of Performance Appraisal," *Across the Board*, 2000, 37(5), 14.

8. S. Wetlaufer, "Who Wants to Marry a Millionaire?" *Harvard Business Review*, 2000, 78(4), 60.

9. H. Lancaster, "Managing Your Career," *Wall Street Journal*, Aug. 31, 1999, p. B1.

10. B. P. Noble, "At Work," *New York Times*, Apr. 17, 1994, p. 25.

11. John J. Heldrich Center for Workforce Development [at Rutgers University] and Center for Survey Research and Analysis [at the University of Connecticut], *Work Trends II: Work and the Family: How Employers and Workers Can Strike the Balance*, [www.heldrich.rutgers.edu], Mar. 1999.

12. "Increase Job Satisfaction Without Increasing the Bottom Line," summary of Randstad North America and Roper Starch Worldwide, *2000 Randstad North American Employee Review*, [www.roperasw.com], July 2000.

13. J. Bainbridge, "Employees Seek to Balance Lives," *Marketing* (London), Oct. 15, 1998, p. 71.

14. The Conference Board, *Work-Life Initiatives in a Global Context* (Conference Report 1248-99-CH), (New York: The Conference Board, 1999), p. 6.

15. M. Berman, *The CEO Challenge: Top Marketplace and Management Issues* (Research Report 1244-99-RR), (New York: The Conference Board, 1999), p. 4.

16. A. Tang, "As Hours Lengthen, Workers Gain Freedom to Set Them," *New York Times*, Nov. 3, 1999, p. G1.

17. C. Handy, "Trust and the Virtual Organization," *Harvard Business Review*, 1995, *73*(3), 46.

18. M. Apgar IV, "The Alternative Workplace: Changing Where and How People Work," *Harvard Business Review*, 1998, *77*(3), 136.

19. R. Reynes, "Programs That Aid Troubled Workers," *Nation's Business*, 1998, *86*(6), 73–74.

20. Bureau of Labor Statistics, U.S. Department of Labor, "Employee Benefits in Medium and Large Private Establishments," table 2 (1997 news release text, summary of *Employee Benefits Survey*), [www.bls.gov], Jan. 7, 1999.

21. The Conference Board, "Child Care Services," *Work-Family Roundtable*, 1997, *7*(4), 1, 3; *Work-Life Initiatives in a Global Context*, p. 11.

22. K. O'Brien, "You Can Print This Corporate Benefit Gray, *New York Times*, June 28, 2000, p. G1.

23. J. Useem, "Welcome to the New Company Town," *Fortune*, 2000, *141*(1), 63–64.

24. John J. Heldrich Center for Workforce Development [at Rutgers University], *Work Trends Fall 1998 Survey: Americans' Attitudes About Work, Employers, and the Government* (New Brunswick, N.J.: Heldrich Center for Workforce Development, 1999), p. 8.

25. C. L. Cole, "Building Loyalty," *Workforce*, 2000, *79*(8), 42–48.

26. L. Saad, "American Workers Generally Satisfied, but Indicate Their Jobs Leave Much to Be Desired, *Poll Releases* (Princeton, N.J.: Gallup News Service, Sept. 3, 1999).

27. M. Buckingham and C. Coffman, *First, Break All the Rules: What the World's Greatest Managers Do Differently* (New York: Simon & Schuster, 1999), pp. 11–12.

28. See, for example, The Gallup Organization, "People Join Companies, but Leave Managers," The Workplace Column, [www.gallup.com], accessed Dec. 2001.

29. P. Schofield, "It's True: Happy Workers Are More Productive," *Works Management* (Horton Kirby), 1998, *51*(12), 33–35. The Sheffield Effectiveness Program is based jointly at the Centre for

Economic Performance at the London School of Economics and the Institute for Work Psychology at the University of Sheffield.

30. C. Cherry, *On Human Communication: A Review, a Survey, and a Criticism* (Cambridge, Mass.: MIT Press, 1966), p. 4.

31. Watson Wyatt Worldwide, *1999 Communications Study: Linking Communications with Strategy to Achieve Business Goals*, [www.watsonwyatt.com/homepage/us], accessed Oct. 12, 1999. This study was conducted in cooperation with the International Association of Business Communicators (IABC) and the IABC Research Foundation.

32. F. F. Reichheld, "Lead for Loyalty," *Harvard Business Review*, 2001, 79(7), 78.

33. E. H. Schein, *Organizational Culture and Leadership* (San Francisco: Jossey-Bass, 1985), p. 81.

34. J. Collins and J. Porras, *Built to Last: Successful Efforts of Visionary Companies* (New York: HarperBusiness, 1994), chap. 6.

35. A. R. Kare, "Work Week," *Wall Street Journal*, Mar. 7, 2000, p. 1A.

36. J. Schu, "Intranets Help Keep Goodwill of Downsized Employees," *Workforce*, 2000, 79(7), 15.

37. Watson Wyatt Worldwide, *1999 Communications Study*, p. 4.

38. R. Abelson, "A Leader's View of Leadership," *New York Times*, Oct. 10, 1999, Sec. 3, p. 12.

39. Handy, "Trust and the Virtual Organization," p. 46.

40. TJ Larkin and S. Larkin, "Everything We Do Is Wrong," *Across the Board*, 1995, 32(4), 33.

41. R. Prickett, "Stateside Statistics Show Significance of Soft Skills," *People Management* (London), 1998, 4(5), 19.

42. Watson Wyatt Worldwide, *1999 Communications Study*, p. 5.

43. E. L. Axelrod, H. Handfield-Jones, and T. A. Welsh, "The War for Talent: Part Two," *The McKinsey Quarterly*, 2001, no. 2, [www.mckinseyquarterly.com], accessed May 2001.

44. R. Freeman and J. Rogers, *What Workers Want* (Ithaca, N.Y.: ILR Press, 1999), pp. 4–5.

45. J. Pfeffer and R. Sutton, *The Knowing-Doing Gap: How Smart Companies Turn Knowledge into Action* (Boston: Harvard Business School Press, 2000).

46. A. Wooldridge, "Come Back, Company Man," *New York Times Magazine*, Mar. 5, 2000, p. 83.

47. Wetlaufer, "Who Wants to Marry a Millionaire?" p. 60.

48. J. Laabs, "Satisfy Them with More Than Money," *Workforce*, 1998, *77*(11), 42.

49. Louis Harris and Associates, *Women and Society Whirlpool Study* (Storrs, Conn.: Louis Harris and Associates, Mar. 1996).

50. The Gallup Organization, "Work and Work Place," *Gallup Poll Topics: A-Z*, [www.gallup.com], accessed July 27, 2000.

51. Hudson Institute and Walker Information, *Commitment in the Workplace: The 1999 Employee Relationship Report*, [www.hudson.org], Oct. 19, 1999.

52. H. Axel, "Employee Recognition Programs," *HR Executive Review* (The Conference Board), 1999, *7*(3), 5.

53. B. Nelson, "The Ironies of Motivation," *Workforce Stability Alert*, 1999, *2*(6), 5.

54. S. D. Friedman, P. Christensen, and J. DeGroot, "Work and Life: The End of the Zero-Sum Game," *Harvard Business Review*, 1998, *76*(6), 119–120.

55. J. M. Kouzes and B. Z. Posner, *Encouraging the Heart: A Leader's Guide to Recognizing Others* (San Francisco: Jossey-Bass, 1999), chaps. 7, 12.

56. Axel, "Employee Recognition Programs," pp. 3, 6.

Chapter Three

1. N. M. Tichy and R. Charan, "The CEO as Coach: An Interview with AlliedSignal's Lawrence A. Bossidy," *Harvard Business Review*, 1995, *73*(2), 76.

2. L. S. Csoka and B. Hackett, *Transforming the HR Function for Global Business Success* (Research Report 1209-98-RR), (New York: The Conference Board, 1998), p. 9.

3. Watson Wyatt Worldwide, *Human Capital Index: Linking Human Capital and Shareholder Value*, [www.watsonwyatt.com/homepage/us], Nov. 19, 2000.

4. Bruce Bassman, Towers Perrin principal, quoted in C. Comeau-Kirschner, "Making Retention Work," *Management Review*, 1998, 87(10), 7.

5. "1997 Survey of Human Resource Trends," *Braun Consulting News*, Winter 1997-1998, 3(3), 4.

6. C. L. Cove, "Building Loyalty," *Workforce*, 2000, 79(8), 43; S. Branch, "You Hired 'Em. But Can You Keep Them?" *Fortune*, 1998, 138(9), 247.

7. J. Laabs, "Pick the Right People," *Workforce*, 1998, 77(11), 51.

8. "1997 Survey of Human Resource Trends," p. 4.

9. "Work Week," *Wall Street Journal*, Jan. 18, 2000, p. A1.

10. L. Wah, "It's No Easy Job to Retain Talent," *Management Review*, 1998, 87(5), 5.

11. M. W. Walsh, "Luring the Best in an Unsettled Time," *New York Times*, Jan. 30, 2001, p. G1.

12. P. F. Drucker, "The Future Has Already Happened," *Harvard Business Review*, 1997, 75(5), 20.

13. U.S. Bureau of the Census, International Data Base, table 094, "Midyear Population, by Age and Sex," [www.census.gov], accessed Dec. 9, 2000; "Where Will All the Babies Go?" *Migration World Magazine*, 2000, 28(1-2), 27.

14. U.S. Bureau of the Census, International Data Base, table 010, "Infant Mortality Rates and Deaths, and Life Expectancy at Birth, by Sex," [www.census.gov], accessed Dec. 9, 2000.

15. U.S. Bureau of the Census, International Data Base, table 094.

16. P. J. Purcell, "Older Workers: Employment and Retirement Trends," *Monthly Labor Review*, 2000, 123(10), 22; M. W. Wilson,

"Reversing Decades-Long Trend, Americans Are Retiring Later in Life," *New York Times*, Feb. 26, 2001, p. A1.

17. U.S. Bureau of the Census, "Projections of the Resident Population by Race, Hispanic Origin, and Nativity: Middle Series" (NP-T5-A, F, G), [www.census.gov], accessed Dec. 14, 2000; "Projected Migration by Race and Hispanic Origin, 1999 to 2100" (NP-T7-C), [www.census.gov], accessed Dec. 14, 2000.

18. S. Greenhouse, "Pension Workers at Highest Level in Seven Decades, *New York Times*, Sept. 4, 2000, pp. A1, A12.

19. H. N. Fullerton Jr., "Labor Force Projections to 2008: Steady Growth and Changing Composition," *Monthly Labor Review*, 1999, *122*(11), 20, 24, 27–28; "Labor Force Participation: 75 Years of Change, 1950–98 and 1998–2025," *Monthly Labor Review*, 1999, *122*(12), 4–5, 10–11.

20. Bureau of Labor Statistics, U.S. Department of Labor, "Tomorrow's Jobs," *2000–01 Occupational Outlook Handbook*, [www.bls.gov], Apr. 19, 2000.

21. D. Braddock, "Occupational Employment Projections," *Monthly Labor Review*, 1999, *122*(11), tables 3, 4.

22. Bureau of Labor Statistics, "Tomorrow's Jobs," chart 11.

23. E. G. Chambers and others, "The War for Talent," *The McKinsey Quarterly*, 1998, no. 3, 45.

24. "Mypay-myway: Monetizing Total Rewards in the Talent War," *Perspectives on Reward Management* (Towers Perrin), [www.towers.com], 2000.

25. Organization for Economic Cooperation and Development, *Historical Statistics 1960–1997* (Washington, D.C.: Organization for Economic Cooperation and Development, 1999), p. 43; *Labor Force Statistics 1978/1998* (Washington, D.C.: Organization for Economic Cooperation and Development, 1999), pp. 86–87, 158–159.

26. J. Tagliabue, "Sprechen Sie Technology?" *New York Times*, May 5, 2000, pp. C1, C21.

27. S. R. Schmidt, "Long-Run Trends in Workers' Beliefs About Their Own Job Security: Evidence from the General Social Survey," *Journal of Labor Economics*, 1999, *17*(4, part 2), S127–S141.

28. M. Dolliver, "It's a Love of Labor," *ADWeek* (Eastern ed.), Jan. 31, 2000, *41*(5), 62.

29. John J. Heldrich Center for Workforce Development [at Rutgers University] and Center for Survey Research and Analysis [at the University of Connecticut], *Work Trends II: Work and the Family: How Employers and Workers Can Strike the Balance*, [www.heldrich.rutgers.edu], Mar. 1999, p. 2.

30. B. Hale, "Staff: How the US Is Reacting to Its Squeeze," *Business Review Weekly* (Australia), [www.brw.com.au], accessed July 2000.

31. "Benchmark Study Reveals Perceptions and Realities About Generational Differences in the Workforce" (Press Release), [www.roperasw.com], Mar. 16, 2000.

32. P. B. Britton, S. J. Chadwick, and T. Walker, "Rewards of Work," *Ivey Business Journal* (London), 1999, 63(4), 46–52.

33. Bureau of Labor Statistics, U.S. Department of Labor, "Employee Tenure Summary," *Labor Statistics from the Current Population Survey*, tables 1, 2, [www.stats.bls.gov], Aug. 29, 2000.

34. "Work Week," *Wall Street Journal*, Jan. 18, 2000, p. A1.

35. Hudson Institute and Walker Information, *Commitment in the Workplace: The 1999 Employee Relationship Report*, [www.hudson.org], Oct. 19, 1999.

36. Families and Work Institute, "Executive Summary," *The 1997 National Study of the Changing Workforce* (New York: Families and Work Institute, 1997), p. 14.

37. John J. Heldrich Center for Workforce Development [at Rutgers University], *Work Trends Fall 1998 Survey: Americans' Attitudes About Work, Employers, and the Government* (New Brunswick, N.J.: Heldrich Center for Workforce Development, 1999), p. 2.

38. Hudson Institute and Walker Information, *Commitment in the Workplace*.

39. J. Pfeffer, *The Human Equation: Building Profits by Putting People First* (Boston: Harvard Business School Press, 1998), p. 74; see also P. Carbonara, "Hire for Attitude, Train for Skill," *Fast Company*, Aug. 1996, pp. 73ff.

40. Watson Wyatt Worldwide, Human Capital Index: Linking Human Capital and Shareholder Value [www.watsonwyatt.com/homepage/us], Nov. 19, 2000.

41. R. V. Gilmartin, "Diversity and Competitive Advantage at Merck," *Harvard Business Review*, 1999, 77(1), 146.

42. N. Shirouzu and Y. Ono, "In Race with Honda, Once-Stodgy Toyota Tries to Rev Up Image," *Wall Street Journal*, Sept. 21, 2000, pp. A1, A6.

43. Daniel Goleman, of Rutgers University's Graduate School of Applied and Professional Psychology, first set forth his views in *Emotional Intelligence: Why It Can Matter More Than IQ for Character, Health and Lifelong Achievement* (New York: Bantam Books, 1995). A convenient summary, focusing on business, is found in D. Goldman, "What Makes a Leader," *Harvard Business Review*, 1998, 76(6), 92–102.

44. National Center on the Educational Quality of the Workforce, *First Findings from the EQW National Employer Survey* (Philadelphia: National Center on the Educational Quality of the Workforce, 1994), p. 14.

45. H. Schultz, "Starbucks: Making Values Pay" (excerpt from *Pour Your Heart Into It*), *Fortune*, 1997, 136(6), 261–272.

46. M. A. van den Bergh, "Message from the President," *Royal Dutch Petroleum Company Annual Report 1998*, Mar. 21, 1999.

47. J. Jesitus, "Engineered for Success: How George Binder Keeps Amgen Healthy," *Industry Week*, July 10, 1999, p. 48.

48. M. Gimein, "Smart Is Not Enough," *Fortune*, 2001, 143(1), 130.

49. T. G. Stephen, "The Relationship Between Sources of New Employees and Attitudes Toward the Job," *The Journal of Social Psychology*, 1994, 134(1), 99–111.

50. N. Stein, "Winning the War to Keep Talent," *Fortune*, 2000, *141*(11), 134.

51. S. Hays, "Capital One Is Renowned for Innovative Recruiting Strategies," *Workforce*, 1999, *78*(4), 93.

52. Nua Internet Surveys, "How Many Online?" [www.nua.ie], accessed Dec. 20, 2001.

53. CyberAtlas, "Internet Appliance Market Worth $5.6 Billion by 2005," [www.cyberatlas.internet.com], Dec. 15, 1999.

54. W. Wood, "Work Week," *Wall Street Journal*, Dec. 12, 2000, p. A1.

55. "Work Week," *Wall Street Journal*, Mar. 28, 2000, p. A1.

56. American Management Association, "Summary of Key Findings," *2000 AMA Survey on Workplace Testing: Basic Skills, Job Skills, Psychological Measurement* (New York: American Management Association, Mar. 31, 2000).

57. M. Leuchter, "Capital One: Fanaticism That Works," *U.S. Banker*, 2000, *111*(8), 25.

58. G. Nicholson, "Automated Assessments for Better Hires," *Workforce*, 2000, *79*(12), 103.

59. Leuchter, "Capital One," p. 28.

60. R. Lieber, "Wired for Hiring: Microsoft's Slick Recruiting Machine," *Fortune*, 1996, *136*(2), 124.

61. C. Fernández-Araóz, "Hiring Without Firing," *Harvard Business Review*, 1999, *77*(4), 113.

62. Hays, "Capital One Is Renowned for Innovative Recruiting Strategies," p. 93.

63. Pfeffer, *The Human Equation*, p. 74.

64. William M. Mercer, Inc., "Mercer's Fax Facts Surveys: Turnover: How Does It Affect Your Business?" [www.wmmercer.com], accessed Oct. 7, 1998.

65. Society for Human Resource Management, "Organizations Are Feeling the Labor Market Squeeze According to New SHRM Survey" (Press Release), June 25, 2000.

66. J. Cook, "Everyday Low Turnover," *Human Resource Executive*, Feb. 2000, pp. 1, 41–44.

Chapter Four

1. "Workers Everywhere Want the Same Things," *Workforce*, 1998, 3(6), 8.

2. Aon Consulting, *The 1999 Workforce Commitment Index* (Chicago: Aon Consulting, 1999), p. 7.

3. John J. Heldrich Center for Workforce Development [at Rutgers University], *Work Trends Fall 1998 Survey: Americans' Attitudes About Work, Employers, and the Government* (New Brunswick, N.J.: Heldrich Center for Workforce Development, 1999), p. 8.

4. J. L. McAdams and E. J. Hawk, "Organizational Performance and Rewards: A Strategic Use of Employee Assets," *ACA Journal* (now *WorldatWork Journal*), 1994, 3(3), 46–59.

5. P. W. Mulvey, G. E. Ledford Jr., and P. V. LeBlanc, "Rewards of Work: How They Drive Performance, Retention and Satisfaction," *WorldatWork Journal*, 2000, 9(3), 8.

6. L. Wah, "The New Workplace Paradox," *Management Review*, 1998, 87(1), 7.

7. J. Laabs, "Satisfy Them with More Than Money," *Workforce*, 1998, 77(11), 41.

8. Randstad North America, "Benchmark Employee Study Uncovers Salary Expectations and Attitudes on Benefits" (Press Release), June 6, 2000.

9. BridgeGate LLC, "Employee Retention Survey Reveals Americans Favor Cash over Flextime" (Press Release), July 26, 2000.

10. "Survey Finds Seven Factors That Drive Employee Commitment," *HR Daily News*, [www.hr.com], June 4, 2000.

11. A. Kohn, "Why Incentive Plans Cannot Work," *Harvard Business Review*, 1993, 71(5), 54–63.

12. "Perspectives: What Role—If Any—Should Incentives Play in the Workplace?" *Harvard Business Review*, 1993, 71(6), 37–49.

Responses to Kohn's *HBR* article, "Why Incentive Plans Cannot Work."

13. N. Gupta and J. D Shaw, "Let the Evidence Speak: Financial Incentives Are Effective!!" *Compensation and Benefits Review*, 1998, 30(2), 28.

14. "Perspectives," *Harvard Business Review*, p. 43.

15. E. E. Lawler III, *Rewarding Excellence: Pay Strategies for the New Economy* (San Francisco: Jossey-Bass, 2000).

16. Lawler, *Rewarding Excellence*, Introduction.

17. S. E. Prokesch, "Companies Turn to Incentives: Pay Linked to Performance," *New York Times*, July 19, 1985, p. D1.

18. S. Hays, "Pros and Cons of Pay for Performance," *Workforce*, 1999, 78(2), 69.

19. R. Ganzel, "What's Wrong with Pay for Performance?" *Training*, 1998, 35(12), 36; J. E. Abuena, "Profits Are Down, So, Boss, Can I Have That Raise?" *New York Times*, Apr. 1, 2001, p. BU14.

20. S. Gates, *Aligning Performance Measures and Incentives in European Companies* (Research Report 1252-99-RR), (New York: The Conference Board, 1999), p. 6.

21. L. Lavelle, "Undermining Pay for Performance," *Business Week*, Jan. 15, 2001, p. 70.

22. A. Rappaport, "New Thinking on How to Link Executive Pay with Performance," *Harvard Business Review*, 1999, 77(2), 91.

23. Watson Wyatt Worldwide, "Key Findings: 2000/2001 Survey of Top Management Compensation," *Executive Pay in 2001: The Land of Opportunity*, [www.watsonwyatt.com/homepage/us], Dec. 19, 2000.

24. C. Rosen and M. Quarrey, "How Well Is Employee Ownership Working?" *Harvard Business Review*, 1987, 65(5), 126–130.

25. J. E. Godfrey, "Does Employee Ownership Really Make a Difference?" *The CPA Journal*, 2000, 70(1), 13.

26. G. E. Ledford Jr., E. E. Lawler III, and S. Mohrman, "Reward Innovations in Fortune 1000 Companies," *Compensation and Benefits Review*, 1995, 27(4), 78.

27. P. J. Taylor and J. L. Pierce, "Effects of Introducing a Performance Management System on Employees' Subsequent Attitudes and Effort," *Public Personnel Management*, 1999, 28(3), 430–431.

28. Watson Wyatt Worldwide, "Stuck in Neutral: The Untapped Potential of Rewards," *Playing to Win: Strategic Rewards in the War for Talent: Fifth Annual Survey Report 2000/2001*, [www.watsonwyatt.com/homepage/us], Dec. 18, 2000.

29. Rappaport, "New Thinking," p. 101.

30. B. J. Hall, "What You Need to Know About Stock Options," *Harvard Business Review*, 2000, 78(2), 121.

31. Watson Wyatt Worldwide, "Key Findings: CEO Pay Study," *Executive Pay in 2001: The Land of Opportunity*, [www.watsonwyatt.com/homepage/us], Dec. 19, 2000.

32. "Lowering the Bar," *Wall Street Journal*, Apr. 8, 1999, p. R1 (special section titled "Executive Pay").

33. H. Axel, "Strategies for Retaining Critical Talent," *HR Executive Review* (The Conference Board), 1998, 6(2), 11.

34. P. Cappelli, "A Market-Driven Approach to Retaining Talent," *Harvard Business Review*, 2000, 79(1), 105–106.

35. S. Boden, M. Glucksman, and P. Lasky, "The War for Technical Talent," *The McKinsey Quarterly*, 2000, no. 3, [www.mckinseyquarterly.com], Feb. 1, 2001.

36. M. A. Champion, "Meaning and Measurement of Turnover: Comparisons of Alternative Measures and Recommendations for Research," *Journal of Applied Psychology*, 1991, 76(2), 199–213.

37. C. Peck and H. M. Silvert, *Top Executive Compensation in 1999* (Research Report 1281-00-RR), (New York: The Conference Board, 2000).

38. B. Leonard, "Continuing High Turnover Frustrating Employers," *HRMagazine*, 1998, 43(11), 22.

39. S. Hays, "Capital One Is Renowned for Innovative Recruiting Strategies," *Workforce*, 1999, 78(4), 93.

40. S. Branch, "The 100 Best Companies to Work For in America," *Fortune*, 1999, 139(1), 128.

41. C. Hymowitz, "In the Lead," *Wall Street Journal*, Dec. 12, 2000, p. B1.

42. R. Levering and M. Moskowitz, "The 100 Best Companies to Work For," *Fortune*, 2000, *141*(1), 82.

43. M. Lewis, "The Artist in the Gray Flannel Pajamas," *New York Times Magazine*, Mar. 5, 2000, p. 46.

44. D. G. Strege, "Employee Strategies for Stock Based Compensation," *Compensation and Benefits Review*, 1999, *31*(6), 41.

45. B. Parus and J. Handel, "Companies Battle Talent Drain," *Workspan*, Sept. 2000, p. 20.

46. National Center for Employee Ownership, "Growth of Employee Ownership Accelerates Rapidly in U.S. and Abroad," [www.nceo.org], May 1997, updated Dec. 2000.

47. Compuware Corporation, "ESOP/401K" (Internal Company Document), (Farmington Hills, Mich.: Compuware Corporation, Aug. 1995).

48. National Center for Employee Ownership, "A Growing Number of U.S. Employees Receive Stock Options: New Estimates from the NCEO," [www.nceo.org], accessed Mar. 18, 2001.

49. F. M. Biddle, "Work Week," *Wall Street Journal*, Jan. 18, 2000, p. A1.

50. Bureau of Labor Statistics, U.S. Department of Labor, *Pilot Survey on the Incidence of Stock Options in Private Industry in 1999*, [www.bls.gov], Oct. 11, 2000.

51. Hall, "What You Need to Know About Stock Options," pp. 123–124.

52. Bureau of Labor Statistics, *Pilot Survey*.

53. L. Shuchman, "New Tool in Tokyo," *Wall Street Journal*, Apr. 8, 1998, p. R9.

54. Starbucks Corporation, "Your Special Blend: U.S. Total Pay Summary" (Internal Company Document), (Seattle, Wash.: Starbucks Corporation, Oct. 1, 1999).

55. "Ericsson Safeguards Its Primary Asset," [www.ericsson.se], accessed Jan. 19, 2000.

56. William M. Mercer, Inc., "Executive Summary," *2000 Executive Long-Term Incentive and Equity Survey.*

57. Heldrich Center, *Work Trends Fall 1998 Survey,* p. 8.

58. Aon Consulting, *The 1999 Workforce Commitment Index,* p. 30.

59. Randstad North America, "Benchmark Employee Study."

60. BridgeGate LLC, "Employee Retention Study."

61. Bureau of Labor Statistics, U.S. Department of Labor, "Employee Benefits in Medium and Large Private Establishments," table 1 (1997 news release text, summary of *Employee Benefits Survey*), [www.bls.gov], Jan. 7, 1999.

62. D. E. Herz, J. R. Meisenheimer II, and H. G. Weinstein, "Health and Retirement Benefits: Data from Two BLS Surveys," *Monthly Labor Review,* 2000, *123*(3), 3.

63. "Executive Summary," *EBRI (Employee Benefit Research Institute) Notes,* [www.ebri.org], 1998.

64. M. W. Walsh, "Luring the Best in an Unsettled Time," *New York Times,* Jan. 30, 2001, p. G1.

65. Heldrich Center, *Work Trends Fall 1998 Survey,* p. 8.

66. L. Saad, "American Workers Generally Satisfied, but Indicate Their Jobs Leave Much to Be Desired, *Poll Releases* (Princeton, N.J.: Gallup News Service, Sept. 3, 1999).

67. Hudson Institute and Walker Information, *Commitment in the Workplace: The 1999 Employee Relationship Report,* [www.hudson.org], Oct. 19, 1999.

68. Bureau of Labor Statistics, "Employee Benefits in Medium and Large Private Establishments," table 5.

69. R. Winslow and C. Gentry, "Medical Vouchers," *Wall Street Journal,* Feb. 8, 2000, pp. A1, A12; M. W. Walsh, "Factory Workers Fight the Squeeze on Health Benefits," *New York Times,* Oct. 25, 2000, pp. C1, C8.

70. Levering and Moskowitz, "The 100 Best Companies to Work For," p. 92.

71. Bureau of Labor Statistics, "Employee Benefits in Medium and Large Private Establishments," table 1.

72. Bureau of Labor Statistics, "Employee Benefits in Medium and Large Private Establishments," tables 1, 11.

73. Bureau of Labor Statistics, "Employee Benefits in Medium and Large Private Establishments," tables 1, 11.

74. Walsh, "Luring the Best in an Unsettled Time," p. G1.

75. G. Morgenson, "Hidden Costs of Stock Options May Soon Come Back to Haunt," *New York Times*, June 13, 2000, p. C10.

76. R. Buckman, "Microsoft Upgrades Perks to Keep Talent," *Wall Street Journal*, Apr. 17, 2000, p. B8.

Chapter Five

1. T. O. Davenport, *Human Capital: What It Is and Why People Invest It* (San Francisco: Jossey-Bass, 1999), p. 143.

2. J. Arapoff, "Human Capital Index: Measuring Your Organization's Greatest Asset," *Strategy@Work*, Oct. 1999, p. 21.

3. Watson Wyatt Worldwide, *Competencies and the Competitive Edge*, [www.watsonwyatt.com/homepage/us], Apr. 1998.

4. Watson Wyatt Worldwide, *1999 Communications Study: Linking Communications with Strategy to Achieve Business Goals*, [www.watsonwyatt.com/homepage/us], accessed Oct. 12, 1999.

5. Aon Consulting, *The 1999 Workforce Commitment Index* (Chicago: Aon Consulting, 1999), p. 10.

6. Randstad North America, "Benchmark Employee Study Uncovers Salary Expectations and Attitudes on Benefits" (Press Release), June 6, 2000.

7. P. W. Mulvey, G. E. Ledford Jr., and P. V. LeBlanc, "Rewards of Work: How They Drive Performance, Retention and Satisfaction," *WorldatWork Journal*, 2000, 9(3), 11.

8. H. Frazis, M. Gittleman, M. Horrigan, and M. Joyce, "Results from the 1995 Survey of Employer-Provided Training," *Monthly Labor Review*, 1998, 121(6), 5.

9. E. Seaborn, "Strengthen Links Between Benefits and Strategy," *HR Focus*, 1999, *76*(6), 13.

10. Hudson Institute and Walker Information, *Commitment in the Workplace: The 1999 Employee Relationship Report*, [www.hudson.org], Oct. 19, 1999.

11. The Conference Board, "More Americans Dissatisfied with Their Jobs Despite Economic Boom" (Press Release No. 4592), Oct. 2000.

12. C. Handy, *The Age of Unreason* (Boston: Harvard Business School Press, 1989), p. 34.

13. S. Branch, "The 100 Best Companies to Work For in America," *Fortune*, 1999, *139*(1), 134.

14. R. Levering and M. Moskowitz, "The 100 Best Companies to Work For," *Fortune*, 2001, *143*(1), 156.

15. Frazis, Gittleman, Horrigan, and Joyce, "Results from the 1995 Survey of Employer-Provided Training," p. 4.

16. Davenport, *Human Capital*, p. 145; Educational Development Center, "Project Overview," [www.edc.org], accessed Apr. 10, 2001.

17. Frazis, Gittleman, Horrigan, and Joyce, "Results from the 1995 Survey of Employer-Provided Training," pp. 4–5.

18. National Center on the Educational Quality of the Workforce, *First Findings from the EQW National Employer Survey* (Philadelphia: University of Pennsylvania, 1994), p. 10; see also National Center on the Educational Quality of the Workforce, *The Other Shoe: Education's Contribution to the Productivity of Establishments: A Second Round of Findings from the EQW National Employer Survey*, [www.irhe.upenn.edu], accessed Apr. 9, 2001.

19. National Center on the Educational Quality of the Workforce, *First Findings*, p. 9.

20. Bureau of Labor Statistics, U.S. Department of Labor, "BLS Reports on the Amount of Employer-Provided Formal Training," table 13 (Press Release), July 10, 1996.

21. "Industry Report 1999" (Abstract), *Training*, 1999, *36*(10), [www.umi.com], accessed Apr. 12, 2001.

22. Frazis, Gittleman, Horrigan, and Joyce, "Results from the 1995 Survey of Employer-Provided Training," p. 5.

23. B. Hackett, *The Value of Training in the Era of Intellectual Capital* (Research Report 1199-97-RR), (New York: The Conference Board, 1997), p. 6.

24. Toyota Motor Corporation, *Outline of Toyota* (Toyota City, Japan: Toyota Motor Corporation, Feb. 2000), p. 10.

25. Nokia Corporation, *The Nokia Way of Learning* (Espoo, Finland: Nokia Corporation, Jan. 2000).

26. S. Hays, "Capital One Is Renowned for Innovative Recruiting Strategies," *Workforce*, 1999, *78*(4), 94.

27. S. Thurm, "What Do You Know?" *Wall Street Journal*, June 21, 1999, p. R10.

28. B. Hackett, *Beyond Knowledge Management: New Ways to Work and Learn* (Research Report 1262-00-RR), (New York: The Conference Board, 2000), p. 5.

29. I. David, "Doing the Knowledge," *Professional Engineering*, 1998, *11*(11), 29.

30. G. H. Anthes, "Learning How to Share," *Computerworld*, 1998, *32*(8), 76.

31. Nokia Corporation, *The Nokia Way of Learning*.

32. R. Cohen, *Managing Knowledge for Business Success* (Conference Report 1194-97-CH), (New York: The Conference Board, 1997), p. 21.

33. T. H. Davenport, D. W. De Long, and M. C. Beers, "Successful Knowledge Management Projects," *Sloan Management Review*, 1998, *39*(2), 47.

34. Brook Manville, chief learning officer at Saba, a provider of business-to-business networking via the Internet, quoted in T. Kulik, *Knowledge Management: Becoming an E-Learning Organization* (Research Report 1283-00-CH), (New York: The Conference Board, 2000), p. 21.

35. Davenport, De Long, and Beers, "Successful Knowledge Management Projects," p. 47.

36. Hackett, *Beyond Knowledge Management*, p. 60.

37. S. Thurm, "What Do You Know?" *Wall Street Journal*, June 21, 1999, p. R19.

38. L. M. Lynch and S. E. Black, *Beyond the Incidence of Training: Evidence from a National Employer Survey* (EQW Working Papers), (Philadelphia: National Center on the Educational Quality of the Workforce, 1994), p. 12.

39. Hackett, *The Value of Training in the Era of Intellectual Capital*, p. 8.

40. "Industry Report 1999," *Training*.

41. Bureau of Labor Statistics, U.S. Department of Labor, "1995 Survey of Employer-Provided Training: Employee Results," table 1 (Press Release), Dec. 19, 1996.

42. Novo Nordisk, *The Novo Nordisk Way of Management* (Bagsvaerd, Denmark: Novo Nordisk, Aug. 24, 1998), p. 11.

43. Wal-Mart Stores, Inc., "Wal-Mart Debuts at No. 7 on *Fortune* Magazine's World's Most Admired List" (Press Release), Sept. 22, 1999.

44. Acer Incorporated, "Acer Group Stan Shih Selected as 1999 International Business Executive of the Year" (Press Release), Nov. 23, 1999.

45. Hackett, *The Value of Training*, p. 8.

46. "Industry Report 1999," *Training*.

47. Bureau of Labor Statistics, "1995 Survey of Employer Provided Training: Employee Results," table 1.

48. Lynch and Black, *Beyond the Incidence of Training*, p. 12.

49. D. Wessel, "How Loyalty Comes by Degrees," *Wall Street Journal*, May 17, 2001, p. A1.

50. Bureau of Labor Statistics, "1995 Survey of Employer-Provided Training: Employee Results," table 10.

51. J. Jesitus, "Engineered for Success: How George Binder Keeps Amgen Healthy," *Industry Week*, July 10, 1999, p. 48.

52. P. F. Drucker, "A Growing Mismatch of Jobs and Job Seekers," *Wall Street Journal*, Mar. 26, 1985, p. 24.

53. D. Kirkpatrick, *Evaluating Training Programs: The Four Levels* (2nd ed.), (San Francisco: Berrett-Koehler, 1998).

54. Hackett, *The Value of Training*, pp. 7–11.

55. M. W. Walsh, "Luring the Best in an Unsettled Time," *New York Times*, Jan. 30, 2001, p. G1.

Chapter Six

1. Indicative of the turmoil of the FASB is the following paragraph (no. 60), found in Financial Accounting Standards Board, "Appendix A: Basis for Conclusions," *FAS 123 Summary* (Norwalk, Conn.: Financial Accounting Standards Board, Oct. 1995): "The debate on accounting for stock-based compensation unfortunately became so divisive that it threatened the Board's future working relationship with some of its constituents. Eventually, the nature of the debate threatened the future of accounting standards setting in the private sector."

2. V. Barocas, *Benefit Communications: Enhancing the Employer's Investment* (Report No. 1035), (New York: The Conference Board, 1993); J. Lineberry and S. Trumble, "The Role of Employee Benefits in Enhancing Employee Commitment," *Compensation & Benefits Management*, 2000, *16*(1), 12.

3. For example, L. Wah, "It's No Easy Job to Retain Talent," *Management Review*, 1998, *87*(5), 5, mentions a Watson Wyatt Worldwide study that found that "companies that communicated . . . benefits had a 13 percent lower turnover rate, on average, than those lacking such a clear strategy."

4. J. Pfeffer, *The Human Equation: Building Profits by Putting People First* (Boston: Harvard Business School Press, 1998), p. 173.

Index